With Reckless Abandon
Memoirs of a Boat-Obsessed Life

With Reckless Abandon
Memoirs of a Boat-Obsessed Life

Capt. Jim Sharp

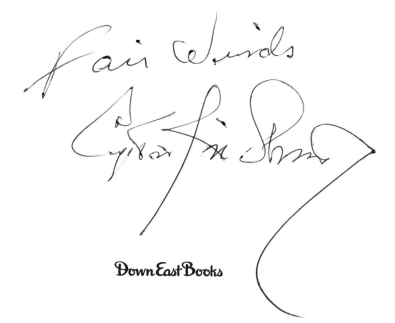

To Mebe & Sharon

Fair Winds

Captain Jim Sharp

Down East Books

Copyright © 2007 by Captain Jim Sharp

Down East Books
www.nbnbooks.com

Distributed to the trade by National Book Network

ISBN: 978-160893-000-5

Library of Congress Cataloging-in-Publication Data available upon request.

Design by Albertson Design

Cover photograph © Benjamin Mendlowitz

Back cover photograph: Steve Lang

Printed in U.S.A.

Contents

Appreciations   7

Prologue   10

Chapter 1: Tough Times and Wet Feet   12

Chapter 2: Off the Deep End   22

Chapter 3: The Maine Idea   34

Chapter 4: A Career Is Launched   44

Chapter 5: Total Immersion   58

Chapter 6 : Musical Spars and a Bad Surprise   69

Chapter 7: Love Affair   81

Chapter 8: Settling In   96

Chapter 9: The Arctic Schooner *Bowdoin*   104

Chapter 10: A Sardine Carrier Comes to Sharp's Wharf   118

Chapter 11: Someone to Watch Over Me   128

Chapter 12: Reckless Abandon   138

Chapter 13: Marry Me, El Capitano   148

Chapter 14: The *Wannie* Comes to Town   158

Chapter 15: Hollywood Comes to Camden   175

Chapter 16: Passengers   187

Chapter 17: A Second Career   201

Chapter 18: Fear Rings My Bell   212

Chapter 19: A Fascinating Freighter   220

Chapter 20: Hammering Out Retirement   230

Chapter 21: Europe Tugs at My Sleeve   237

Chapter 22: The Lady's Birthday   246

Chapter 23: The Tears of '88   254

Afterword   265

Addendum   267

Appendix: List of Vessels Owned by Captain Jim Sharp   269

Appreciations

I would like to extend special thanks to: the late Captain Marge Pratt, whose boundless enthusiasm and never-spared words of encouragement would, when my fire started to smolder, be right there with the rekindling; Spencer Apollonio for his endless editing, a task that stretched his patience to near breaking and dog-eared his old *Webster's*; Virginia Thorndike, who would nudge me with her optimism and invigoration; Joseph E. Garland for showing me how to do it with gusto as he did in *Adventure, Queen of the Windjammers*, and many other volumes; Shelly Johnson for her words of wisdom for a novice writer; Johanna Calderwood, who said, "Forget about composing, spelling, and the like—just write it down!" Thanks to Llewellyn Howland III, Peter Spectre, and Fredrick Gunther for guidance and encouragement.

The last is best—my endearing wife Meg, whose infinite patience has made all things possible in my life.

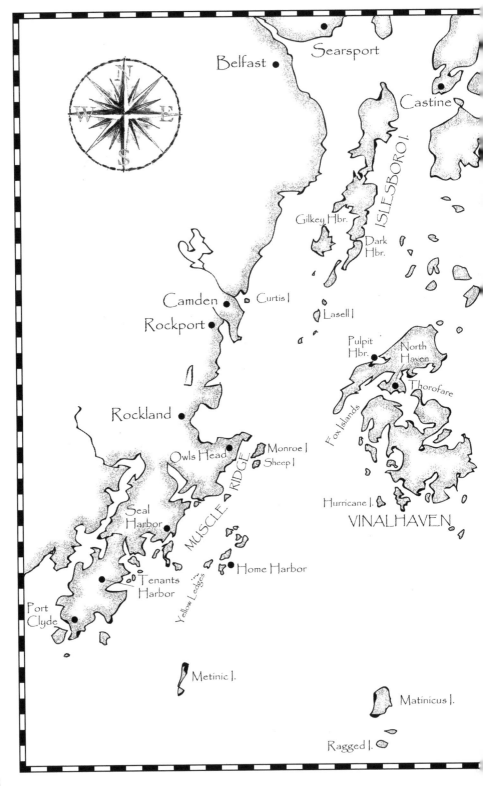

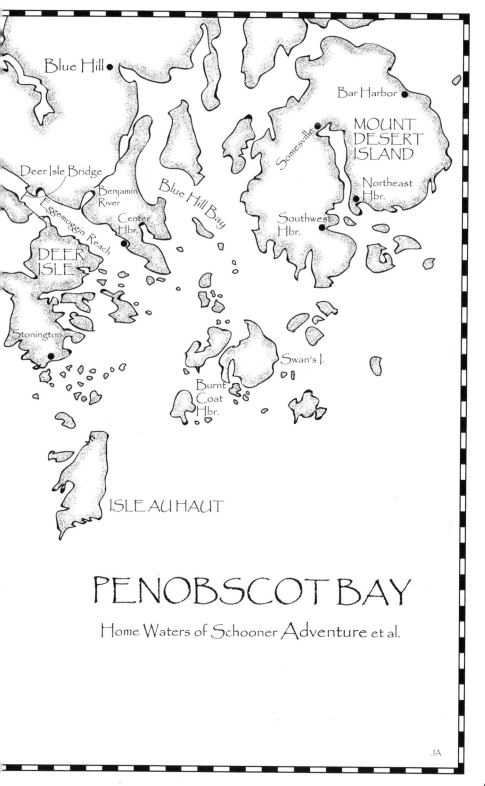

Blue Hill

Bar Harbor

MOUNT
DESERT
ISLAND

Somesville

Deer Isle Bridge

Benjamin
River

Blue Hill Bay

Northeast
Hbr.

Eggemoggin Reach

Center
Hbr.

Southwest
Hbr.

DEER
ISLE

Stonington

Swan's I.

Burnt
Coat
Hbr.

ISLE AU HAUT

PENOBSCOT BAY

Home Waters of Schooner Adventure et al.

JA

Prologue

'Tis always the same image. . . that old dream repeating. Always there is the schooner's bow—long, narrow, and powerful, rearing, gamboling as she parts the wave crests in the Gulf of Maine. She does it so easily, offhandedly, and with a swish, almost as a ballerina on toe. Then in her wake, she trails a jumble of white froth curling, a cascading wake left endlessly far astern.

Once again, I am perched on the main crosstrees, nearly 90 feet above the tumbling seas. From here I gaze down on the lift and fall of the knife-like stem as my old vessel cavorts below. All about me are the great curves of the schooner's sails, the white canvas stretched into symmetry by a typical sou'west "hat full o' wind."

In my dream, the old vessel is reaching east for all she's worth, halyards and sheets reverberating from strain, and with a hiss and a roar we blast through the lee of Monhegan. Then, we poke her up to the northeast, running like a gliding eagle past Owls Head Light. The blue of the water, the green of the hills, and the gray ledges and rocks of Maine unfold now into one of the most beautiful sailing grounds of our world, our home waters—Penobscot Bay.

We keep her nose to it until, fetching in by Curtis Island, the headsails are doused, the wheel is spun, and she curtseys into the wind. The anchor chain, with a plume of rust, roars out the hawse. She settles on her anchor, sails all aflutter, and she rests.

We have just nestled down in the cradle of the place where the mountains meet the sea. Here, in the snug harbor of the tiny town of Camden, in 1935, in front of the broad green lawn of Library Park, the Maine windjammer fleet was born. From my masthead perch, the prettiest town of Down East Maine spreads out before me. Up the harbor, at the foot of the rushing Megunticook Falls, sailing vessels have been coming and going for centuries. Just a splash downstream and to the west is the place that became known as Sharp's Wharf, home to the many boats this addict could never resist owning. They all lived here once, magnificent schooners—*Adventure, Bowdoin, Stephen Taber, Roseway*—the tugs and yachts, freighters and fish boats. The list was near endless.

But just give me the *Adventure*, the last and finest of the Grand Banks fishing schooners. She was my center, a place of pine decks and oak planks, of tarred cordage and soft, woven duck, of pioneer spirits in their thousands who sailed with me. Here was my world, my life—a life so fine that it would have seemed impossible to achieve, save for in a dream. And yet, it happened.

Captain Jim Sharp
Camden, Maine
December 2006

Chapter 1

Tough Times and Wet Feet

had no idea that my father, who had become stricken with a long-lasting and tortuous illness, was being helped to his bed for the last time. It was the middle of what was soon to become the long, oppressive summer of '53. Having just completed one year of college, I was busily engaged in an unusual summer of cultural studies at the University of Oslo. I'd gone to Norway comfortable with the understanding that Dad was recovering. Instead, when I returned home, I learned that Dad would no longer be coming downstairs.

Mother gave me the choice of continuing my studies or running my father's personal finance company, a family business in the suburban Philadelphia community of Upper Darby, Pennsylvania. I chose the latter. For one thing, I wasn't a very good student. For another, what would I do with a certificate in business administration and not the foggiest idea of where to hang it? So, dressed in a second-hand blue serge suit, I assumed the duties of the office where my very elderly and mostly crotchety Aunt Connie, my father's sister, was then managing.

I did enroll at Temple University night school, but with the preparations for my father's passing, learning all I could about the business, and supporting my mother, I had little time for studying. I found night school an incredible chore. The five nights a week were soon reduced to four, and then to three. I transferred to the Wharton School for two evenings, and finally I only took those subjects apropos to the finance business on one night a week.

I soon discovered how just gloomy and forlorn was this business of finance. Our customers would come in with pleading, pained expressions on their faces and tell me every problem from which they were suffering and how they'd become mired down in such desperate straits. Sometimes it was real—sometimes it was a two-dollar sideshow. I would console the unhappy borrowers, and they would depart with a fleeting relief and a few bucks in their wallet. Then, on the date due, in order to recover the money, I would have to listen to a whole new list of reasons why they hadn't met their obligations, why they couldn't pay now, and perhaps why they couldn't ever repay their loan. In spite of my feelings, I doubled the volume of the business in four years. The future looked promising, but was this any way for a fellow to enjoy living?

Between customers, I would sit at my desk behind a partition, reading a book or playing my practice guitar and gazing out the window across 69th and Market Streets, Upper Darby, Pennsylvania, where the Red Arrow Terminal was home to a fleet of buses, streetcars, subway trains, and taxicabs. The business was named Terminal Finance Company in honor of the bus terminal, but the "terminal" part seemed a perfect fit for my mood. If I opened the window, the smell of the exhausts, the cacophony of horns, the screech of subway wheels, the hubbub of voices, and the tweet of police whistles would rain in, washing away my sanity. I used to gaze out over the buildings and mutter to myself, "There has got to be more to life than this!"

My father had brought me up imbued with his love of small powerboats, music, travel and a lust for life that few enjoy. In his twenties, he'd been a professional musician. After college, he had his own band and then moved on to be first-chair trombonist with Fred Warring and his Pennsylvanians, playing, traveling, and touring all over the world. As the family expanded, Mom prevailed upon him to give up the fame and fortune of the Roaring Twenties (and, with one of the best bands in the country, lucrative it was) and settle down to fatherhood on the eve of the Great Depression. In spite of the hardships of the business world, Dad, through his Scottish parsimony, provided well for the family. He and Mom dragged us (my sisters and me) all over the United States, three times to Europe, and to many other foreign countries, seriously infecting us with his own wanderlust.

I should add that all this happened after an unfortunate event that created profound changes in all our lives, an event that I would spend the rest of my life doing my best to ignore. In 1937, at age four, while playing with sister Chris at the beach in Ocean Gate, New Jersey, I contracted polio in my entire lower body. Chris also became infected with the virus, but was able to throw it off with few aftereffects. Not quite so lucky, I was left with an emaciated, shortened right leg and very little muscular dexterity. The leg would continually collapse under me. I couldn't run with the other kids, and the simple act of walking had the look of an acrobatic exercise.

Then, when I was twelve, a talented, forward-thinking orthopedic surgeon performed an experimental procedure that he had contrived. He transplanted two of the three unaffected muscles in the back of the leg and, by tying the ligaments to the kneecap, was able to create sort of a "Rube Goldberg" muscle to straighten the leg. Now, being on the wrong side of the leg, these muscles not only stretched the tissue in an odd way, but my mind had to get used to the leg snapping straight when I would think to bend it.

As the disease had bent the leg bones, the doctor had to break the leg in three places to lengthen and straighten it. Then, he lengthened the heel cord by severing it in half and periodically stretching it by driving wedges into a hinged slit on a damnable plaster cast that went from my toes to my waist. I spent one entire hot summer in that itchy thing, scratching my 148 stitches by stuffing a stick, coat hook, or back scratcher down inside the cast.

The next year was spent on crutches, braces, and canes. It was all terribly embarrassing to a teenager about to enter junior high school, but I finally came out the other end with a half-decent walking capability, albeit with a stiff leg and a decided limp. Years later, I would discover to my amusement that landlubbers seem to delight in a limping seaman. Those who have the nerve to ask are aghast when I explain, trying to hide the twinkle in my eye, that a shark bit the leg in '02 on a voyage 'round the Horn!

Perhaps the most telling result of this childhood illness was its impact on my general approach to problems. I developed a kind of stubbornness, and a seeming recklessness that refused to acknowledge the damn leg a handicap. Years later, I discovered that I could climb a ship's rigging quicker than most because my upper body was so powerful, for I had insisted that my arm muscles would make up for what I lacked in legs. Although my disability did keep me from doing sports in school and although it made me cripplingly shy around girls, it also kept me out of a foxhole in Korea.

Shortly before Dad died of cancer in 1953, he had sold the last and largest of his beloved yachts, a 30-foot Chris-Craft sedan cruiser built in 1941. I had grown from kid to teenager going "down to the boat" on weekends and vacations. One of my fondest early memories was the day I stole my father's skiff and pretended to play sea captain. I must have been all of ten, maybe eleven years, old, and after having helped him with the construction of that small rowing boat in the basement the winter before, felt like I had uncommon rights to the thing.

A couple of broom handles mysteriously disappeared from mother's closet, and then I pilfered one of her bed sheets to fashion a square sail. I sailed, as if in command of a Cape Horn square-rigged clipper ship, straight across the treacherous waters of Dredge Harbor, New Jersey. I set off before the breeze and had an exciting sail the length and breadth of that pond-size harbor. Then, when I fetched up on the beach at the lee side, it dawned on me—I now had to row all the way back upwind! That moment vividly illustrated why my father had powerboats. I thought all sailors must be demented. It was not until some years later that I understood the principle of beating to windward, and then became a hopeless sailing addict.

Desperate for my first sailboat, when I turned 20, I convinced my school chum Don Sager to go with me to buy an old 20-foot plywood-built sloop. I had located the boat in a barn upcountry, where it had reposed for at least the prior 10 years. We were some excited! She was on a trailer of more rust than steel, with two flat tires and a mountain of dirt, straw, and barnyard junk that had to be moved to get at her. The boat was covered inches thick in dust and bird droppings and had gobs of little treasures down inside, left there by the various animals that had come and gone. Still, the price was right and we were happy. The seller, for some odd reason, seemed more than overjoyed!

We took her home, painted her up, got the old, rusty engine running, gussied-up the interior, and even hung little kerosene lamps in the cabin. Proud of our first boat, we named her the *Bay Wolves* and we took her to Gaskill's Dock on Brant Beach, Long Beach Island, New Jersey. This is the marina where in the early 1940s, my dad and I had first cruised when I was a little tyke. We held our breath when the crane picked up the *Wolves* and set her overboard. Looking like a swan in the water, she quietly, surreptitiously started leaking in great gulps. Ignoring the inrush of water for the moment, we went to work and rigged the absolutely enormous mast. It was built of steel and weighed what seemed like half a ton. The former owner must have broken the original wooden mast and then he overbuilt this one as if he intended to sail through another '38 hurricane. I could almost hear him saying, "Well, laddie, this mast won't break."

The old *Wolves* leaked a little bit (our denial) or a lot (the reality), but with great confidence and new-found knowledge about such things, I said, "She'll soon swell up and be tight as a jug!" We tied her up in an assigned slip, and that evening, wrung out by exhaustion, Don and I blew up our air mattresses and unfolded our sleeping bags. We bailed again, and again, and then crawled into our bunks to dream of sailing into a peaceful sunset.

Instead, about two in the morning, sailing through a terrible storm, I awoke with a start. A strange feeling of panic gripped me as I tried to sit up. I couldn't rise. Was I paralyzed? Instead of snapping bolt upright, my sleeping bag sank atop a collapsing mattress. Cold water, shocking and chilling, was filling in around my buttocks. As I came to my senses, I real-

First learning experience on a wooden knockabout sloop. (author's collection)

ized the "terrible storm" was only the motion of our air mattresses float-ing around the cabin with us aboard, bumping and thumping against the centerboard trunk. Don woke up and we accepted the obvious. It was time to bail yet again!

By the next day the leaks had slowed down not at all and another les-son had been learned — plywood does not swell like planking. With heavy hearts, we unrigged and unstepped that unwieldy mast and hauled the boat out of the water again. We lugged her back home, put her in the ga-rage, turned her upside-down, and, in the middle of a hot summer, ground all the paint from her bottom and completely encased it in fiberglass. Dumb and unthinking, we did it shirtless. The fiberglass dust got into our skin, sticking to the perspiration. Even now, remembering back to the 'glass dust, I start to itch. Well, in 1953 fiberglass was a comparatively new boat-building material. The centerboard trunk was rebuilt. We threw away that old engine and mounted a Johnson outboard on the side of the hull. Little did we realize that old outboard would often be doused in the sea as the vessel rolled.

Don and I and friends sailed the *Bay Wolves* for many years, mostly around Toms River, New Jersey. That old boat bent our learning curves into pretzels, and I only once suffered the terrible embarrassment of cap-sizing her. At the time we were bound down Barney Google's Bay — as we called Barnegat Bay — and a very obvious weather front was approaching. I had been reading books about weather fronts and concluded this one would be full of wind. So, with all nautical prudence, we furled and lashed the mainsail. My old high-school buddy Fred went forward on the fore-deck to run down the jib and put the anchor out.

Just before Fred was able to stow the jib, the wind and rain roared down. He had struggled the sail halfway down, and it was flapping and thrashing in the fresh gale. I, in a panic, was shouting, "Throw out the blasted anchor, for God's sake!" He grabbed the anchor and proceeded to throw it through the jib, putting a large hole in the center of it. Fortu-nately, he did have the foresight to make the anchor line fast, but when the anchor fetched up, its line was running out through our sail.

That didn't much matter anyway because the anchor never had a chance to hold. The breeze was so strong it blew the boat off sideways, and the wind, pressing against that enormously heavy steel mast, rolled us down, filling the cockpit and cabin with cold salt water. Fred's wife, Tammy, who had never learned to swim, was seated in the cockpit. We were all hanging onto the swamped boat, wind roaring, mast stuck in the mud, bread, brassieres, and blankets all bobbing up from the flooded cabin when Tam turned and queried, "What do we do now, Captain?"

I think I yelled something like, "Save my guitar!"

A good Samaritan came along in a powerboat after the squall had passed and towed us into Forked River for a session of "beach and bail." We had to come back a week later and move her to her dock in Toms River. The poor old outboard had been done-in with that sinking, and though we fussed over her, coaxed her, and changed her plugs, we had gone only a couple of miles when she died a quick and permanent death. Of course, there was no wind, and of course it had to be late in the afternoon with the sun going down, and mosquitoes coming out. Can there be anything worse than a hungry New Jersey mosquito? We had to paddle some five miles back to the Island Heights Marina. One cannot swat while paddling; one can only curse while paddling. Our backs were black with the critters feasting at the bloody trough. We finally arrived about four in the morning wishing for a transfusion to replace what they took.

The *Bay Wolves* was fun, but I needed more. In the wee hours of the evening, especially in the dead of winter, rather than go sit in a bar with beer-drinking friends, I would putter around in the shop my father had set up in the basement. There, I built a 14-foot wooden Sunfish. It was only a little too big to get up the curved cellar stairway. We pushed and pulled, jerked and jigged, and, just like the jokes you see in the comics, that beautiful, shiny paint job, so lovingly, carefully applied, had several deep scratches in it before the launching. I called the vessel the *Crab*. She was as slick as a wet seal and would sail rings around the *Bay Wolves* in most any breeze.

The addiction for this sailing thing now grabbed me like life itself. To gain more experience, I recruited friends and we would sail at every opportunity, fair weather or foul, aboard a variety of racing or cruising yachts in the Toms River area. In the coldest part of a dark February, we'd welcome the chance to freeze our buns off ice-boating. It was never enough. Because ice could be an iffy thing, I invested in a new Penguin-class sailing dinghy. With the 'Guin, I went "frostbiting" in the dead of winter on the beautifully polluted Schuylkill River, dodging the ice cakes and listening to the roar of the cars whizzing past the Philadelphia Art Museum. No doubt about it, the fine points of sailing are best learned while racing, half drowning, or freezing. Of course, the little Penguin only fed my habit. A bigger boat was the only cure!

In the summer of 1959, Fred and Tammy and I decided to charter a schooner and spend a week cruising on the Chesapeake Bay. So, gathering my guitar and Fred, his wife, and his banjo, we, and three other friends, set out for John's Army Surplus Shop on Market Street in Philadelphia. There we picked up a full-size Air Force red-and-white-striped parachute. Although we were sure this old schooner was no racing machine and had never been graced with anything like a spinnaker, we decided it would have one this trip! Tossing the chute into the car, we drove to Whorton Creek, where we were to meet the owner of the 42-foot *Sea Cloud*. She was a homely looking cruising type, but she sported almost indestructible guardrails all around, and had a large cabin with lots of room for the six of us. The owner wanted to know just who, in this motley gang, was to be captain and I stepped forward. "You do know the rules of the road, don't you?" he queried. I assented, but wasn't sure exactly what he was talking about and was very grateful when he didn't pursue the inquiry.

He gave us a quick shakedown, seemed satisfied, and cast off our lines. Well, occasionally rubbing her keel on sand and mud, we bounced that old schooner all around the Chesapeake for a week. We set the parachute as a spinnaker, tying off the hundred or so lines all over the vessel like some huge spiderweb and sailed exaltedly under the Bay Bridge, running with this huge red-and-white bulb over our unsightly bow. Cars on the bridge stopped to watch in disbelief. We made music in Annapolis, survived a gale of wind in the Choptank, visited the maritime museum in St. Michaels, and had a generally fantastic cruise. Eventually, we got the schooner back to its owner in one piece and I was already looking ahead to whatever adventure would follow. The boat that came next changed my life.

Chapter 2

Off the Deep End

Fresh from my experience in the Chesapeake, I convinced two other friends that we all needed a boat of our own, a big one, a fancy sailing machine, one that would be all-consuming and a challenge of the first magnitude. As my pal Don had now enlisted in the service, it was Joe Erwin and Bill Herd who would be limited partners in the purchase of a classic yawl named *Malabar XI*. She was a John Alden original, 52 feet overall, and replete with fourteen bags of racing sails, fifteen winches, a huge mainmast, a great bowsprit, a boomkin, a four-cylinder inboard, and yards and yards of varnished woodwork to maintain. Mr. Alden had her built as his own boat back in the 1930s when vessels were crafted with great care and pride. And—I was captain!

My first act was to rig our spring line on the wrong side of a lifeline stanchion when backing out of the dock in Mamaroneck, New York, and I promptly broke that expensive bronze casting. Only a little daunted, we motored down the East River through Hell Gate, out by Sandy Hook, and then, in an increasing easterly breeze, headed south along the New Jersey shore. I knew well that the Jersey shore can be a hellacious place with an easterly blowing, but I figured this was one big and able vessel. It was time to get "out there" and, like real mariners, find out what the hairy-chested knew. At least I had sense enough to seek a good offing, rather than be caught too close to that dangerous New Jersey surf. We went offshore all that day and all night long, and by morning when the gale was blowing itself out, we were lost. We were also wallowing in seas that were running 15 to 20 feet high.

My first great pride, the Alden-designed Malabar XI, *crosses Biscayne Bay in a wholesail breeze. (author's collection)*

Under shortened sail the vessel was rolling hard and we were taking quite a thrashing. The whole crew was seasick and, although I did not get sick, there was a time when my tummy rebelled. I had to clean the engine's filters in the middle of the night. So, in the bowels of that engineroom, stretched out prone with the bulkhead jammed into my gut, my head jammed under the exhaust manifold and my nose jammed in the bilge, gasoline fumes soon started my stomach into a series of flip-flops. I got back up on deck just in time to avert disaster.

When dawn broke, with everyone exhausted and demoralized, and our new boat looking a shambles, we finally set more sails and got underway for Atlantic City. Our first problem: where in hell is Atlantic City? There was only an empty horizon all around and we must have been 30 miles offshore. Well, one would figure if you go west, you'd eventually run into land, so off we went in that direction. I knew it would be humiliating, but I figured a little caution couldn't hurt and demanded of the first fishing vessel we saw to give us the course to the Atlantic City breakwater. He offered it, exuding sympathy and shaking his head.

Eventually, we did manage, without too many more incidents, to get up Delaware Bay and pass through the Chesapeake and Delaware Canal and into the tranquil Sassafras River. This was to be our homeport for the next three years as *Malabar* cruised Chesapeake Bay, raced with the fleet, and taught us the ways of a classic yacht. Of course, there was never enough time for sailing, and all my waterborne activity was promptly followed by a return home to the mentally deflating office of Terminal Finance Company, Upper Darby, Pennsylvania.

Disenchantment with the business world flourished like a malignancy, and I lived to get out of the office and down to the boat. Then a crazy notion flew into my head. We would sail around the world! My old friend Don Sager was now out of the service and trying to decide what to do with his life. Oh, the picture I painted, the gushing adjectives I used to embellish visions of the tropical paradises we would visit in the next two years. Don was easy to convince. His major problem, so he thought, would be convincing his wife, Jocelyn. They had been married only a short time, but we went at convincing her with verve. Jocelyn was hesitant and sensible, but we had inexhaustible enthusiasm and gradually we wore her down. She finally saw there was no hope for it, and agreed to go along as well.

Our plan was to sell *Malabar*, and I would purchase a double-ended, ketch-rigged, ocean cruising boat. Then it would be plan, plan, plan our blissful cruise over the next two-plus years. We spent hours and hours researching sailing routes, equipment, and places to visit. I went to Don's tiny apartment almost every night while we listed every blessed thing we would need. In the midst of all this, suddenly, somehow I came across an ad in some magazine for a 120-foot, three-masted schooner called *Amphitrite*. She was built entirely of teak and was for sale for only $20,000. A new idea now entered my ever-active imagination. We could buy this vessel, convert her for passengers, and set up shop offering windjammer cruises in the Bahamas. Simple when you say it fast! Don's wife thought this was a much better idea than the "world thing." The only trouble now was that the vessel was in the Canary Islands. Ah, but that seemed only a bump in the road!

"Okay," I said. "I can go over and survey it and then it's only a matter of sailing her home—and it's all downwind from there!"

I immediately started researching her history. Writing to the owner for details, I found she was built for the Guinness family of England, had silver doorknobs and hardware, etched glass and mirrors, a fieldstone fireplace in the saloon, and a long list of accoutrements. Prodigious! And, all the owner wanted at the outset was one-half as a down payment. It sounded too good to be true.

I made my arrangements, bought my ticket, and set the date to fly to the Canaries to inspect this vessel. But, just before I went, the cerebral light bulb finally came on and I got the idea to call the harbormaster in Las Palmas. I rang him up looking for info on this three-masted vessel *Amphitrite*. I think he knew he was on the spot because he was pretty evasive. He did confirm the vessel was there, lying at the dock. He did confirm that she was for sale, but gave me very little more information.

"Oh, by the way," he said just before hanging up, "there was a man here from California a few days ago who looked her over." I bamboozled the man's name and telephone number from him before we hung up, and immediately dialed California. Then I talked to a man who had lost a bundle over this boat, but was willing to give me the straight scoop.

It seemed that the owner had been using the vessel to run drugs or contraband into Morocco or Algiers. He was caught and incarcerated. But, he managed to escape, boarded his vessel, and high-tailed it for the Pillars of Hercules. The authorities gave chase, but he was already in the Atlantic and headed for the Canaries. They, with their speedy gunboat, overhauled and strafed him with a machine gun (the bullets of which were still in the hull) and towed him to the dock at Las Palmas. Before leaving they disassembled the engine and impounded the sails and rigging. He would not escape again. I was told that he paid off the authorities somehow and made his way back to England, sans ship. His scheme was to offer the vessel for sale, collect a deposit, renege on the sale because, of course, he had no right to sell it, and pocket the deposit. Trying to bring an action internationally would have been a terrible hassle and would cause anyone to just write it off! My friend in California had fallen into the trap, and it had cost him plenty. Bless his soul—his cooperation saved me much more than plane fare.

The *Amphitrite* episode was only a temporary disappointment. Gathering up our courage, we went in search of another vessel. Curiously, the next one that popped up happened to be at Hog Island, Nassau, Bahamas. How convenient! She, the *Cruise Del Sur*, was a burdensome, three-masted training ship built for Elcano, the Spanish school of seamanship. The vessel was then owned by Huntington Hartford, the wealthy heir to A & P stores, but he had no idea what he would do with her. I inspected the ship, and we started to dicker in what we considered big bucks and he considered chicken feed. It just didn't matter to him if he sold her or not, and we never were able to pry an answer from him.

In the meantime, I decided I needed more experience in the windjammer business, so I hustled on over to Watson Island in Miami to apply for a job with a windjammer company there. Two vessels were tied up, and I approached the one named *Cutty Sark,* a Baltimore Clipper type with raked masts. I jumped on the rail and asked to speak with the mate. My courage was bottoming out in the pit of my stomach. I was praying that the vessel's owner would be elsewhere because, only a few days earlier, I had put an application into the Board of Pilotage in Nassau for certification to run a large vessel (the *Cruise Del Sur*) in Bahamian waters. I knew that soon, very soon, this application would be aired in the *Bahamian Gazette* and that my prospective employer would not be pleased when he learned what I really had in mind.

The mate appeared and growled, "What's with you?"

I sheepishly answered, "A job."

"Can you do, like, anything at all?" he growled.

I had glanced around the deck and saw, besides many other things in disrepair, that there were several old sails that were ripped and torn. I had just finished reading a book on repairing commercial sails, so I took a deep breath and mumbled something about being a sailmaker. "Ah huh, sure," he said doubtfully. Then, picking up the corner of the topsail and putting his finger through a small hole, sneered, "And what would you do with this?"

Without hesitating, I said, "I would star-stitch it!" Well, I guess they were desperate enough to hire most anybody, and stars or not, I got the job. Working away at sewing sails for the next couple of days, I made friends with the crew, learned to avoid the mate, kept my head down and my ears open. The *Cutty Sark*'s foresail was too far gone to repair, so they had borrowed a spare foresail from the other vessel, the *Mandalay*, a grand 120-foot, Alden-designed, two-topmast schooner. Of course, that vessel had plumb masts, and the *Sark*'s masts had lots of rake. Obviously the *Mandalay*'s sail would never fit, but they still planned to use it. As the only sailmaker aboard, I was asked to pass judgment on its serviceability.

"Serviceable," I said. The mate got a gang together, and with a few profane words, they went hot and heavy at bending on that sail. I glanced up from my work just as they were seizing on the mast hoops and, to my horror, realized they were lacing up the foot of the sail on the gaff—bending it on upside-down! I knew better than to tell the mate he was doing it all wrong so I grabbed one of the crewmen going by and told him. He knew the mate better than I, he having been aboard almost a week, and his response was, "You don't expect me to tell him do you? No way, mister!"

The *Cuddy*—as they called her—was bound out the next day. Happily, I was transferred to the *Mandalay*. I later found out that they finally rebent that sail right-side-up after they sailed with it for four days with its boom dragging back and forth across the deck. A few days of outfitting these schooners taught me a boatload about how not to run a vessel. Our mate arrived for final outfitting on the *Mandalay,* and we prepared to sail for the Bahamas, where charter business awaited. We were to load our passengers in Bimini, as the Coast Guard would never allow this gang to take passengers from any U.S. port.

I thanked my stars I was not on the *Sark* now, as our mate turned out to be a great guy, a real Polish count, an experienced seaman and a reasonable human being. The other deckhand, Freddie Huntington, and I more than willingly followed Count Christopher D. Grabowski's orders and snapped-to, ready to show the captain, who would be arriving soon, that we were a crack crew. Soon after, however, we were to learn that we were wasting our efforts. The skipper was an old Norwegian fellow with a destructive drinking problem. One of the captain's favorite expressions was, "You make me so mad I could scratch out my own navel." Of course, this and other expressions were colored with all imaginable profane blessings.

As we steamed down through Government Cut headed for sea, all hands were called to set the mainsail. The captain, to teach us a lesson on discipline, decided not to use any of the automatic winches for setting the sails. We were a small crew and that mainsail was some heavy. Well, we started on throat and peak, Freddie and I on one and the mate and cook on the other, and we stalled out with the sail about one-third up the mast. The four of us then ganged up on the throat and we hove and hove while the captain shouted obscenities in both Norwegian and English. Switching between peak and throat, we finally got that sail raised. By that time, the cook had fainted, Freddie and I were frothing at the mouth, and the mate had sat down in complete exhaustion. The skipper, in a fit of great disgust, went aft. Muttering and swearing to himself, he got a little nip or three from his bottle and waited for us to set the rest of the sails.

After the lowers were set, Freddie went up the foremast and I the main to set the topsails. I can still remember the sight she was, breasting the Gulf Stream, cleaving the seas, waves all blue and white on top, cascading this way and that! 'Twas glorious to be up in the rigging and away from the deck. 'Twas glorious to hear the sound of the breeze in the rig instead of all that Norwegian profanity!

Arriving at Bimini with the wind onshore, the skipper dropped the anchor a bit too late, we backed up on the sand, and she started to thump. The skipper then hove the anchor up and proceeded to drive the vessel ahead at full throttle. She stuck fast and, as he tried backing and filling with machinery roaring at full throttle, the old engine started to overheat and eventually blew a head gasket. We called for a tow to get us off.

Our passengers were flown over from Miami to Bimini, and we sent the small launch in to pick them up. As the overloaded boat returned, she poked her bow into the cresting waves, taking solid spray. By the time we helped our guests up to the deck, water streaming from their clothes and luggage, they were dripping like divers fresh up from the great deep. It was not a good beginning. Out came the rum swizzles. They would be the cure-all for spoiled food—the refrigeration was working poorly and many things tasted poorly—and we had a great number of deck leaks. With enough rum swizzles, however, the passengers soon forgot the inconveniences and just about everything else.

Early in the cruise, we encountered a little gale of wind. While reefing the mainsail, the skipper took a line from the reef cringle to the end of the boom for an outhaul. Neglecting to take the necessary turn around the boom, he pulled right from the first leach cringle and tore the entire lower sail panel all to pieces. From then on, we had to permanently double-reef the mainsail and sail like a gull with a broken wing until we could have it repaired. As if these things were not enough, in an alcoholic rage, the skipper took exception to the mate and, for no substantial reason, ordered him off the deck. One passenger fell from aloft where he should never have been allowed to go, and had to be taken ashore for medical attention. Out came the rum swizzles again. There was a host of other incidents, but the crowning blow came when we started back for Miami in the night crossing of the Gulf Stream and the skipper proceeded to get drunk and passed out under the galley table.

With the mate ordered off the deck, it was up to Freddie and me to get the vessel home to Florida. We figured we were up to the task because, of course, "it ain't my boat" as Freddie would say, so we could afford to take chances. We made a perfect landfall at Fowey Rocks Lighthouse, corrected our course for Government Cut, and as we were steering through the breakwater, the skipper woke up and came on deck. He took command and brought the vessel in with a flourish so that, when the owner came aboard at the pier, he suspected nothing.

We had no more than tied up when I was called aft and an ultimatum was delivered by the vessel's owner: "You, Sharp, joined my ship under false pretenses, and I'll give you thirty seconds to get off my vessel."

That being my intention anyway, I welcomed the news. "I'm on my way, Cap," I said. I didn't have to buy a copy of the *Bahamian Gazette* to know that my own application for a charter license had been aired in the news. Needless to say, the Bahamian government turned down our application. I often wondered how much my short tenure aboard the *Mandalay* had to do with that decision.

Unsatisfactory as it was, this brush with the cruise business opened my eyes to a way of life far removed from the Terminal Finance Company, Upper Darby, Pennsylvania. In fact, it tickled my determination to move *Malabar* south, snuggle into Florida waters, and start chartering. I set up the finance business to be run "absentee," and purchased the shares of my two *Malabar* partners. Then, with my friends Don Sager and Freddie Huntington, I swung off from the Sassafras Boat Company in Georgetown, Maryland, and pointed *Malabar*'s bow south. "Here we go," I told my pals, "embarking on a new 'era' in our lives, and I only hope it's not spelled 'e-r-r-o-r'!"

Down the Inland Waterway we went, sometimes sailing, sometimes motoring, and sometimes both. The old boat fetched the bottom and stuck only six times. Hey, that's not too bad with a draft of seven feet! We got a berth on Pier Three at Dinner Key, Coconut Grove, Florida, hung out our shingle, and said, "Come on, charter parties!" Unfortunately, it was by now the first of July 1961 and the height of the off-season. We got jobs working on other people's boats and did what we could until we could book a charter and make our first million. We ate lots of peanut butter and pasta that summer, but by and by the season came on, and we managed to get a few customers.

Then came the winter. The wind began to blow, and the Gulf Stream was waiting to dish out all of its pleasantries to us. On one of our early charters, we had four men who were gung ho to cross the Stream. I warned them it was too rough and that we should wait for better weather, but they, of course, wanted to see "how it really was." We entered the Gulf Stream with wind and sea both against us, killing our headway and forcing us north. We were more than a day and a half trying to cross 40 miles of Gulf Stream. In the middle of the night we took a knock-down with such force that the guys in the bunks in the main cabin, starboard side, flew through the air and joined those on the port side without even touching the floor. A couple of them, with sick and pasty looks on their faces, asked me very seriously if anyone else knew we were out here.

I assured them in a wry, none-too-comforting tone, "No. Not one soul knows we're here, and there is no way to contact anyone!" This, of course, was back in the "old" days when there was only an AM radio, no GPS, and not much of anything but a compass. We took a second wave that night that completely filled the self-bailing cockpit and, when the water drained away, there was a fish flopping around at my feet. "Breakfast!" I exclaimed. Our passengers saw no humor in it and were a pretty sorry-looking sight when they desperately inquired about airline flights back to Miami from West End.

The old *Malabar*, with her seven-foot draft, was really too deep for the shoal water in the Bahamas, but I was too stubborn or too stupid to care. The first time we approached Bimini, I carefully lined up the harbor entrance according to the cruising guide and with a little flood tide stood in for the buoy. A long, bony Bahamian in an outboard skiff ranged alongside and, with a big yellow-toothed smile, said, "Hey, mon, you need pilot? I Henry. I pilot you in!"

Mustering confidence, I declined, saying it looked passable to me from here. "Many shoals grab your keel, mon," he retorted. "You follow me, mon, an' I lead you over de bar."

Hoping to get some free advice, I asked, "How much water is there over the bar at this tide?" He, being a little craftier than he looked, replied, "Oh, plenty water dere for you, mon. For two beers, I take you safely in. I find you de deep spot. How much do you draw?"

I somehow felt the question of "how much" should come before the statement "plenty water dere," but I lied and said that our draft was eight feet so we would have a foot to spare. I agreed to the price of two cold ones. By and by, the old keel started bumping on the hard sand. I backed off and scolded the so-called "pilot."

"Hey, Henry. I thought you said there was plenty of water through here for me!"

"Funny, mon. They' was plenty water dere last week, mon! I took big ship in."

We found our own way to the deep water and drank the cold ones, washing down our first lesson on native expertise. Whatever the dangers posed by our boat's relatively deep draft and the Bahamas' relatively shallow waters, I found a certain magic there. Who could forget anchoring at Wardwick Wells, diving in the gin-clear water, picking up a couple of lobsters, and spearing a grouper for dinner! We all loved to go diving on the reefs. There was the time I sat up on the crosstrees of the mainmast watching hundreds of hammerhead sharks run before the vessel as *Malabar* dragged her heel across the Bahama Bank. Of course, I still have the horrors when I think of crossing the Yellow Bank in the late afternoon with the sun in our eyes, wind blowing, sea running, and we straining to see the coral heads and scared to death of slamming into one. Our passengers, oblivious to the danger, thought it romantic.

Overall, ours sure seemed like an idyllic life. In those days, I was brown as a berry and more in the water than out. Despite the problems I'd had in my initial attempt to get a Bahamas passenger license, I was still in the market. What's more, Don and I were also on the lookout for a larger vessel that we'd use to sculpt out a career for the two of us.

Back in Upper Darby, Pennsylvania, meanwhile, the finance business had been running on an absentee basis for more than a year, and the customers were beginning to realize that my two secretaries were the only ones in attendance. The girls would always say, "Oh, Mr. Sharp just stepped out for a minute." But the ruse must have been obvious, as the office was burglarized one night. After that, the girls started to get skittish. I had to fly home now and then to appease and encourage them. Things quieted down after a while and they continued acting out the charade. You need secretaries with spunk if you want to go sailing!

Chapter 3

The Maine Idea

The year 1963 was a lean one. In order to keep eating between charters I worked on other boats in the Miami marina where we were based. One day, while I was sanding and varnishing on a big powerboat, a lanky stranger came walking down the dock and struck up a conversation. He introduced himself as captain and owner of two large commercial passenger schooners on the coast of Maine. By coincidence, and just to add to my résumé, I had studied and passed my Coast Guard license exam the previous year and now, age 30, was able to brag about having a sail license. We had a long talk about how ancient his captains were and how he was looking for some young blood to take their place. Soon enough, he offered me a job as mate on one of the boats and, remembering how slow the previous summer had been in the charter business, I jumped at the chance.

I knew a little bit about the Maine coast schooners because, back in 1957, three high-school buddies and I had signed on an old vessel called *Adventure* for a week's cruise on Penobscot Bay. We had heard somewhere that these boats carried a lot of single girls, so we picked out one of the largest schooners, hoping for a good ratio. It was a great time. Captain Dayton Newton smoked a pipe, wore a pea coat, talked sailors' talk, and sang sea chanteys. We four squeezed into a cabin they called the black hole of Calcutta. It was a dark little place with a leaky deck, tucked in behind the mainmast, but we didn't care as we were much more interested in having a beer and exploring the female possibilities aboard.

The poor old boat needed paint. The food was good but the galley was none too clean, and she was certainly what you would call rustic—very rustic! As it happened, I found myself much more impressed by the rocks and islands of the Maine coast and the seamanship involved in wrestling that 122-foot Grand Banks schooner around the bay than I was by the female population aboard. I spent many an hour quizzing the captain and picking his brain. But, never in my wildest dreams did I suspect, while drifting around Penobscot Bay, that the old *Adventure* would prove to be my eventual destiny.

Having hired me, my new employer and his wife quickly formulated a great plan in their heads. They had two fully grown, lively Dalmatians and a big station wagon with springs that bottomed out under the weight of many bags of dog food and schooner gear piled aboard. I was to hitch my new boss's car to a long trailer loaded to the gills with even more equipment and drive from Fort Myers, Florida, to Maine. By moving a dog, there was just enough room to squeeze my sea bag on the passenger seat and lash my fold-up scooter on the trailer. After securing *Malabar* with a live-aboard tenant for the summer, I was ready to leave. I wasn't too sure who was more excited, the dogs or me, but we three were off.

On my way north, I stopped in suburban Philadelphia, where I had a tiny third-floor apartment. There I spent a couple of days checking in with my secretaries at Terminal Finance Company, and then roared on to the top of the world, Camden, Maine, where the owners took over the caravan. It was the middle of May and the middle of mud season. I was fresh from the islands and brown as a Brazil nut, and it snowed the next day! Snowed—in May. Welcome to Maine!

The two vessels were the schooners *Mattie* and *Mercantile*, and they were still in their winter berths in Stonington, a fishing village a bit farther Down East. Before I had a chance to think about the snow and the cold, I was dropped off at a deserted and grim-looking shipyard. Nearby on an island just beyond the channel, a fog signal droned every minute, all day and all night. It was cold, foggy, depressingly gloomy, with piles of dirty plowed snow creating many a spooky-looking sculpture, and the yard was closed tight as a drum. I could find not a soul around, it was dark as a pocket, and I had to move aboard this old schooner built in 1881.

All I could do was commiserate with hundred-year-old ghosts. I built a smudge in the ancient black iron galley stove, but the stovepipe was filled with soot, it wouldn't draw, and the rascal immediately filled the vessel with thick black smoke. I, choking, had to go on deck until it all cleared out and, for a week thereafter, my sleeping bag smelled like a dead campfire. Well, off and on, I sure did some serious pondering about my beautiful varnished yawl in the sunny southland.

I stayed aboard outfitting those old schooners for nearly two weeks. It was quiet, and depressing. To alleviate my grim circumstances, I lured my old high-school buddy Don Leahan to drive miles out of his way on a business trip to New England. I did this by conjuring up the magical mystique of spending a night on a fancy schooner yacht in Maine. Don arrived in a fervor of optimism, shouting "Sharp, where the hell are ya?" He, all decked out in his Brooks Brothers business suit, was ready to be escorted to his accommodation by some sweet-looking young receptionist. To his chagrin, he pee'd in a number-ten spaghetti can, brushed his teeth in the morning with concentrated orangeade, and, quickly taking his leave, was muttering under his breath all the way to his car. As he spun around, tires squealing, he spat from the open window, "Sharp, you jerk, I'll never let you forget this one!"

Under the owner's tutelage, I painted without sanding, repaired without bedding compound, rigged with nothing but hardware string, and caulked seams with old used manila line. The decks leaked so badly that I hung aluminum trays over the bunks with little hoses to carry the water drizzling through the decks off into the bilge. I could do anything as long as it cost almost nothing. I did all I could to justify my three dollars an hour and considered it a real learning experience. Social life consisted of watching the shipyard crew roar out of the yard at quitting time, spinning and squealing the tires of their pickup trucks on the causeway road to the mainland.

Then, I saw a flyer nailed to a telephone pole for a dance at the local Grange hall. That hall was only a couple miles away, but never fear, I had my totally unreliable fold-up scooter waiting in wings. This was one of those rigs that folded the front wheel and handlebars into the body so it was then luggable as a suitcase, but lots heavier. The beast would sometimes embarrass me and fold up on its own without warning, and the dance night was one of those times. I got her stopped just in the nick—a second before the crash—and refastened the anti-folding strut. I tuned her and gassed her, even spoke kindly to her, and she declared she was ready.

Then, infected with overpowering excitement, I scraped the schooner dirt off, shaved, and tried to get myself all gussied up for the first time in over a week. Came the hour, I, perched aboard that scooter, roared with the yard crew at quitting time across the causeway road towards town. Wow, I was off to the dance—real people—and music! Then she hesitated. I opened the throttle wide. She hesitated only once more and quit. I pulled and pulled on the starter rope, but she had passed on to the great beyond. I tossed her into the ditch and walked back to that gloomy old shipyard.

After my questionable experience with windjammer cruising on the schooner *Mandalay*, I was looking forward to a grand and glorious summer with these wonderful old commercial vessels sailing the coast of Maine. A crew arrived from Camden and we moved the boats to their summer berth. In getting parts and equipment for the final rigging, I had occasion to go to the Camden Shipyard and met a man working in the parts department. He was a tall bean-pole of a "Down Easter" with a nasal Maine accent. He had an incredible dry wit, and a comfortable, warm, welcoming attitude. This was Orvil Young. He was a master boatbuilder and had worked on these very same schooners back in the days of Captain Frank Swift, who had originated the Maine windjammer fleet in 1935.

As the outfitting wound down and the sailing season approached, I could see that the owners, in my opinion, left a lot to be desired in the world of employers. Now, my Scottish nature demands that I remain on the conservative side of the line that separates the thrifty from the spendthrifts. These guys went way beyond me on the side of the thrifty. Normally, I admire this quality, but when running a business that involves the public, there are places where you must yield to your customers' safety and comfort and spend a little extra.

In deference to the hired captain, I will say he probably learned from Captain Swift, who started the Maine fleet during the Depression, when you could buy a schooner, sails, and rigging, including captain, for $300. Then the going rate for a week's cruise was $20, and the captain earned for the week a two-passenger wage. But, that was then and now is now. It had come to my attention that the Great Depression had ended some years earlier, and I wondered if and when my employers would come to this realization.

I was to go out as mate aboard the *Mattie* for Captain Fred Morey, the hired skipper, who was pushing eighty salty years and had to squint to see anything beyond the bowsprit. He was a man of few words, most of which were unintelligible. I tried hard to humor the skipper, and we got along famously. After all, he did have gobs of experience in sailing vessels as he'd spent all of his life at sea. I loved to hear him, after a nip or two in the main cabin, tell stories of the old days.

Like many of the Maine windjammers, the *Mattie* was (and remains) a pure sailing vessel. If there is no wind or when in a crowded harbor, the schooner uses an engine-powered yawlboat tied under the stern to maneuver. It was the mate's job to jump in this boat and answer to the captain's instructions whether to go faster, slower, left rudder, or right, to stop and reverse, or get out of the boat and go get coffee. I expected that some system of communication between captain and yawlboat operator would necessarily be indispensable.

Not so with Captain Fred. From the wheel on the quarterdeck where he stood, he would turn and, half facing me, would mutter something that sounded like an Indian campfire chant. At the same time, he would curl and uncurl his fist in my direction and leave his intention to my imagination. If I hadn't already humored Captain Fred and gotten into his good graces, we would have had a parting during those first three or four days. It was a perpetual panic outguessing old Captain Fred. One time, when returning from one of our cruises with a deckload of passengers, the skipper decided to carve a new channel between all the moored boats in the center of Camden Harbor.

Poor old Fred—once committed, his anxiety level and blood pressure went up and he started firing orders in my direction, one after another, in a confusing jumble. By and by, he hit a boat on the port side and it came scraping down the topsides of the *Mattie*. The strain of the collision brought up short its mooring line, and forced the boat around our stern, where it gave me a pretty good bump on the side of the yawlboat. Old Fred was still hollering his Indian war chant and waving his arms in the air. I had a good grip on the towing bitt when the second moored boat came thumping and bumping down the starboard side. Remember, Captain Fred's eyesight was not the best, and that old curmudgeon hit five boats before we finally got to the dock. But then you have to figure, he *was* still getting Depression wages.

I then went on to work on the *Mattie*'s sister ship, the *Mercantile*, for most of that summer, but I still remember old Fred, red faced, hollering and gesticulating at the new and confused yawlboat operator one Monday morning when he hit a lobster boat. He had the misfortune of catching it on the starboard bow where the storm anchor fluke reached down below the rail and hooked the cabinhouse on the fish boat. With a great ripping and tearing, it picked the house right off and stayed hooked while the *Mattie*, like a fat duck, casually continued on her way out the channel. Fred never hesitated. When they got out beyond the island and into the bay, with the lobsterboat's house—windows, spotlight, and all hanging from the anchor, he quietly said to the mate, "Go forward and kick that thing overboard!" That's the way it was in the old days. Now, if the Coast Guard got wind of that, you would never live long enough to fill out all the forms.

Soon, Captain Ross Eaton arrived to take command of the *Mercantile*. One glance at the stooped, round-shouldered figure silhouetted on the pier head told me he was just like old Fred, another ancient mariner. But Captain Ross was different. He had clear blue eyes, a sharp mind, and a humble, professional way about him. The owner didn't trust him to take the vessel and decided that, in spite of his skipper's qualifications, he would "Show him the ropes." I later found out that Captain Ross had one of the largest licenses in the U.S., a license that encompassed all waters, sail or steam, and included pilotage in every harbor from Eastport, Maine, to Brownsville, Texas.

Here was a true master mariner. He had a marvelous way of giving orders with the quiet confidence that exuded proficiency. You can always tell a master when he shows his colors; he always does it in a quiet, confident voice. The novice, unsure of himself, has to rant and rave and try hard to embarrass the recipient of the order. Captain Ross had had three double hernias and was well up in his seventies, but you could tell that he would immediately understand and be in control of almost any situation.

Unfortunately, our owner was blind to the skipper's ability, so he went along on our first week's trip, elbowing that grand old gentleman away from the wheel and shouting orders to cast off the lines on the foredeck with a voice that could deafen the tourists on Main Street. He assumed an entirely different air than when he and I worked together on the outfitting. His voice was two or three octaves higher, but his ego must have climbed by multipliers. I said to myself, "This isn't going to work 'tween us for long."

We set sail, fore and aft, to the sound of the owner's orders that greeted us like fingernails on a chalkboard! I finished coiling down and was cleaning up by the fore mast and running the swab under the windlass when he asked me to adjust fore staysail sheet. Leaning the mop handle against the foremast, I proceeded to uncleat the fore staysail sheet. Then, with the screech of a snowy owl, and over the heads of all the passengers, he screamed, "You lame-brained idiot. Don't lean your mop against the foremast!" I was so mad, my eyes were crossing. I decided then and there I was going to quit this damned old leaky tub when, to my amazement, Captain Ross Eaton walked forward and quietly apologized for the owner's behavior.

I was already sold on this gentle mariner, but that little message settled it—I decided to stick it out. After a couple more days, the light finally dawned on my employer that Captain Ross could handle his little schooner. He finally took his leave from Friendship Harbor, but he misjudged our speed when coming into the anchorage, and I got my chuckles. With the headsails down and stowed, we were still making five or six knots with just the fore and main when he signaled to me to drop the anchor. I glanced over the side and figured we had too much momentum, so I looked questioningly back towards the wheel. Again and in a panic this time, he roared, "Let her go."

That chain roared out the hawsepipe, the anchor hooked into that good mud in Friendship Harbor, the chain fetched up, tore the hawsepipe (the fitting in the bulwarks through which the anchor chain runs) right out of her, shook up the knightheads, and broke part of the bulwark planking. That hawsepipe rattled down the chain, "kersplashed" into the bay, and I felt kind of warm and fuzzy all over. Captain Ross brought the vessel home at the end of the week and made a landing so professional you could have fended off with a marshmallow. Our owners were on the wharf taking lines, giving orders, and screeching their heads off.

To enhance profits, there was a rigid policy of saving some food from each meal during the week for the final dinner. These leftovers were then offered as our cruise's final meal. 'Tis a grand way to impress your passengers on the last meal of the trip—let them go home remembering the leftovers! We, the crew, all ate so much, the leftover pickings were picayune. The result was that Cookie was ordered to hold back on all the food he gave the crew, especially the milk. The nerve!

Well, Cookie was in our camp. He held back the milk all right, and lots of other stuff, hiding it for the crew alone, and the passengers either went hungry or were forced to stop at the market ashore to stock up on junk food. It had been accepted policy that as soon as we hit the dock in Camden, the owner's wife would come aboard and pack up all the leftover food she could find in the ice chest to take home. That meant the crew had nothing to eat over the weekend. With cook and crew in cahoots, that official policy was soon trashed. We had the most choice part of the steer hidden away for our sandwiches, and our poor owners just couldn't understand why the larder was so empty all the time. Never underestimate the inventiveness of a hungry crew!

Looking back, 1963 was a terrific summer. Captain Eaton taught me well—not just the piloting, but the philosophy and attitude of a master mariner. He had a way of injecting us with a strong sense of responsibility and commitment and we never felt the needle. Come seven in the morning, we were to be on deck for wash-down. Of course, many nights were spent in late conversation with the female passengers, so seven came early sometimes. Our living accommodations were meager and the four of us, captain, cook, mate, and deckhand, shared the fo'c's'le in upper and lower bunks.

The Captain would turn on his radio to catch the news about 0645. About 0650, he turned the volume up just a little. At 0700, he would start to clear his throat and sometimes hum a little tune. At 0710, quietly, ever so quietly, he would say, "Boys, do you think it's about time?" At 0725, "Boys, you have to get the deck washed up before breakfast!" and we would finally roll out of our bunks. It was kind of a game we played, and he, well—he had us figured! He was usually to windward of the likes of us. Any of us monkeys would have broken an arm for him, and gladly.

The Maine season was short, the boats were old and often in questionable condition, and there was lots of black fog. Experiencing only the *Mattie* and *Mercantile*, however, probably limited my horizon. The *Mattie*, built about 1882, was so weak and leaked so copiously that they didn't dare use her centerboard. A shoal-draft centerboard coaster without that board will hardly sail to windward. Being caught on a lee shore, particularly if the old yawlboat was taking fits, would be downright dangerous.

The *Mercantile*, built in the early 1900s by a couple of farmers on Little Deer Isle, was built for a life of perhaps 12 or 15 years and she took the grand prize for hog. That term is used to describe a vessel that no longer has sheer or is losing its shape. In other words, she no longer came up on both ends like a saucer, but was so weak that the bow and stern sagged down in an unhappy frown. The poor *Mercantile* went through the water dragging her stern like an old dog with rheumatism. They used to sing, "There's so much hog to the *Mercantile*, they're serving pork at every meal." Her crew, including yours truly, spent many a weary, gut-wrenching hour sailing and pumping and sailing and pumping. Of course, a total rebuild was possible and it did happen, but that wouldn't be for many a year.

Maintenance on these old boats was constant and gear failure was certainly a worry. I remember one time I was standing next to the fore mast when the whole nest of topping lift blocks and cable let go from the masthead and came crashing down next to where I was standing, leaving a huge scar in the deck. The ironwork on the block was just worn through from years of chafing, dangling there and being ignored. The little yawl-boats, indispensable as the schooners' only power, suffered greatly for the want of more than a cursory maintenance program. A college-age employee looking for an easy, glamorous, not-too-taxing summer job almost always ran them. It's a credit to these old captains that they got around most of the rocks most of the time, and did it as well as they did.

As the cold fall of 1963 settled into Maine, I didn't feel overly enamored of the now dreary Maine coast or the poor old broken-down boats. I was some glad to get back on *Malabar*, my beautiful varnished little yacht, and to settle down and do some more serious chartering. I was convinced that the Bahamas was the place to run a windjammer cruise. I exclaimed to my friends, "Anyone living above the Mason-Dixon must be out of his gourd!"

It was not until a few short weeks later that I began to realize how much the rocks, the pine trees, the afternoon sou'westers, and the attitude of the real old-time Maine people like Captain Ross had gotten under my skin. Still I gloried to see blue water and sunshine, and porpoises playing around our bow. We had a couple of charters with some time in between, and then a few days off to catch up on paperwork. Then somehow I got wind of the fact that the *Stephen Taber* was for sale.

Chapter 4

A Career Is Launched

The twenty-two-passenger schooner *Stephen Taber* was built in 1871 and was even older than the already decrepit Maine windjammers I had worked on. Constructed only a few short years after Lincoln was shot at Ford's Theatre, she was the oldest pure sailing vessel in the United States still in continuous operation. I was just thinking of going north to have a look into the ancient vessel when, to my horror, Terminal Finance Company was robbed again! I had to catch a plane home because this time it was an armed robbery. Upon arriving in Upper Darby, my office manager, Eleanor, still a bit shaken, described the crime. It had been late in the afternoon when a man walked in with a gun and pointed it at her, frightened them all half to death, and then got away with all of $75.

Eleanor, brave soul that she was, continued on, but the other girl, after being scared out of her wits, had quit. So we interviewed and hired a new secretary to round out the crew. I suggested to Eleanor, "Here, take this police whistle and if anyone comes and robs you again, when they leave, open the window and blast the whistle with gusto at the policeman who is almost always directing traffic down on the street." She thought it was a good idea and we would certainly catch the thief as he descended the stairs and exited the building.

Well, I thought, since I had already come so far north, I might as well take the time to drive up through Maine and look at the old *Stephen Taber*. Of course, this was the dead of winter—what a great time to be boat shopping, in Maine's deep freeze! The *Taber* was wintering in East Blue Hill, covered with snow and looking pretty forlorn. The owner, Cy Cousins, said apologetically, "You're a mite too late." He had accepted a deposit and was expecting the vessel to head up to the westward in the spring to cruise Long Island Sound. He told me right out that the price was $18,000 and then, with brazen Maine moxie, asked me what I would have paid for her. I said to myself, "These Down Easters are pretty darn direct." So I hemmed and hawed and kind of suggested $14,000. But, none of this really mattered now. I swung over to Sedgwick to see Captain Buds Hawkins, who had just completed the building of a fabulous new schooner, the *Mary Day*, for the Maine windjammer business.

I was charmed at this meeting because we were in Captain Buds' boatbuilding shop, standing in six inches of fresh wood shavings. A big barrel stove was radiating waves of heat that literally baked your front while your backside and feet froze. He said, "Join me for lunch?" When I gushed, "Sure," he took a hammer and came down with a thump on the top of that barrel stove, making a nice six-inch dent into which he threw a hamburger patty. The grease running down the sides soon burned off in a puff of smoke, and the hamburger, properly seared, was divided in half with a wood chisel.

What an incredible personality was this talented, vibrant sea captain! We became fast friends and chewed over all aspects of the windjammer business for the next three or four hours. Man, did I feel privileged! I explained what Cy Cousins and I had discussed. Captain Hawkins, a guy with a big open heart and a guru among the windjammer skippers, suggested that if I could baby the *Taber* along, and not spend too much money on her, sailing her slow and easy so she wouldn't fall apart, I might, in three years, get my money back. Since he had owned the *Taber* for years, he was familiar with all her failings. After lunch, I headed back to Philadelphia to be a businessman in my blue serge suit for another week or so. Then I high-tailed it for Florida where *Malabar* had six weeks of charters waiting.

Don and I felt like we were making progress, bringing in some money and paying some long-overdue bills. My skin was brown again and we managed through dumb luck to avoid all the coral heads. Don had tuned up the engine so the *Malabar* was running well, and we spent almost two months of blissful sailing in the Bahamas. When we returned to Miami, I went to the post office. There, I found two cables, three telephone messages, and several letters. Cy Cousins was calling and writing to tell me that the option on the *Stephen Taber* was running out and that he felt his buyer was going to renege. Next, was a carrot from the buyer—would I accept a half-interest in the *Stephen Taber* and run the boat for him in Long Island Sound that summer? Third, the finance company had been robbed yet again!

I called Cy Cousins first—a sure indication of where my heart lay. He explained that his buyer couldn't find a captain to run the *Taber* and his option was running out in a few days and he would be forfeiting his deposit of $2,000. Next, I called the prospective owner, who offered me a position as captain on the *Taber,* and a large block of stock in his company and a piece of his planned new schooner, which was then in the design stage. Last, I called Terminal Finance Company. This time, armed robbers had entered the office, made the girls lie down on the floor, and tied them up! Again, they made off with only a little over a hundred dollars since we would always hide all heavy-duty money in a particular envelope in the back of the files where the unwelcome would never be able to find it. When they left, my spunky manager, Eleanor, jumped up and grabbed the police whistle and blasted the alarm over and over out the open window. She told me later everyone in the street, police included, only looked up at her, wondering why that crazy woman was blasting that whistle and making all that noise. In the meantime the robber quickly escaped. I secured *Malabar*, jumped on a plane, and headed north again.

"Enough is enough," I decided as I crossed 69th Street from the Red Arrow Terminal, dodging the traffic in my tight necktie and blue serge suit. "Enough"—as I entered the Morton Building and climbed the stairs to Terminal Finance Company. Eleanor agreed that enough was enough, too, and said she didn't want to suffer through this entire trauma again. She wanted to retire. Then and there I made the decision to starve if I must, to struggle if I must, to be poor if I must, but that life is too short for such grief. My mom by now had passed and, since I had only myself to worry about, I could afford some reckless abandon. I was determined to go sailing! So, contacting Ellis Finance Company and Household Finance Company, two of my closest competitors, I said, "Look over the books and make me an offer." Three days later at HFC, we were signing papers.

Then, I telephoned Cy Cousins. It was good to hear his Down East Maine accent. "Ayyahh," he said in his no-nonsense manner, "The other fella' lost out, and I have his deposit. Where do you stand?"

"Well, Cy, it's getting late, spring is almost here, and I can't quite afford what we talked about before," I said, testing the waters.

He retorted, "It's the end of March, and ya ain't got time to dickaa! What's your offaaa?"

"Twelve," I blurted out.

"Done!" he said, and I headed for Maine.

With at least eight hours of driving and twelve thousand doubts resonating between my ears, I mulled it over endlessly. First, I was complimenting myself for nailing down such an exciting and thrilling summer business, then berating myself for the insanity of the whole thing. The old *Stephen Taber* was 68 feet on deck, with another 20 feet of enormous bowsprit. To me, she had damn near as much mystique as the *Constitution*. She's a vessel with a personality that infected everyone, a ship on which many a novice captain had cut his teeth.

Built as a North River brick schooner, the *Taber* had carried sand, cement, and brick to help build the city of New York. Good heavens, she was already old when the last century rolled over! And, I owned her! Every rotten timber! Every squeaky block! Every leak in the deck! A mammoth, schooner-rigged centerboarder, she carried two great anchors on the fore deck and had no power except a little push boat to bring her great bulk into the harbor. She was 22 feet wide, had two heads, and was fitted to carry twenty-two passengers. Her crew included the captain, mate, cook, and deckhand. "Well, by God, I've really done it this time," I said as I drove to Maine. "I just bought the old *Stephen Taber*!"

Back in the early 1960s, we were charging only $95 a week in the off-season and $125 in season, including food and linens. On my first cruise, I had the intimidating sum of six whole passengers, and three of those were referred by my friend and competitor, Captain Buds Hawkins. So I decided to invite some friends who not only would be fun to have aboard, but also would willingly help out with all the chores. That grand, incredible "Down Easter" Orvil Young and the talented folksinger Gordon Bok were among the welcome dignitaries who were my guests. I hired a nice plump cook named Bessie, a mate called Joel, and a deckhand, David, from Rockland. I invited Louise, a gal that stuck in my memory and who'd been a passenger on the *Mercantile* the prior season, to come to Maine and do my bookings.

It was a fantastic summer. I was enthralled with the old *Taber*, her sailing qualities, her mystique and majesty. In spite of the "go easy" warning by Captain Hawkins, I sailed the old girl hard. Too hard at times, I guess, but she seemed to love it. I know I did. I remember one time we were beating down the west bay in thick fog, light air, and almost zero visibility. I heard a roll of thunder and immediately perked up my ears. Something told me to douse the jib and let go the foresheet.

While I was slacking the fore, the nor'wester hit us hard and fast. The wind jumped out of the fog, increasing from 10 knots to 40 in a heartbeat, and it came roaring down from the northern mountains with a deluge of rain. My mate Joel started to slack the main sheet to the new breeze. I ran aft and spun the wheel and told him rather forcefully to cleat the sheet. This gave her a chance to point up and weathercock. The fat old *Taber* heeled down farther than you would like in a centerboarder and came up into the wind with her sails shaking and thundering and the rigging reverberating through the hull. When the squall had passed and things calmed down on deck, a portly passenger appeared at the main hatch with the tears streaming down her face and pleaded, "Are we saved?"

The old *Taber* leaked a mite when I would put the wood to her in a breeze. One day when I was too tired to pump in the evening, I woke up in the middle of the night, put my feet to the floor by my bunk, and found to

Sailing since 1871, the oldest pure-sail vessel in the U.S., the schooner Stephen Taber *struts her stuff. (author's collection)*

my horror that I was up to my ankles in seawater. There were my sneakers, tacking, and jibing, floating around between my legs. First things first—I went to the head! Upon finishing, I unlocked the door and pushed it open. At the same instant, a passenger, coming to do her thing, opened it from the outside. She was embarrassed, startled, screamed, and slammed shut the door, turning the button—the one on the outside securing the door from blowing open at sea—and ran back to her cabin. I was locked in the head in a sinking vessel at two a.m.! Ah well, I did have the knife that all sailors carry on my belt and was able to carve my way out of that situation and get to the pumps.

How I loved sailing the old *Taber*! It was an experience rich in learning, replete with music, Down East culture, and social interaction among the passengers. In short, it was the best thing I had ever done in my whole life. I was sold completely on the windjammer business. Besides, at the season's end, I had cleared close to $14,000 profit after paying only $12,000 for the vessel. Hallelujah! I thought I was in clover.

In preparation for an old-fashioned Maine winter, I tied the *Taber* up at Wayfarer Marine in Camden, storing everything in a good, dry barn, and draining all her systems. I then made arrangements for Gordon Bok to live on board, ship keep, write music, and drink coffee for the cold months. And his coffee could wash the hair off a dog. I knew the vessel would never freeze up as long as he had a pot of that atomic mud radiating on the stove. Waving goodbye to the old *Stephen Taber*, I packed up and, with a tear in the eye, headed off to Florida.

Somehow, the Bahamas now seemed like paradise lost. The islands had been recently handed over to the Bahamians, and the Brits were no longer in charge. Now, the only way to get things done with this new outfit was to slip payola to the authorities. There was always too much drinking, carousing, and artificial atmosphere. It all went against my grain. I know they call the islands "paradise," but I couldn't get the Maine people out of my head. They were honest, hardworking, forthright, a solid type of individual possessed of a true pioneer spirit. It was during that Florida winter of 1964 that I realized it was Maine that was the "true paradise."

Meanwhile, my attractive, easygoing office reservationist seemed to stay in my thoughts. We kept in touch and Louise, looking for a job, agreed to meet me in Coconut Grove, where she got an apartment and a position as a secretary. My friend Don found himself trying to develop a boat-repair and refrigeration business, and I seemed to find plenty to do locally, courting the secretary and chartering in home waters. Still, I was very anxious to throw my whole self into the schooner scene in Maine and, since the *Taber* was so old and so limited in capacity, I decided the only thing to do would be to build a new vessel just as Captain Hawkins had done.

This would be my life! I chose the design of a ship I had long admired and had even built a model of some years before—the schooner yacht *America*. A replica of the *America* would propel me into the upper echelon of the windjammer world and the classic yachting world in one grand jump. The *America* was large enough to provide a good living (hopefully) while allowing me the reward of doing what I loved. No one had attempted a replica of this famous vessel, but I would! I was ready! Although I was on the threshold of becoming licensed by the Board of Piloting in Nassau, ensuring a way of life in the Bahamas, I curtailed my chartering, abandoned the idea, and confined activities to Florida, where I'd be better able to work on plans and a prospectus.

I then hired Charlie Wittholz, a soft-spoken and highly experienced naval architect, to develop the design. Because he was reputed to have connections in Washington with the Coast Guard, I hoped that Charlie could assist me through the myriad of approvals from the government. By now, Bob Douglas, of Martha's Vineyard, captain and owner of the new square topsail schooner *Shenandoah*, and I had become friends. We spent many an engaging hour in *Malabar's* main cabin that winter discussing and cussing the Coast Guard bureaucracy. Bob had built his vessel speculating on eventual certification but, when the Coast Guard refused, he was buried in appeals.

Watching the pain that Captain Bob Douglas was going through, I began to realize there was no hope. Bob, to prove his vessel was sound and seaworthy, and in a desperate attempt to pry a certification from the Guard, ran a season giving free "Santa Claus" cruises. Even after Bob had proven the vessel's ability, certification was still not immediately forthcoming. I could see that kind of expense involved in my project was beyond me. If the Coast Guard would not come up with criteria for the certification of my plans, the magnitude of the debt I would incur from building the *America* would bury me. To no avail I argued that the newly certified schooner *Mary Day* had already blazed a trail over the route to licensing. But when I explored this issue, the bureaucrats told me she was considered "an administrative oversight."

The Coast Guard hassles, appeals, and conferences continued all through the winter months of 1965. Reams of plans, trips to Washington, volumes of paper, and thousands of bucks later, I came to a dead end. I got nowhere. I was at my wits' end. Then, one day, in an off-handed way, Captain Bob Douglas mentioned the old *Adventure*.

I said, "Hey, I know her. I was aboard her in 1957, chasing girls." Bob Douglas and I started discussing the attributes of the schooner *Adventure*. She had a certificate of inspection, a large passenger capacity, represented an established business, and in spite of her many desperate needs, she had great potential in other ways. We hashed over the news that Captain Newt—the same captain she had when I was aboard in 1957—had put her aground a year ago and swore he would run her no more. I wrote up a business prospectus indicating that with her capacity of forty-four passengers, she would be in a good position to support herself and earn a bit extra for rebuilding and refurbishing. I got all fired up about going after her that spring.

Before that, however, there would have to be a survey. The *Adventure* was then in Boothbay Harbor, Maine. Of course, it was March and colder in Maine than in Greenland. Of course, there had to be snow and ice all over everything. I went down the backward hatch—one designed so that it opens forward so the precipitation would conveniently cascade below—and found the floorboards lifted and a pump and an axe there; the pump to keep her afloat and the axe to chop away the ice so the pump could get at the frozen bilges.

The decks, the hatches, the ventilators, the mast boots, and the bottom planking all had the same malady—they were leaking. I must have been high on the euphoria of owning a Gloucester schooner since all I could see was this vessel rebuilt and gloriously beating to windward down Penobscot Bay. Here we go again! I started rationalizing all the reasons why buying this old schooner really did make sense. So she drew 14 feet of water and there was only 9½ at low tide going into Camden Harbor. I could wait until half tide. So her rig was cut down; in time, I would completely rerig her. So she leaked profusely; I would caulk her old hull up as "tight as a tick."

I placed the fateful call to Don Hurd, business manager for Yankee Schooner Cruises, the company that owned the schooner. "Hello, Don, this is Jim Sharp.... [pause]... Is the *Adventure* for sale?" Of course, I knew it was, as they had no captain for the coming season. I was also aware that the three partners who owned the schooner had not spoken to each other in over a year. As a result, the vessel was suffering. We started to dicker and after the smoke cleared away, I had a verbal agreement at $18,000.

My God, now I owned *two* old leaky schooners in Maine! It immediately occurred to me that I couldn't run both at the same time. What's more, the latest purchase was a 134-ton vessel and my sail license was limited to 100. I could not even run her without an upgrade in tonnage, and that took a year of sea time to satisfy the Coast Guard! I should have had my reckless head examined. Instead, sailing on cloud nine, I went back to Florida to get my affairs in order. I was moving to Maine and going sailing, come hell or high water!

How much could I get done in a month? Well, the flies had no chance to land on me over those thirty days of April. I put *Malabar* up for sale. I advertised and sold her in only a few weeks. I persuaded Louise to marry me and come to Maine. I contacted Orvil with a proposal to go partners in the *Taber*. I framed a proposal for a captain and cook for the *Taber* and tentatively approached the mate of former years who had never been a captain but possessed a sail license sufficient for the *Adventure* to return as her erstwhile first mate. With all this done, I packed a trailer with my sailing skiff, tools, and all manner of equipment I thought I would need in the windjammer business, and loaded my station wagon to the roof.

The *Adventure* had spent the winter in cold storage at Boothbay Harbor, so my first chore was to tow her to Rockland, where most of her gear was stored. I rented a little house on Amesbury Hill in Rockport and started to think in terms of a wedding. Then I got the brilliant idea of anchoring the *Adventure* in the middle of Rockport Harbor and accommodating the wedding guests on board the schooner. This put a little more pressure on my spring schedule, but it sounded very alluring to the gang of friends who would be attending the ceremony.

I then went to have a long, serious discussion with Orvil Young. If there was anyone in this world I would without hesitation approach as a partner, Orvil was that man. It wasn't long before I offered him a 50 percent share in the *Stephen Taber*. Conservative in the old Maine way, Orvil said he would have to "mull it over." I thought it best not to press him at the moment and turned my attention to the *Adventure*.

The only way I knew to get the schooner from Boothbay to Rockland was to hire a small oil transporter called *William McLoon* to tow her. I hired a local high-school kid to help, and we went to Boothbay to ready the schooner. When the *McLoon* arrived, we made fast the hawser, dropped our lines, and were soon underway. At the wheel, gazing over the great expanse of deck, feet and yards of it stretching by what seemed like a mile up to the shapely bow, I stood euphoric. She had come to life for the first time at my hand. *Adventure!* With emotions soaring, my fist tightly wrapped around the solid spokes of the wheel, I proudly guided and she followed obediently.

The former owners of *Adventure* had a friend in the aluminum screen door business and, along with the many other nautical transgressions they showered down on this poor vessel, they had fitted each cabin with loose-paneled, noisy aluminum doors. Every time you slammed one of them, she would rattle her panels for ten minutes. They were horrible! I knew, with the myriad of things I had on my agenda, if there were doors on the cabins I would not take the time to build new ones. At the same time, I knew if there were no doors on the cabins, I would be forced into building new ones. I gave my crewman a screwdriver and instructions to take off each cabin door and bring it up on deck. With the appearance of each door coming out through the hatch, I promptly, gleefully, raised it over my head and without looking back, heaved it over the side.

By and by, the captain on the *McLoon* called me on the radio and said, "Hey, what in hell's going on back there? Why're you throwin' all them doors overboard?" When I explained, he said, "Well, hell's bells, save the rest of them for me and I'll take them off your hands." I told him that I didn't want to see them in the same county with me and continued sending them all to Davey Jones.

Once we tied up in Rockland, work began. We built new, matched, varnished wooden doors. We attacked the leaks in the deck and gussied-up the interior for our summer cruise passengers and wedding guests. Donald Hurd, upon hearing of the nuptials, gave me an old, upright, foot-pedal pump organ for the ceremony and for future use on the schooner! We naturally had to revamp some of the accommodations to make way for such a generous donation. I cut her capacity down from forty-four to thirty-seven, enlarging the main cabin and adding an extra head in the process.

I engaged some of my old high-school buddies to lug that old organ high up a long hill to the Bok outdoor chapel for our own unique ceremony. After the reception I bamboozled them into taking it, by small boat, back out to the *Adventure* anchored in Rockport Harbor. Rocking, rolling, straining, and hefting, they managed to get it aboard and stowed below into the new space provided. Then, at least half of the twenty-five or so guests who stayed aboard that night suffered in painful silence listening to the creaking and groaning of the old schooner as she rolled to the Penobscot Bay ground swell. Those who were awake had drunk little. Now they were slightly seasick and groaned about the lushes who, tanked up on champagne, were now snoring loudly in competition with the schooner's creaking and groaning.

The wedding was a grand success, but I had no time for a honeymoon just then and turned my attention to hiring a crew for the *Taber*. Orvil was having fits about leaving his job at the state liquor store, where he had benefits and security, and going instead into my apparently reckless scheme as a schooner captain. I desperately wanted him. For one thing, I knew Orvil was a master boatbuilder and I needed his expertise. I also needed his calm, deliberate approach, his honest Down East ways, and the intangible horse sense with which he was deeply imbued. Besides, his liquor store job represented a tremendous waste of his incredible talent. Although he did not as yet have a captain's license, he exuded confident ability and, without a doubt, he could do the job. His wife, Andrea, was on my side and put the pressure on him with her subliminal female silence. Finally, Orvil became my partner in the ownership and operation of the old *Stephen Taber*. I cheered!

With both boats safely in Camden, we kept the name Yankee Schooner Cruises for our business, hoping for some recognition by past passengers. I had already tentatively hired a captain and his wife for the *Taber*, a captain-cook combo who were friends from my charter connections in Florida. They were anxious to get started with their new Maine experience and, when I called and told them about Orvil, they were getting packed to come north. It was a little awkward as they digested the fact that Orvil would be sailing with them as mate. I assured them he was a great guy and they would love him as I did.

When I had approached the former mate on *Adventure* to sign on for another year, he groused and growled, but was finally persuaded to be the legal captain. He was, however, to sail as mate for all practical purposes. His captain's license would enable me to get my sea time this season and satisfy the bureaucracy. I made the proposal attractive enough and he, with some reservation, agreed. I made it very clear, however, that he understand from the get-go, I was going to sail the old schooner strictly my way. He was a good worker and he accepted his position aboard without further complaint. My old reliable second mate from *Taber* days, David Wheaton from Rockland, enthusiastically signed on to the *Adventure* as well.

Things were coming together, at least for the moment. Having long since forgone a honeymoon, Louise would cook with a helper named Rose. By the end of May, the schooners were mostly fitted out, and we moved the *Adventure* into Camden Harbor on the top of the tide and slid into our berth at Wayfarer's shipyard where the lineup consisted of *Adventure*, *Stephen Taber*, and Captain Hawkins' *Mary Day*. Our other competitors in those days were the *Mattie* and *Mercantile* on the other side of the harbor and the three-master *Victory Chimes*, which sailed out of Rockland Harbor.

What a thrill it was to be in Camden, Home of the Windjammers, and a part of the whole scheme! I was young, blond, had a mustache, smoked a pipe, played guitar, had a great partner, enjoyed people, had lots of energy, a sense of history, was an enthusiastic sailor, and just loved these old vessels. By now, too, I had found an iron determination to make this a workable career.

"Hey, look out, *Adventure*," I said out loud, "here we come!"

Chapter 5

Total Immersion

Well now, who would ever have believed Mom Sharp's shy, freckled little kid with the awkward leg would have been embarking on his first cruise as captain of a Gloucester fishing schooner? But there I was, white-knuckled on a chilly spring day in 1965, working that engineless vessel with her 14-foot draft out of Camden Harbor on a necessary three-quarter tide. I was attempting to turn her around in her own 122-foot length, spinning that four-foot wheel and shouting a series of orders to a deck-load of young boys on a two-week working-training cruise.

Our great State of Maine wanted to charter *Adventure* for a summer training cruise for Mainestay, a program for underprivileged boys—boys from broken families, dropouts, and reform-school kids. Typical of the bureaucracy, the State wanted to come the first of August, the most expensive time and the height of our season. I was so aghast at the way the State squandered money that I turned them down and insisted they come at the beginning of the season when I could give them a large discount and keep the costs for the taxpayer to a dull roar. They finally agreed.

When the boys arrived, they were accompanied by three "counselors" who soon decided they were out for a free windjammer cruise and did very little counseling. My crew and I got stuck with the job of keeping the kids in line. In a firm voice, I handed down a series of strict laws right from the beginning: There would be no smoking except in designated places. There would be no profanity. There would be absolutely no fighting. Everyone would willingly stand a watch and work on the ship.

The old *Adventure* needed lots of fix-me-ups, and so she really made a great platform for this kind of training. We lined the kids up on the halyards and hove up that mainsail, foresail, jumbo, and jib. We taught them sailing nomenclature, basic marlinspike rope work, a smattering of navigation, chart reading, etc. They were very inhibited at the outset and most were quiet loners. An infraction of the rules would cost them privileges and a second offense would see them sanding the paneling in the main cabin or, worse yet, chipping rust from the anchor chain.

Consequences were something they didn't understand. We had two boys who started to fight, not once but twice. When it happened the second time, I grabbed them both by the shirt front, lifted them to their toes, jammed their heads together, read them the riot act, and put them both in the grungiest bilge under the floor in the main cabin with scrapers and scrubbers. Four hours later, they came up friends and were good buddies from then on.

We were two weeks on the training cruise, and the counselors did almost nothing. I screamed and hollered at the kids and put them through their paces until I was hoarse. I insisted on discipline and had to threaten bodily harm if they didn't listen. I got almost all of them working as a team by the second week, but the most rewarding part was the last day of the cruise. To see those boys interacting with each other, trusting each other, relying on each other for the first time in their lives and collecting names and addresses of newfound buddies they met aboard was my recompense. Some, as they departed, actually had tears in their eyes.

A lot of those boys came around the bend on that cruise, and I heard from many of them years later telling me it was one of the valued experiences of their lives. The old *Adventure* loved it, too, as we got layers upon layers of old paint off the beautiful fiddle-back and bird's-eye maple paneling in the main cabin. At first it resembled an archaeological dig, but when the grain of that beautiful original paneling started to peek through, the boys decided to take pride in their work. They became enthusiastic and went at refinishing that woodwork just to see the result, accepting the effort, not as penalty, but as reward for being a part of the creation of

Adventure *as she appeared during the last days of her fishing career with her deck stacked high with dories. Furled just ahead of the foremast is the "jumbo." The riding sail—the boomless, three-cornered sail on the mainmast—was much easier to handle than the conventional mainsail, dispensed with once the vessel's powerful Cooper-Bessemer engine was installed. (photo: John Clayton)*

the finished patina. It was a hard slog with those types, but in the end it turned out to be one of the most satisfying things I have ever done. I had to wonder what tribulation they found back home.

Adventure had needs galore. Her rig had been cut down in the last days of her fishing career because the men were all getting close to seventy years and didn't want a huge mainsail to manhandle. Then they sold her in '53, straight from her fishing career, and to the same gang I bought her from in 1964. Those owners had been operating a smaller vessel called *Maggie*, a schooner about the size of the *Taber*, which had sunk just before they acquired the *Adventure*. *Maggie* was in such poor condition that they abandoned her, but took her sails and rigging and put them, without alteration, right on the *Adventure*. As a result, the big schooner had only about 2,900 square feet of canvas! That was about half as much as she should have.

With her wings clipped, *Adventure* sailed like a half-tide rock until the wind piped up. With a breeze of over 20 knots, however, she would start to show her stuff. Although I knew I could expect great things from this hull, I should have had more sense than to push her in a hard breeze. But I couldn't help it. One arm hooked into the rigging, hanging on and watching her smoke along, parting the sea and hearing the bubbling, foaming quarter wake stretching all white and frothy far astern was definitely a narcotic.

One day, crossing Isle au Haut Bay, the breeze came on and the old *Adventure* surged up over 10 knots. She hadn't sailed that fast in years as the former captain never pushed her. We had our little yawlboat towing back aft on a long hawser. Since we had no davits to haul her out of the water, the yawlboat was vulnerable and, at this speed, she would soon be towed under. Sure enough, the water started pouring into her. I shouted to the mate to get the jib off the schooner and then got my loyal deckhand, David, to shinny down the yawlboat's tow line.

Like a monkey, he slithered down the line, was drenched by the little boat's bow wave, but managed to get one leg at a time up over the rail and climb aboard. While he was recovering from that superhuman effort of half falling and half rolling aboard, I tossed him a bucket. Then he bailed, throwing water in a great panic, dipping that bucket over and over as fast as he could, and he saved the boat! He got a solid round of applause from the passengers and crew for that dangerous mission. We managed to dry the boat out so quick, the engine never swallowed so much as a pint of salt water. When it was all over, I realized that none of us had even thought to suggest a life jacket to our hero.

That day, we were heading into Stonington to pick up a mess of lobsters for our weekly evening cookout. Once each cruise and a highlight, we would go to a deserted island for a "spiny bug bake" (schooner lingo for a lobster feast). We would lug about seventy-five or a hundred angry lobsters ashore and cook them in a big metal trashcan over an open driftwood fire, covering the pot with seaweed to keep in the heat. After about twenty minutes out would come the critters all red and steamy, spread out right on the rocks, with drawn butter, corn on the cob and/or potato chips, and a little white wine.

Earlier that morning, my hardworking galley slave, my wife, rising at 4:30, would have stoked up the wood fire in the stove and baked seven pies for dessert. At the same time, she would bake bread, rolls, and/or pancakes with the morning coffee, all from scratch, and all on a big, old, black, cast-iron, wood-burning stove with none of the fancy modern frills such as an oven thermometer. The pies would be kept warm over the stove and then later passed out in profusion on the beach once the gorging of the crawling things was accomplished. What a feast!

The cook's job was the hardest on the vessel, a lot harder than being captain. The captain, still at anchor, can, if the weather is wet or foggy, roll over and wait snoozing in his bunk half the day or so, until the weather clears. Not so the cook. Even if the passengers were up and noisy until midnight, or if the anchor dragged and woke everyone in the middle of the night, the cook still had to be up and at it on time. Passengers wanted their vittles. They would put up with leaky decks, small cabins, lack of running water, and cold bathing, but they had to eat. No excuses! And those vittles had to be first-class!

My poor, tired spouse and I agreed, "We want the best. Expense doesn't matter. The best!" We wanted everyone to gain poundage during their week aboard. I learned from the lack of food on the *Mattie* and *Mercantile* a few years back that when passengers go ashore and tell their friends about their windjammer cruise, the second question they are asked is, "Well, how was the food?" The answer offered should be, "Fantastic! I couldn't believe it. I gained ten pounds! And the cook did it all on a wood-burning stove!"

You sure can't buy advertising that good anywhere. I insisted we have gobs of second helpings ready for the devouring, so much so, that we had to throw food out at the end of the meal. Our motto: "Never, ever, run out of anything! Always have food left over at each table and always put extra desserts out at night so people can gorge themselves on a late-night snack. Have too much—stuff 'em! It's the only way."

That first summer of '65 was a wild one. The *Adventure* was so rough and needed so much to make her reasonably acceptable for our passengers that we were constantly cleaning, painting, and decorating, while also attempting to retain the nautical ambiance of a Down East schooner. It was work, work, work, on weekends, all week, and never-ending. Understanding the idiosyncrasies and personality of a big schooner was enough to tax my gray matter. Just getting comfortable bringing her home into Wayfarer Marine, Camden Harbor, was challenging. We had to dock among a bunch of fancy expensive yachts and parallel-park her in a 125-foot space. She was 230 tons displacement, and getting all that weight stopped within a few feet was quite a trick.

When we returned to Camden at the end of each cruise, I arranged with Orvil to have the *Taber* go in first, as she was much smaller than *Adventure*. Then we used his yawlboat, towing on the bow, while my yawlboat towed backwards on the stern. In this manner, we could stop the *Adventure* abreast of her berth, and finally move her sideways into her space.

Parking the *Adventure* was always an adventure. Not only was she heavy, but deep-draft fishing schooners don't like to move sideways. We never hit another boat, but it was close at times. As our final docking maneuver, my mate would throw the heaving line for the bow lines while I would toss the stern line from aft by the wheel. The heaving line, with its monkey fist—a special knot enclosing a weighted ball to project the line—had weight enough so it would carry quite far. One day, I tossed my heaving line a little too zealously as we approached our berth, and it carried right through the plate-glass window of the marina's wharf office and

Adventure *thunders across Penobscot Bay, reeling off 14 knots and loving it.*
(photo: Neal Parent).

landed—*kerr-plunk!*—on the secretary's desk. Barbara Dyer came roaring out from where she was working and shook her fist at me. I guess her desk was a bit glassy. I, with deep apology, paid for the window.

Unfortunately, in the height of the summer, dissension struck the *Taber.* Her hired captain decided that running these old boats on the coast of Maine was not his cup of tea after all, and he and his wife commenced to complain. Orvil, with expansive patience, tried to appease them, but to no avail. In the dead of night, they abruptly up and left. Luckily, Captain Bob Condon from South Brooksville, an original Down Easter, was waiting in the wings. He and Orvil could swap Maine lore, constantly charming the passengers with lively, tall stories, all told with a true Maine twang. However, now we had to find a cook. Andrea, Orvil's wife, was working at the bank to preserve some semblance of stability in the family finances and decided to take a week away from counting money and go to counting pancakes in the galley. This gave us a little time to hire another *Taber* cook.

Cooks, schooner cooks particularly, are a breed unto themselves and good ones are not easily found. Our replacement cook drank himself into oblivion and we found him swinging on the fore boom at two in the morning on sailing day, singing his head off. We sent him over the hill forthwith. Luckily, my good wife Louise dropped everything and volunteered to run over and do breakfast on the *Taber*. I then went to Rosie, Louise's co-cook, who was wrestling stacks of pancakes, and asked her to cook on the *Taber* for one week until we could find a replacement. She refused, saying that I would make her stay over there, and nothing I could say would convince her any differently.

It was then that I found out Rosie and my mate were kindling a little romance. No wonder she was refusing so adamantly. My wife and I agreed

Adventure's galley—a place for everything and everything in its place. (author's collection)

that in order to be absolutely fair about this, Louise would stay as cook on the *Taber* for half the week and, as I told Rosie, we would then switch so she would be off the *Adventure* for only two-and-a-half days at the tail end of the week. I felt we were bending over backwards to accommodate an important member of the crew.

Rosie didn't agree. When the two schooners met up in mid-week at Swans Island, Rosie refused to make the swap. I said, "Now, Rose, we have done all we can, and you are going to the *Taber*. That is an order! Ignore it and you are going home." She still refused, so I relieved her of her duties until I could put her ashore on an island with transportation. Now, with two schooners and only one cook, I was in a pickle. Upon mulling it over, we decided Louise had better stay and finish the week on the *Taber*, and I assured her I would work out something, somehow, on *Adventure*.

Back on the *Adventure*, despite my best efforts to control the situation, my unhappy cook Rosie started complaining to all the passengers and soon a thick and heavy cobweb of gloom settled over the decks. We had a passenger doing her second week. She was a game person with lots of imagination and a passion for the experience of schoonering. I went to her and begged her to cook for the rest of the week and I would refund her fare. She, out of loyalty, said she would agree if we found someone to help her. I next went to my loyal deck hand, David, and asked him to canvass the female passengers to seek help wherever, as I was desperate. He came up with an Indian woman who agreed to try the galley in exchange for her passage fare refund. We talked it over, and for their first meal they decided to prepare our delicious fish chowder for lunch, as it wouldn't be too hard to make and it would probably be a big hit. I went on deck, hove up the anchor, and got under way. The mate, with a sour face, jumped into the yawlboat and started her pushing at the stern of *Adventure*. Thus began what was to be one of the longest days of my life on the schooner.

The whole passenger complement was now buzzing with worries of no food, bad food, and an ogre for a captain. I stood stone-faced at the wheel and, as there was no wind, we pushed with the yawlboat all that day until we came into North Haven. Not one passenger on the ship would approach me. The noon chowder turned into a calamity. They had forgotten to add the fish and produced a potato soup! The mate was sullen and took Rosie's side. Things were becoming psychologically and gastronomically unglued. We had three overweight, elderly women passengers at a table in the galley loudly expressing their displeasure to all in earshot for miles around and expounding on how they were going to go ashore to have dinner. No doubt there would be no decent food fit to eat on this vessel tonight. Attitudes, temperament, and morale of passengers and crew were abysmal.

About four in the afternoon, while crossing Isle au Haut Bay, with my expression exuding chiseled determination, a young teenybopper, whom I had been kidding and who had been obviously having a blast of a trip, came up to me and said, "Captain, I wanted you to know that, in spite of everything, I'm having an awesome time and this is just the best vacation!"

I melted! Right there, I melted!

Conferring with the cooks as we entered the Fox Islands Thorofare, it was decided to cook the roast beef for supper. Everyone was very hungry, and the aroma of that beef, wafting out the hatches and across the deck, would be tantalizing. I anchored in North Haven, called the mate to bring the yawlboat to the gangway, and loaded aboard my mutinous cook with all her gear. The mate ran her ashore where they could say their goodbyes, with Rose all in tears.

I went down to the galley and slid in alongside the three big ones. The roast smelled divine. "Ladies," I said, "the yawlboat is ready to take you ashore!"

"Oh, Captain, what do you mean?"

I could almost hear them salivating from the delicate aroma of woodstove steer. Together they expostulated almost in a harmonious chorus, "We have decided to stay aboard for dinner after all, and we're looking forward to it very much!"

I responded, "All right, ladies, but there is a requirement that will be put on your attendance for the remainder of this voyage. I don't want to hear a ghost of a complaint from any one of you, not a suggestion of complaint, or you will be taking all your meals ashore. This is my only warning!"

They knew I was serious and were on their good behavior for the remaining two days. After that week, my wife continued to do all the cooking by herself for the rest of the season on *Adventure*, but we had to hire five more cooks for the *Taber*. A new one almost each week! It was a terrible trial, but I said to Orvil, "Don't worry. Someday we will look back at this merry-go-round of weekly cooks and get a good laugh!" In spite of everything, we just could not locate a good one. Orvil's wife, Andrea, leaving the bank, took over the following year. She soon took her place among the fleet as the guru of the galley. Thank goodness!

Chapter 6

Musical Spars and a Bad Surprise

Thanks to her cut-down rig, when the wind was light, the old *Adventure* was slow as a toad swimming in a bucket of tar. Captain Buds Hawkins on his new schooner *Mary Day* would sail rings around me. He used to say, "The winner buys the drinks, 'cause the loser feels bad enough already!" We would often sail to the same harbor and frequently raft up together for a big-time hootenanny. I would bang on the guitar, Buds would saw fiddle tunes on the violin, and passengers would gather around and belt out the oldies. Buds' two young boys would always insist I sing "Barnacle Bill the Sailor" (a benign version), a favorite for them. In spite of the fact that the old schooner was kind of rough, '65 was a very successful season and come September we tied the vessels up to the wharf at Wayfarer for the long, cold winter.

I knew I was asking for a pile of work, but I had to somehow restore the rig. There was no other way. Here was a magnificent Grand Banker that sailed so poorly only because she was starving for more sail. Her hull was beautifully sleek, with a fine entry and long run, deep, and a well cutaway forefoot. She should sail! At the end of the '65 season, I stowed the sails for the winter and went to the shipyard in Rockland and had the masts taken out with their antiquated steam crane. We lay the mainmast down on blocks at the yard and secured the foremast overboard alongside the hull. Then I took the little yawlboat and pushed the schooner back to Camden, tied her up, and returned to Rockland to tow the foremast back.

My idea was to play "musical spars." I would purchase a new 92-foot mainmast, which was about the size she had when new. Then I would put the old mainmast, 77 feet of it, into the fore hole. Next, I'd whittle the old foremast into a main boom of almost 60 feet, and the old main boom into a 42-foot main gaff. I planned to store the old main gaff until I someday could make it into a topmast. There was an old greasy, abandoned set of launching ways in Camden and, at high tide, I pulled the foremast up as far as I could and let the tide fall. Then I hitched my old station wagon to that mammoth mast with a one-inch nylon line, rove it through a snatch block, took a hitch on the spar, and put the pedal to the metal.

The car surged ahead, the nylon line stretched out all a-humming and vibrating until the wagon poked her front bumper into the dirt bank at roadside and stopped dead. The old spar came zinging up about 15 feet on the greased timbers. I backed and shortened the line and took another hitch, repeating, the Chevy groaning and complaining, over and over until I had her all above the tide, the whole two-and-a-half-tons of her. That spar was 18 inches in diameter, over 70 feet long, and quite rotted where the ironwork went through the masthead. Had I known how awfully poor that masthead was, I might not have sailed her so hard. Naw, I would have done it anyway! Eventually, I would whittle her down to become the new main boom 12 inches in diameter at the middle with a taper at both ends. This should have been a daunting task but, for some strange reason, I couldn't wait to "have at it."

Then, I met Cappy. What a fortuitous bookmark in my life! He came hobbling down through the parking lot on two crutches and stood there watching me saw a slash scarf in the buffalo rail where the anchor had chafed it thin. I was so intent on my work that I hardly noticed this powerful man with a sculptured face and aquiline nose. He got my attention when he grinned and spoke, "Hey," he said, "that ain't no way to put a splice in that buffalo rail. That should be a proper ship's locking scarf."

I said back to him, returning the grin, "If you are so damn smart, come up here and do it yourself!" And he did! And he worked with me for almost fifteen years. Erland Quinn—Cappy—was of island stock, tough as nails, had always built boats, and possessed that old kind of Maine hardworking grit which was fast disappearing in this couch-potato world. A couple of years prior to that meeting, Cappy had had a devastating head-on accident with a Greyhound bus in fog, which landed the engine of his car in his lap, right on top of both his legs. The docs said he would never walk again, but they didn't know to whom they were talking. As he gradually got stronger, I gave him more and more to do. He loved it and, in spite of his limping around, could do more in a day than most could in two.

We made quite a pair! He would be hobbling on one end of a big piece of three-inch planking, and I would be struggling with *my* bum leg at the other. We limped and wrestled those planks, working together through the freezing winters on endless schooner projects, and he would go captain fancy yachts in the summers. I always said if I could choose a grandfather, it would be Captain Erland Quinn, a tough Eagle Islander who used to say, "The Lord ain't made a day so cold that I couldn't work hard enough to stay warm." And we had some cold ones in Maine—and I loved that man.

During the winter of 1966, with Orvil's expertise, Cappy's sage advice, and a young guy hired to help me, I proceeded to tear out the *Adventure's* break beam—the main beam in the deck—and the decking around it both fore and aft. There were too many leaks, too much rot in the decks, and something had to be done. This was the deck she was built with in 1926 and it had lasted for thirty years of fishing, enduring gales of wind and monumental seas and the slopping of tons of fish and fishing gear all over everything. The deck had a right to leak after all that! So, redeck, recaulk, and renew the beams, and all that kind of stuff. Simple, huh?

The rain and snow were falling on my tools, so we built a plastic house over the opening in the deck. This was an innovation. No one in Camden had ever tried this one before, perhaps because sheet plastic was only recently invented. It worked so well—keeping the tools dry, breaking the wind, warming things on deck, and shedding the snow—that I continued the structure until it reached bow and stern.

I lay down new planking on the main deck forward and got out a new break beam, a 25-foot oak timber almost a foot square with about an eight-inch crown. After I ran it through the enormous ship's bandsaw over at the lumber mill, I dragged it with my venerable old station wagon on the snow to the top of the hill above the wharf, gave it a push over the brow, and down it tobogganed to the parking lot below. We put a dollop of snow on the rail of the schooner as a lubricant, muscled one end of the timber to the rail, slid and shoved her aboard, then fit and bolted the new break beam across the middle of the deck. Now it was *only* a matter of replacing, spiking, bunging, caulking, paying, planing, and finishing the rest of the decking fore and aft of the beam.

I ordered my new mainmast from the West Coast. It was designed at 92 feet long, 20 inches diameter, and was shipped from Oregon through the Panama Canal to Boston, where Pigeon Hollow Spar Company had a 100-foot-bed wood lathe. They turned it, put the taper to it, and shipped it by tractor-trailer to Rockland. It was heralded as the largest mast to arrive there in 50 years, and it stuck way out in front and way out in back of the truck with red flags flapping everywhere. It was a beautiful stick, with hardly a season check and good, solid heartwood all the way aloft.

Now, I had to get to work and lay out the sail plan and rigging diagram, and develop all the details to restore *Adventure*'s rig to its original grandeur. I researched the Gloucester fish boats six ways from Sunday, through the Mystic Seaport Museum, the Peabody-Essex Museum, and the historical societies of Gloucester and Cape Ann. My new mainsail would have 3,150 square feet of number four canvas duck, more than the entire sail plan of the old *Maggie*. This would be the biggest mainsail in the U.S. In this part of the world only the Canadian *Bluenose* had a larger one. *Adventure* would have close to 5,000 square feet in all four lowers. Bohndell, old-time sailmakers of Rockport, would make the new sails plus all stays, shrouds, sails, and related rigging. I laid the two masts together and proceeded to measure up for the ironwork and build the wooden crosstrees, trestle trees, bibs and bolsters, cut the tenon, and treated the new wood with linseed-oil preservative.

Going back to the main boom project in the early spring, I snapped lines on the old 18-inch-diameter foremast and cut into her with a broadaxe and adze until she was 12 inches square, straight and true, and almost 60 feet long and tapered at each end. Then, I skillsawed off the corners till she came to eight sides, adzed off the eight corners to sixteen sides, draw-shaved off those corners to thirty-two, planed off those corners to sixty-four, and then planed it round. Alas, next I got bursitis in my shoulder! Then, grabbing the aspirin bottle, I did the same procedure over again on the old boom until I, with help from my crew, shaped the new 42-foot gaff and got busy sawing out the jaws and fitting the ironwork on these spars. Meanwhile, Orvil was hard at work chinking up the *Stephen Taber*'s deck. I remember saying at one point, "Orvil, isn't it too bad that both Bob Douglas and Buds Hawkins have new schooners and they miss all this fun?"

Where all the energy came from, I can't imagine. I slaved for days over those two enormous masts laying side-by-side at the shipyard in Rockland, fitting the ironwork, bolting up gear on the mastheads, applying the new rigging, and then excitedly pushed the schooner down from Camden to Rockland. There, under the old steam-driven crane at the shipyard, my new masts would be stepped. My heart was in my throat when the bang-crash crew in the yard picked up my new mast weighing out at three-and-a-half tons. The mast was slick with oil and grease preservative, and they swung it out over my new deck without giving proper allowance to the stretch in the strop that was holding the mast. It fell almost four feet when the line stretched out but, incredibly, did no damage. We lowered it gently to its place on top of the keelson and, just before it landed, I reached in my pocket and threw my last thirty-five cents into the mortise socket. I knew it was traditional to put a gold doubloon under the mast of a new vessel to ensure lucky voyages, but who could afford such an extravagance after a winter of expensive outfitting?

I held my breath as the crane operator next lifted the foremast. You would think he would have learned about the stretch in the strop. No way; he only half learned. That mast came down two feet onto my deck water tank and created a great dent in the shape of the top, reducing its capacity by many gallons.

Spring of 1966 finally came, and the pressure of our cruising schedule was looming large before us. Wayfarer Marine then dropped a bomb on our docking arrangements when they emphatically hinted we should find a different place from which to run that summer. Although we would still be welcome in the winter, they wished to reserve the entire wharf to their expanding seasonal yachting business.

We arranged to meet with the Camden selectmen, and they immediately turned down our request for summer dockage. They unanimously framed their opinion: "The schooners do nothing for Camden. They take the people away from the town so the tourist dollars are not spent here." What craziness! I couldn't believe their attitude since the schooners are the major part of a driving force of what puts this town on the map and gives it its character. Captain Hawkins, Captain Orvil Young, and I had to petition the townspeople to arrange to berth us at the public landing.

I was elected to stand up at the town meeting, before the entire assembly of town folk, in the beautiful, Victorian Camden Opera House. There I described the dockage scheme we had cooked up.

If the town would furnish wharf, floats, and dredging, we would compensate the town with docking fees. That revenue would pay back the cost of the project in eight years. The money we would pay, plus what excess the municipality could collect by charging visiting yachts mooring fees, could go far to stuff the town coffers. What's more, in the future, revenues would be available to fund harbor projects. Most importantly, the plan would allow the schooners to continue to sail from Camden Harbor and enable the town to retain its title as "The Home of the Windjammers."

As we suspected, our petition was approved with an overwhelming majority. The townspeople were very much in favor. The dredging was done and the moorings arranged. *Adventure* moved to the center position, *Taber* rafted along inside, and the *Mary Day* on the outside. What a spectacular sight for the little village of Camden. These three big schooners were majestically gracing the most prominent position of our pretty little harbor, right there at the foot of Library Park! The new arrangement was not only functional, but also photographically perfect.

Adventure was the first to grace the new mooring arrangement. She looked like a white swan! I had taken the time to grind off the old, horrible, gooey, rough, and scaly black color she had in thick layers on her planking. Then I gave her a couple of coats of fresh, smooth white. It made her look even longer and far sleeker. She looked positively regal dressed in white. It definitely accented the high noble bow and long sweeping sheer.

Elmer Collemer, one of the last master boatbuilders in Camden, had worked most of the winter and had almost completed a new 16-foot yawl-boat for me. She was some handsome! The old yawlboat that had come with the *Adventure* had a Chevrolet engine that had been underwater too many times, and the boat was too big and heavy to conveniently haul out on my newly designed stern davits. I needed something more powerful, lighter, and with diesel dependability. I chose a design developed by Captain Bob Douglas, a beautiful model with a plumb stem and traditional wineglass stern, one that would hopefully skip along the water while the schooner was making seven knots and that we could haul out without dumping. Now, that was a real trick in design.

The yawlboat, even with her modest 68 horsepower, was a very necessary, integral part of the schooner's equipment, equally as important as the mainsail or masts. She would help to get us out of trouble, provide power in a calm, and carry passengers ashore for necessaries and/or emergencies. The yawlboat's wiring, painting, finishing, and tuning were still on the "to do" list, but she was close to ready.

I was hard at the other "to-do" list, stretching the new rigging, hanging spars, and doing a multitude of final outfitting chores, when my summer crew arrived. Mark would be my mate and brothers Pete and Mike, my crew. One fine spring day, they climbed over the rail with duffel bags and a spring-loaded enthusiasm to go to it. Fine boys, each and every one of them. I was so overwhelmed with a literal boatload of things to do that I hardly gave them time to stow their gear before putting them to work at a thousand different projects.

We worked like dogs until the passengers arrived at the gangway. I remember that just four days before our first sailing, I was in the old shed sawing out the jaws for the main boom from a 10-foot-long piece of three-inch oak, and, as I was wrestling this enormously heavy piece of timber by myself, shoving it through the big ship's bandsaw, Freeman Brewer, one of the yard crew, came through the door, asking me what on earth I was doing at this late hour. I tried to explain in as few words as possible and he, knowing my sailing date, just walked away shaking his head and saying, "Jim, you'll never make it!"

I said, "Freem, you might be right."

We made it! But our sails were lying in a pile on deck. Monday morning, after a big breakfast, I announced to the passengers, "Hey, how many of you good people have ever had the chance to bend sail on a bona fide Gloucester fishing schooner?" They knew there was no choice if they wanted to go sailing. But they were good sports and when I kidded them, prodded them, egged them on, all turned to and they followed with verve. With the mainsail bent on, we then taught them to furl it—a harbor furl—neat and precise as a freshly ironed shirt.

Though enlisting our passengers to help out might have been a little unorthodox, most everyone thought it was an exciting thing to do, and it made each of them feel like a genuine part of the crew. The more schooner chores we provided for our passengers, the better they liked it. Duties included cutting up vegetables for the galley, swabbing the deck, coiling lines, furling sails, and even mundane things like taking a trick at the wheel.

Out on the bay, we all ganged up on the halyards and raised that new 3,000-square-foot mainsail and, wow, was that thing big and some powerful! The new sail plan really made the vessel go. I was "jumping up and down" excited and looking forward to racing my good friend and competitor, Captain Hawkins, on the *Mary Day*.

It was a wonderful summer, that summer of '66, full of passionate sailing and schooner lore. Orvil and I had both gotten our Coast Guard license endorsements, and Andrea, his wife, and Louise, my wife, were cooking. We had a great, young, giggly mess girl named Pam Seekins, who had a wonderful way of conning help from everyone around her. She made everyone laugh with her shy but infectious and carefree titter and added much to the spirit in the galley.

"All hands—gang up and give me a decent harbor furl!" (photo: William MacDonald)

My crew was as agile as monkeys and scampered everywhere about the ship, from aloft in the rigging to "alow," cleaning the heads. Even without topmasts, the *Adventure* was a majestic sight sailing down the bays with that huge mainsail. She was in proportion now, and the new mainmast made all the difference. *Adventure* was the tallest thing around. Gingerly, on that first outing of the new season, I headed for Eggemoggin Reach and the only bridge anywhere on the coast under which we had to sail. The Deer Isle bridge was an 85-foot-high fixed span and, if my planning was accurate, *Adventure* would have just enough clearance to pass beneath. I was going to try it cautiously and with great trepidation at the lowest part of the tide next morning.

That night, we lay anchored just around the corner from the bridge in Bucks Harbor. I tossed and turned in my bunk in restless sleep, suffering a wild and all too vivid nightmare. Just as we were committed to pass under the bridge with only inches to spare, a monstrous oil truck came down the hill and started to climb the road to the center span. Both he and my schooner would obviously arrive in the center at the same moment! Would the weight of that truck make any difference in the height of the bridge? Would she sag down in the middle? I woke up just as we struck and my new masts came crashing down on deck, likely killing dozens. I was in a cold sweat and shaking all over!

The next morning when we went through for real, we first had to scandalize the mainsail, i.e., lower the gaff because it stuck up above the masthead, and one of my crazy crew volunteered to sit on the main masthead with a yardstick to measure our clearance exactly. I was sure we would make it, but the illusion as we approached had everyone on edge. Sure enough, as soon as we were committed and there was no turning around, just as in the dream, a tractor-trailer came up the ramp to cross the bridge. We had plenty of room at this tide, but our measurement indicated that it would be damn close at the top of the high water. With my imagination going wild, I started to mull over an innovative design for a fitted topmast that could easily slide down and be temporarily housed when sailing under that Deer Isle bridge.

As I became more fascinated by the *Adventure*, I resolved to begin re-searching her history. Soon I went poking around the junk shops in Glouc-ester, gathering lore, and I decided it was time to visit the old boat's fishing captain, Leo Hynes. He was still quite active and lived outside Boston, in Melrose. After researching some of his escapades, I went knocking at his door. The door opened and this stocky, commanding figure stood before me. I hesitantly said, "Hello, I'm Captain Jim Sharp, owner of *Adventure*."

Leo's face lit right up and he bellowed in a voice that was obviously quite used to giving orders, "Hey, Lil, put on the coffee pot. Captain Jim is here!" Leo knew all about what I was doing with his old vessel and encap-sulated my hand with two enormous, rough, strong paws with ten grip-ping fingers that conveyed an eager acceptance of this stranger coming through the door. The coffee pot went on the stove and Lil, with a heart as big as a house, served scones. The couple gave me an overwhelming welcome I'll never forget. They were Newfoundlanders and the finest kind of "salt-of-the-earth" folk.

The old captain then sat me down and, in an off hand, quiet, and modest way, regaled me with great tales of his experiences on the *Adven-ture*. The telling went on and on into the late evening, yet it was obvious we were only scratching the surface of his experiences. Then he told me of a journalist named John Clayton who had sailed on *Adventure* six times to the Grand Banks on fishing trips and recorded everything on film—both movies and stills—while also keeping a diary of every happening.

Leo said, "Captain Jim, you've got to see that stuff. I'll arrange it!" It gradually dawned on me that the *Adventure* had an extensive and in-credible history to tell the world. It seems that as a result of the uncanny expertise of Captain Leo, she caught more fish, made more money for her owners, and was more successful than any vessel of any type until her retirement in 1953. Leo made more than three-and-a-half million dollars in fish with this vessel in only twenty years, and that was back when a mil-lion was a lot of bucks! My old boat had been the all-time high-liner of the Gloucester fishing fleet!

Suddenly I found myself energized in a way that I had not expected. I had to see those films! I had to record what this unpretentious but powerful man was quietly saying. I had to write it down and preserve this history for the public. I got the names of the few, very few, fishermen still alive that had sailed with Leo. When I could find them, I contacted them for interviews. I started collecting photos and artifacts to display aboard.

Wherever I went, the name *Adventure* kept coming up, time and time again. Leo and Lil welcomed me over and over with my tape recorder and, after we had a Scotch or two, or sometimes three, the stories would pour forth. Leo had dumped enough seawater out of his boots to fill an ocean. Yet, when he told a story, it was straight from the shoulder. He didn't have to embellish or exaggerate to make it interesting or to make your hair stand!

During one visit, Leo took me to John Clayton's for an after-dinner slide and movie show. We sat in the recreation room in John's basement, and he and Leo started to swap stories. John kept getting up to get another drink. The stories became more magnified. We were looking at the slides and soon some of them were upside down. John quickly changed them at first. Then, after a few more toots, he didn't bother to change them at all. We just cranked our necks off sideways and went on as if nothing was out of the ordinary. Then he showed us the movies. Here were reels and reels full of magnificent color frames, colossal real-life stuff of my old vessel fishing on the Grand Banks! I was on the edge of my seat—those films were an unbelievably exciting record of dory trawling, an industry that had spanned hundreds of years and was the backbone of the economy of New England.

I was at about the high point of my excitement when our projectionist forgot to connect the take-up reel, and the film deposited itself—hundreds and hundreds of feet of it—on the floor. I was heartbroken for fear the priceless film would be ruined. It was to be many years before I ever asked to see that film again.

Chapter 7

Love Affair

Gloucester fishing schooners were rigged to sail hard and stand all the North Atlantic could dish out, summer and winter. Their hulls were shaped to hold a hundred thousand pounds of fresh fish, and to speed the catch to market. Since the first vessel home would get the most attractive price for her catch, a vessel the size of *Adventure* would crowd on about seven or eight thousand square feet of sail. They carried a huge jib topsail, an enormous fisherman's staysail and gaff topsails on both masts.

A schooner's rig was called "bald headed" when no topmasts were fitted, and this more conservative rig was typical in the winter months. It was snug and low, adapted for the terrible gales that prevailed through the cold winter on the Grand Banks. I, however, was simply a summertime sailor. I'm not conservative when it comes to sailing and, even after playing musical spars and the addition of a proper-sized mainsail, I desperately wanted all the kites. After all, *Adventure* was still, technically, sailing under a "winter rig."

Topsails or no, the old girl could still step as soon as the breeze came on, and one day back in 1967, she showed her pedigree to the newly created yacht *America II* in the filming of the reenactment of the first America's Cup Race in 1851. Rudy Schaefer, of the beer company, grabbed hold of my idea to build a replica of *America* and he was able to do it with plenty of money and pizzazz. He could afford it far better than I. He had the boat constructed in strip-planked fashion using kiln-dried oak, a non-traditional method, but a beautiful result. That is, it was fine until after the

Adventure Sail Plan

1. Mainmast	11. Leach	21. Peak Halyards
2. Main Topmast	12. Clew	22. Throat Halyards
3. Main Topsail	13. Foot	23. Stays
4. Main Topmast Staysail	14. Tack	24. Shrouds & Ratlines
5. Main Gaff	15. Luff	25. Chainplates
6. Main Boom	16. Foremast	26. Bow
7. Mainsail	17. Foresail	27. Stern
8. Throat	18. Fore Gaff	28. Davits for Yawlboat
9. Head	19. Jib	29. Starboard Side
10. Peak	20. Jumbo	

launching, when all that dry oak started to soak up water, swell, and go all out of shape, eventually jamming her rudderpost and creating havoc in the deadwood and keel.

A Hollywood movie company blew like a tornado into Maine, chartered most of the windjammer fleet for background, and proceeded to re-create the famous race at Cowes, England, where, in 1851, the yacht *America* outran the fleet and brought home what would ever after be known as the America's Cup. The movie would be called *Sail to Glory!* The *Adventure* played the part of the British schooner-yacht *Brilliant*, one of several British contestants. The *Brilliant* happened to have been a three-master, but that mattered not a hoot to Hollywood, and new nameboards were screwed over *Adventure*'s name. Our job was to sail hard and fast while being defeated by the *America II* which, if necessary, would use her big engine.

Now the movie company had, from the hodgepodge of Camden schooners, matched up eight vessels about as different as political opinions, each with their own diverse capabilities in terms of speed, sailing qualities, and crew ability. Optimistically, they lined us up like ducks in a row for the start. Of course, it was only a very few minutes before we looked like a pack of wild ducks after a buckshot blast. The *Mary Day* and I immediately ranged way ahead of the fleet. The director couldn't get his "take" and called us all back for a restart. The plan now called for the *America II* to come from behind and sail gloriously through the fleet, passing us all with ease.

It took almost an hour to tack and jibe all those schooners and get back in line. For the next take, the *America II* was to run her engine and barge the line quickly. They missed their cue, however, and again we scattered. The director's voice came over the radio, "Slow down the *Adventure*. . . more power on *America*. . . slow down the *Adventure*."

What a fiasco! I tried to slow down by pinching upwind, but that put me way to windward. Then, when I ran back down on a broad reach to rejoin the fleet, I had a snoot-full of headway and zipped past everyone else like they were anchored. The third take was the same pattern, except this time the old sou'wester picked up on the flood tide and it started to blow a right smart breeze. The director got on the radio and called for more and more power on *America II* until her captain retorted, "She's wide open now. I've got no more." Now, in this little "breeze o'wind," the *Adventure* really started to strut and we were reeling off the knots in spite of the fact we had no topsails.

The orders again came over the radio, "Slow down the *Adventure!*" But this time, knowing where I'd end up, I decided the hell with it. The old girl surged up over 10 or 12 knots and, to the gross indignation of the director, the *Adventure* passed the *America II* with all the drama and hoopla of the original Cup races! Black smoke poured from under *America's* stern, confirming that her engine was wide open the whole time. Then, the director's voice dripping with frustration, came again over the radio, "Slow down the #*^## *Adventure!*" It was transmitted with so much insulting vehemence, I calmly answered, "Sorry, Cap, they never did put any brakes on these Gloucester schooner-boats!"

After the brief experience with moviemaking, knowing the *Adventure* could go even faster, I invented a temporary, tryout-kind of topsail. I took an old yacht jib, cut it in half, and sewed it together into a funny-looking triangular excuse for a sail. I tried setting it, using the old main gaff from the former rig for a top mast, but the result looked more like a worn out shopping bag than a topsail. So, I got a spruce tree and whittled out a full-sized topmast, 42 feet long, fitted and properly shaped, and with all the mechanical gear to enable me to strike it when going under the Deer Isle bridge. Then I had Bohndell build us a properly shaped topsail. At last! The result was so beautiful that I decided to complete her outfit by adding a fisherman staysail.

Not to be outdone, Captain Buds Hawkins now put topmasts on the *Mary Day*, and she just looked exquisite with all that sail. She was faster, too. To keep up with Hawkins, I hoisted an old oversize jib on my triatic stay—the wire support that ran between the two masts. In effect, this sail was a main topmast staysail, a sail that was way up high where the wind was and, sheeting back to the very stern, it pulled like a mule in light air. Everything was fine until one day I passed the slow-moving *Victory Chimes*, aka the *Jingler*.

For a variety of reasons, I had become a thorn in the side of the *Jingler's* skipper, and on this day, I guess the old captain was still angry about our latest disagreements. He took one look at the *Adventure*, called the Coast Guard, and reported me for having an *illegal sail*. Sailing vessels baffled the Guard. They knew not what they wanted for criteria for certification of wind ships, and had no idea what this new animal called a main topmast staysail was all about. There were no sail plans for these old schooners and the Coast Guard manual had no definitions for this kind of sailor lingo, so my sail was not illegal, just unknown. Still, they had to justify their existence, so they wrote me a letter saying: "Thou shalt add no additional sails to the *Adventure's* plan unless so authorized by the Officer in Charge, USCG."

The *Adventure* now carried just over 6,000 square feet of canvas, and what a sailing machine she was! "Exhilarating," "awe-inspiring," "rousing" would be apt words to describe the feeling that would envelop me when we would push out of Camden Harbor on the first sail of the season. What a thrill to call out the gang of crew and passengers to turn to and heave on our halyards and hoist that vast mainsail. After a long, cold winter of hard work, the massive power of that mainsail in a fresh breeze of wind would feel like a religious experience.

As the *Adventure* came alive, I could feel the energy in her timbers as she got down to business. She would heel over, wetting a couple of strakes on the leeward side, and my gaze would roam up and down the enormous mainsail as it took shape with the press of a fresh morning breeze. The horsepower of her much-increased sail area would soon overcome the 230 inert tons of her hull. I stood next to the wheel on historic decks. The spokes were checked and worn from years of harsh weather and from the rough grip of the many hands of Gloucester fishermen who came before me. The old deck under my feet was worn to half its original thickness

Schooner Adventure—*she's a long, lean, and handsome vessel. (photo: E. L. Boutilier)*

from the "red jacks" (sea boots) of the fishermen who had guided this vessel through storms and calm, danger and tragedy, exultation and death. Her men had made and lost fortunes since her creation in 1926 as the last and greatest of the Essex-built Grand Bankers.

How many eyes, I often wondered, had looked searchingly into the opening of the binnacle an arm's length in front of me? There was mounted the ancient compass, its card printed not with degrees but with the points and quarter points as was the custom in the old days. Sailing the *Adventure* was to me like sailing a living museum. It was all hemp rigging, deadeyes and lanyards, and heavy canvas. I gloried, too, in the great height and patina of those enormous wooden masts. At the head of the main topmast, the vessel's highest point, a fluttering pennant seemed to touch the blue of the heavens. Of course, there was no sound to our going save that of the hiss of the water sliding along the stout oak hull. She sailed enwrapped in her past, her phenomenal history! She infected me with her soul and made me her slave.

And now that you know where I'm coming from, I'll come back to earth. The old *Adventure* is certainly one of the all-time great sailing vessels. She was cut of the same cloth as the great Grand Bankers like the *Bluenose*, *Gertrude Thebaud*, *Columbia*, and *Puritan*, but gave up the extreme racing lines for sensible fishing performance. Captain Leo Hynes, who set all records in *Adventure* and fished in her for more than twenty years, also commanded the *Gertrude Thebaud* on a few trips. The *Thebaud*, aka the "white-winged flyer" and considered the most successful racer of the Gloucester fleet, was a disappointment to Leo. He said she was so long, big, and unwieldy that she would blow off and start to sail again rather than heave-to so the fishermen could fork their catch aboard. A little more short-ended, the *Adventure* would sit like a duck hove to, while the men came and went in their dories. Even so, *Adventure* showed her heels to many over the years, not just the yacht *America*, but to *Ernestina*, *Pride of Baltimore*, *Spirit of Massachusetts*, *Harvey Gamage*, and others.

One fine summer day, Penobscot Bay was all abuzz. *Shenandoah*, the topsail schooner from Martha's Vineyard, was approaching. Captain Bob Douglas had decided to make a trip to our area on a little cruise to Down East Maine. I made radio contact with Captain Buds Hawkins on the schooner *Mary Day*, and we decided to beat out together to Matinicus, rendezvous with *Shenandoah,* and then have a little race up to Islesboro Harbor. The wind was fresh from the sou' west and gave us a good chance to compare three very different ships. When we came upon *Shenandoah* between Matinicus and Monhegan, the *Mary Day* tacked under her bow and ran with her, while we jibed over behind her, looking for good pictures.

It was a magnificent sight. *Shenandoah* foamed along on a broad reach with her square sails set perfectly, and everything in her sail locker hung out and pulling like a team of mules. The *Mary Day*, meanwhile, ran out ahead, topsails arching against the blue sky. Last in line, the *Adventure* surged forward on the groundswell, her 60-foot main boom sheeted way off, single topsail set over that 3,100-square-foot mainsail as the breeze strengthened. *Adventure* was gaining steadily. Soon, we were waving at the passengers and crew of the rakish clipper eyeball to eyeball. I was just a little proud of the old girl. Then we passed in front of the *Mary Day* and turned to square away up the bay. We jibed the foresail over, increasing our lead as we ran "readin' both pages"—sailing wing on wing. The wind had strengthened even more now and was blowing at over twenty knots. I was eavesdropping on the other skippers' conversation on the marine radio when it was suggested that Pulpit Harbor should be the end of the race.

"Hang on," I said, "Islesboro is just ahead. What is the all-fired need to go to Pulpit Harbor anyway?" But, in spite of my anxiety, they suggested that we jibe over and run for Pulpit instead of Islesboro. I said, "Jibe! In this breeze!" It would be no sweat for the *Shenandoah*, as her mainsail is much smaller and the rake to the masts would dampen the jibe. The *Mary Day* had a smaller mainsail as well, easier to sheet in and bring over. But *Adventure* had a huge main and a long, heavy boom. I was not happy.

Leo Hynes was sailing with us. He often enjoyed a week of September sailing to reminisce and tell stories, and made at least six different trips with me. What a joy it was to listen to his tales of the fishing days at sea. He was standing by the wheel when the change of course came over the radio. I turned to him and said, "Leo, I am not at all excited about jibing over in this breeze."

"I know," he answered, "but if you take the time to tack, you'll lose the race." Well now, we can't have that! I got a gang on the seven-part mainsheet and we heaved the old thing in until the boom was about centered, took a turn, and when she came over with a bang, I let run the sheet till it smoked on the cleat. That 42-foot gaff, 70 feet aloft, came over with a crash and fetched on the lee rigging. . . *craaaccckkkk*. Ten inches of solid gaff broke clean off just beyond the jaws and hung like a broken wing from the masthead.

Fortunately, there was no damage to the topsail or the main. I ordered the mainsail down. Then we stowed the topsail, unlaced the gaff, and put the broken pieces on deck. We then raised the main by the throat, tied off the peak halyards, and sailed on with a jib-headed main. Yes, my competition then decided to change their minds again and we all jibed over once more, to anchor, after all, at Islesboro!

Cappy (Erland) Quinn was back in the shop banging on an old skiff when I got him on the ship-to-shore phone. I begged him, "Cappy, would you go up in the loft, get that green oak stored there, saw it in strips two inches square and 14 feet long, bale it up and put it on the first ferry to Islesboro in the morning for me?" Good old Cappy, he got right on it, and we picked up the stock promptly on the eight o'clock ferry.

We laid out the broken gaff and fished it up with the oak strips, then took the manila main topmast staysail sheet and seized it round and round the gaff, pouring salt water on the line to shrink it so she'd be tighter than three men could pull each round turn. Then we bent the mainsail back on and raised the whole mess aloft. Finally, we were ready to raise our anchor, and join our competition for a little race, downwind around Turtle Head and a hard beat up to Pulpit Harbor. The run to Turtle Head was no sweat but, when we got on the wind, the bend in that gaff was horrific. We kept her nose to it, though, and were first to Pulpit by an easy margin. I turned back to help *Shenandoah* locate the entrance to the harbor since Captain Bob Douglas was unfamiliar with it, and by the time they came up, night had fallen. A hootenanny ensued, so a great day was had by all.

So there you have it. With a breeze o' wind the old *Adventure*, even with a broken gaff, is hard to beat. She is fast off the wind for a deep-draft, heavy keelboat, but on the wind she is just a joy to sail. She will really charge to windward, will almost never miss stays—you have to abuse her terribly to miss stays—and when she is really performing at her 12 or 14 knots, she'll make your blood race. Of all the vessels I have sailed, be it as captain, crew, or passenger over all these multi-decades, and I've sailed a fleet of them, none can hold a candle to the old *Adventure*. As proof, witness what I will always remember as "the Portland Breeze."

It was just eleven forty-five when we looked over at the lighthouse on Curtis Island and waved to the keeper of the dwelling. He was cutting the grass around the base of the green glowing light, the aid to navigation marking the entrance to Camden Harbor. Stopping the mower, he watched in fascination as our big main topsail was unfurled and sheeted home. This was one of those perfect Maine mornings. A promising nor'wester was making up, an ebb tide, and a good "chance along" was at hand to make many a quick mile to the west. I gave her a long mainsheet.

As we foamed through the tumbling seas making eight or 10 knots, the wind built into a damn decent breeze. By the time we slid down the Muscle Ridge Channel, we were about as excited by that "hat full o' wind" as we were by the lunch of multiple servings of delectable fish chowder. A bit later, by the time we fetched Mosquito Island and sheeted in, squaring off for Old Man Ledge, we had all the wind we wanted. The spray was blowing horizontally across the foredeck. The *Adventure* was rearing and cavorting, sails and rigging all straining, and you could tell she just loved it. The old schooner was showing off like a redneck racing his new pickup.

It was just like we were "drivin' home from Georges" with the old girl dancing along at close to 14 knots. Pemaquid Point dished out a great

Adventure *blasts ahead of* Shenandoah *during an impromptu race up Penobscot Bay.* *(author's collection)*

williwaw that rushed down on us and made the old topmast bend alarmingly. I shouted to scandalize (cast off) the topsail halyard and relieve the strain and then, for the next two hours, we kept up our speed with just the lowers. The wind lightened up off Seguin Island and we reset the topsail for the run through Casco Bay. The waning afternoon brought less wind and from Halfway Rock to the narrows at Peaks Island we slowed again to eight knots. After arguing for right-of-way with the local ferryboat at the entrance to Portland, we rounded up and found our anchorage. Although we were all sunburned, windburned, and tired, a 75-mile run to Portland in a little over six hours proved that none can hold a candle to my old *Adventure*.

Of course, a big schooner has to stop as well as go. The *Adventure* had two very heavy anchors, one on each rail forward. One was the lunch hook, our light-duty anchor weighing about 800 pounds, and the other was our storm anchor, a moose of a thing, weighing in at about 1,200, hooked to a great pile of inch-and-a-quarter stud-link chain. The windlass was driven by a 1902 Fairbanks six-horsepower "make-and-break" donkey engine with a hand-operated clutch and a multi-gear reduction to haul in the chain. We named her Big Bertha the Bull Dog, and when she ran she shook the whole foredeck like a Force 7 earthquake. Her bark was equal only to her bite should you happen to get your fingers caught in the heavy,open flywheel or in a link of the chain flying around the old wooden windlass barrel.

Big Bertha was outrageously independent and would only run when psychologically in the best of moods. I would often have to extract her igniter, which predated that grand invention known as the spark plug, brush it up with a fingernail file, prime her cylinder with half a shot glass of high-test gasoline (spilling just about half on deck), tickle her battery connections, and in a firm but quiet voice just out of earshot of the passengers, praise the Lord from the heavens to the earth's core. Then I would grab that cussed crank and throw all my weight into the roll. She would take off, hitting on her one and only cylinder three times in a row, and then settle down to random firing with an inspiring beat that caused many a rhythmic dance step among the passengers. She had a crack in her piston from which a puff of smoke blew at each ignition, her crankshaft bearing was in nine pieces, her gas tank leaked as did her water tank, and she had a tendency to toss her chain from the drive-wheel sprocket. But she was a dear old thing!

And how we loved her! When she worked, she was a joy as she saved us many hours of labor at the old hand windlass that brought in only a half-link of heavy chain per stroke. However, the handwriting was on the

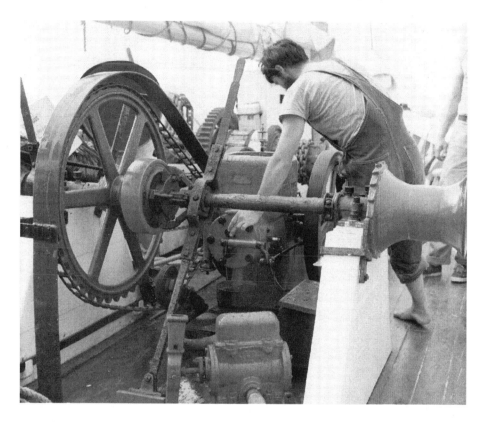

We called her "Bertha"—a 1902 Fairbanks-Morse that powered our anchor winch. She often gave us more fits than starts, but she was a dear old thing, and we loved her. (photo: Mike Carr)

wall. I could see I needed one of two things: a mechanic to completely rebuild old Bertha, or another Bertha. But where would I ever find a 1902 "Bulldog," especially one with Bertha's personality?

Well, as chance would have it, one day while I was poking around the Stonington shipyard, I spied, submerged under a great pile of old wood, boat parts, and just plain junk, the familiar look of a flywheel. Holding my breath, I moved the junk from the front of the engine, and there was Big Bertha's twin sister. Built from the same casting, it was a clone! I ran to the office of Fred Billings and caught him just waking from his afternoon nap. I said, "Fred, what are you going to do with that old building in the back corner of the yard and all the junk piled up to the roof in it?"

"Haul it all to the dump," he said with conviction.

I described the donkey engine and said, "I'll give you fifty bucks for that old engine."

"That's a deal," was his immediate response.

Then I could see his mind turning over, regretting the impetuous answer, and he explained that he'd better ask the present owner about getting rid of it, but he was sure there was no problem and it wouldn't matter a hoot.

Upon asking him who the present owner was, I was set back on my heels when he blurted out none other than the captain of the schooner *Victory Chimes*! Now, since I was not this captain's favorite person, I suggested that Fred not disclose who was inquiring, and I gave him two weeks to clear the issue. On my return, Fred pocketed the fifty dollars and, from his sheepish attitude, I could tell he never made the effort to contact the owner. Before anything could change, I gathered my crew and we dragged that 800-pound engine under the hand crane, got it airborne, and laid it gently on a piece of plywood over the engine box in the middle of my cherished yawlboat. Our center of gravity had just become dangerously high, but we felt that if we had to jettison the engine, we could let her go on a line and marker buoy and return with the schooner to salvage it.

The transfer was successfully accomplished and I put the engine in my shop for overhaul that winter with installation scheduled for the spring. By gee, now that was some fine engine! She had plenty of compression. Her bearings were all happy. Even her gas tank was tight. Perhaps I wouldn't have to praise the Lord to get her rolling. Then the registered letter arrived in the mail. The captain was suing me for the return of his engine. I had to hire a lawyer to tell him that we did indeed have a donkey engine and, if he could prove that it was his by supplying us with engine number, serial number, horsepower, manufacturer, color, and description, and other details, we would compare this information with the engine we had purchased.

As things developed, he couldn't even tell us the model or year. The following summer brought us again to the shipyard where again I happened across Fred Billings. He said sternly but with a grin, "Jim Sharp, you get the hell out of my place. I've had nothing but trouble since you yarded that 'make-and-break' out'a here. We've had a string of fancy lawyers trying six ways from Sunday to figure out how to sue me. At last count there was seven of them, all frothing at the mouth for their commission." I wasn't too worried, as Fred's adequate stomach was reverberating, trying to hold down the giggles, even as he tried to sound alarmingly serious at the same time. As for me, I smiled broadly and muttered a tongue-in-cheek apology—and the old engine remained with me.

Chapter 8

Settling In

Although we thought we had solved the issue of both winter and summer dock space for the schooners, "parking space" in Camden's lovely harbor remained at a premium. As the 1966 season diminished beneath gray skies and falling leaves, we found ourselves again at Wayfarer's dock for winter storage. I had a rented shop on the premises and could conveniently work on the endless off-season tasks required by our old vessels.

An autumn gale was approaching, so I had strung out five bow lines in anticipation of a hard breeze. At the height of the storm, Orvil called and asked if I wanted to put more lines out. I suggested I had sufficient gear to hold her, but he said I should go and look. There was one hell of a chungo—groundswell—waltzing in around the point, and with each wave, the *Adventure*, with all of her enormous weight, would heave on the wharf pilings and the whole dock would sway in and out as much as a foot.

Working in the rain and sleet, I strung out two more bow lines and then called the yard to bring their bulldozer down and dig her blade into the frozen turf. Then we put a chain from the front of the dozer to a bridle around the *Adventure*'s foremast. The marina operator was much more content when his dock stopped racking, but the experience must have made quite an impression. The following spring, we received a notice that Wayfarer could not offer any dockage, summer *or* winter, to the schooner fleet.

Orvil and I were already contemplating the problem of how to find a permanent year-'round berth of our own and we looked longingly at what was always referred to locally as "the old Swift property" across the harbor. The location attractively abutted the public landing and was then leased by our competition, the schooners *Mattie* and *Mercantile*. I said, "Slim"—the nickname I used because Orvil was so tall and slender—"we should buy that property and have our own dock!"

He said, "Forget it. That would be impossible, as it belongs to one of the very wealthy 'townies' and that guy never sells anything he owns."

"Well," I said, "no harm in trying, and since it is next to the town landing, it sure looks tempting!"

I was friendly with the publisher of the local newspaper at that time and asked him to casually inquire of a Realtor but, of course, not to mention a word of it around town. The current renter had been leasing the property for years and would no doubt have first refusal. The Realtor came back with a big, fancy price. I halved it once or twice, and shaved off a bit more, and counter-offered. Curiously, at just about this time, the property owner suffered a mild heart attack. The event apparently changed his attitude to a number of things, and he decided to liquidate some of his holdings. We dickered a bit more, through the agent of course, and darned if the owner didn't accept my offer. Neither owner nor agent breathed a word of the negotiation to the lessee. That was how, in late 1967, our schooners gained a permanent home at the wharf at 20 Bayview Street in Camden, a place that would soon become known as Sharp's Wharf.

Unfortunately, neither the *Adventure*—with her nearly 14-foot draft—nor the *Taber* could then use the wharf because there wasn't enough water. So, we looked forward to the day when we could do the needed dredging while we berthed for another season at the town floats in deeper water. Of course, dredging required plenty of permits but was on the schedule for the winter of 1968–69. As it happened, this wasn't quite soon enough. I thought that I had smoothed things with our wharf tenant, but I soon learned otherwise.

Reality dawned at the end of the first trip of '68. We were bound into the inner harbor and *Adventure* was picking up her skirts and making her way through the numerous, closely packed moorings en route. We were committed to our usual berth at the town float, and there was no room in which to turn around. Now, quite suddenly, we discovered our competi-

A proud captain and a proud vessel—once my wharf had been dredged, we could park the Stephen Taber *(and the* Adventure*) right alongside. (author's collection)*

tor's vessels were tied to the town floats rather than their usual berth at the wharf.

There was always tension when bringing the *Adventure* home, and this was a surprise I surely didn't need. "You tell him to move that damned old rotten pile of green wood before I get there, because I'm coming on in, and I'll split that thing in half if it is still occupying my berth!" I was so mad that I was shouting in the microphone and the speakers in the harbormaster's office were probably reverberating with distortion.

The wharf lessees knew well enough that the *Adventure* wouldn't float at the wharf, but they convinced the town fathers to insist that I go to my own dock and that they would move their schooners to the facility that Captain Orvil Young, Captain Buds Hawkins, and I had developed for the town following the vote at town meeting. The town had given me no in-kling of its edict, and I was some awesomely hot! Luckily, the harbormas-ter was well aware that a major tiff would occur, and he called me as we approached. So, when we finally rounded the point, I could see the crews on the offending boats scrambling, casting off lines, and getting ready to move back to the wharf. That fall, with the needed permits in place, I hired the dredge, scooped out the new berth, and moved *Adventure* and *Taber* happily to my wharf.

I then turned to, rebuilt the broken-down dock, filled the shoreline with blocks, rock, cribbing, and anything I could find to build up the wall. I planked over the wharf and connected it to the public landing. It was a gradual process, but it was satisfying to have my own permanent facility. It took more granite blocks to complete than I could afford, so I had to im-provise. In the old offices of Captain Frank Swift was a huge, leftover iron safe, about six-feet high, four-feet square and very empty. It was a mam-moth, heavy and extremely solid. "Why not?" I thought to myself.

We named the safe the Impenetrable Big Moose, and my crew and I pried, rolled, and struggled her out on the street, put a chain around her so she would not get away, hooked her to an oil truck, and gave her a push and pull down the alleyway to the wharf. The truck slowed her down, but when she reached the flat land, she settled into the gravel and rolled no more. We then put her on the other end of the truck and dragged her haltingly on skids of plank to the water's edge. Carefully we shoved the Impenetrable Big Moose into the tidal zone and declared her a granite block. Although rusty and barnacled, she is still there for all to view. I am, to this day, continually accused of keeping my millions in her steel shell under the wharf, where the pollock swim in and out.

During those first seasons with the *Adventure,* I learned her ways and her needs. With her enormous weight and the absence of an auxiliary engine, there was no way to stop in time if you came unexpectedly upon an ob-struction, be it a moored boat, a rock, or an island. What's more, I soon learned that the big schooner required a half mile to do a U-turn and equally that much to stop. The boat's 14-foot draft only added to the challenge and, during the summer of 1967, the reality of the boat's draft was brought home to me in dramatic fashion.

That summer, we had stopped at Eagle Island in the middle of Penobscot Bay for one of our fantastic lobster bakes. The next morning we set sail, hove up our hook, spun her on her heel, and reached off to the west. The new sun was lighting the Camden Hills in the distance and we were making knots in the fresh southerly as it ruffled up the bay. With a fair offing, we rounded Channel Rock and placed ourselves safely between Bear Island, Bear Island Ledge, and Channel Rock. Still, I now had to pinch—sail closer to the wind than desirable—to clear Three-Fathom Ledge, which is clearly marked on the chart. Pinching slowed our speed from the 10 knots we had been making on the reach, to about four and a half. Suddenly, she struck! *Adventure's* bow came lifting up out of the water; she ground to a rumbling, splintering, reverberating stop. *Arruuuggg.*

I walked forward and could see the rocks under her forefoot with the kelp fanning back and forth. My heart sank. So much for the three fathoms of Three-Fathom Ledge—18 feet—plus a half tide—five more feet. Dropping the headsails, I walked back and turned off the radio. I could see two schooners on the other side of the bay, and I didn't want to have to explain. Soon, Captain Bob Quinn came along in his lobsterboat. He was out early hauling his traps.

"I know just what rock you are on," he said, "That 'un is mischarted and many a keel has left paint on it. Thay's only about four feet there when 'tis low water." He fished lobsters on all the ledges here and knew the area like the back of his hand. We were stranded there for over six hours while the tide went and came again, and we finally floated off. Everyone across the bay could see us with our big mainsail still standing, and we were dead in the water all that time.

We kept a watchful eye on the bilges, but thankfully she was not leaking. I was sure, however, that the worm shoe—the vessel's outer false keel—was all splayed out like a well-used corn broom. That weekend in Camden Harbor, I dived with a saw to trim the splinters back and inspect the hull as best as I could. There was considerable damage, but I had to live with it until our annual haulout in the spring. Feeling it was my civic duty, I wrote and notified both the Coast Guard and the National Geodetic Survey—those responsible for making charts—requesting they name the rock we'd hit Sharp's Ledge. It was 10 years before they changed the charts. They didn't use the name.

That was by no means the only time I struck a rock. The *Adventure's* keel inadvertently found quite a few mistakes on the charts, and I made a few of my own, but none were as serious as that one. The splinters from this event were to plague us all season. We had to be careful and avoid the lobster buoys. Normally, the schooner's smooth hull and her lack of a propeller would just brush off the lines to the traps. But now, with the host of slivers on the keel, the pot warps would catch. On one cruise, we went into Stonington, a fishing town where the traps are like mines strewn in the middle of the channel, and we must have had 40 traps clinging to her bottom.

Barely moving because of the drag, we anchored and all the buoys from the traps came floating up, surrounding the schooner in an array of unmistakable, colored declarations of our guilt. The fishermen came out in their boats, sputtering and cursing, yanking the traps from under our hull and trying to untangle the knotty snarls of gobs and gobs of line. The language they used was a major embarrassment. By the look of it, we were less than popular with the Stonington fishermen.

No matter what the occasional problems, these big schooners had me hooked. Their history, their honesty, their nobility—these were my intoxication. Imagine my surprise, then, when in '67 I realized I had one heck of a wandering eye. Not for other women, for my parents had pounded a strong sense of fidelity into my moral compass, but for almost any sweet, sexy-looking little vessel with an irresistible, traditional rig and a handsome sheer line. How easy it was for me to fall in love with such boats. I was drawn as if by magnetism to all kinds of wonderful, homeless boats, sailing or power.

One day, towards the end of the 1967 season, I received a call from Al Norton of the shipyard at Seven Hundred Acre Island, telling me of a 42-foot, 1902 Herreshoff yawl named *Cat's Paw*, then owned by a wealthy gentleman on Islesboro. Al begged me to take her since her owner, unable to bear the thought of selling the boat, was planning to burn and destroy her for the dollars he would get for the lead in her keel.

This was just the kind of blind-luck opportunity one dreams of and never sees. Al had tried to explain to the gentleman that it would be a crime to destroy such a treasure of a classic yawl. Having been maintained without regard to expense, she was in absolutely exquisite condition. Al pleaded with the owner, saying that, with a little time, he would find someone to take her for the price of scrap lead and maintain her to keep her sailing.

The yawl's owner was amazingly attached to his boat, for he had owned it, sailed it, and loved it for the last 40 years. He, with his family, sailed many a mile, but now they had grown and gone, so he was alone. Eventually, Al won him over, but he couldn't bear to see the vessel go, didn't want to handle any money, wished never to see her again, and would not deliver her or be present at the delivery. He insisted no one know his name and didn't want any knowledge of the new purchaser.

The gentleman's winter address was Number One, Park Avenue, in New York City, and with a flare of creativity he had built a small shop in the back of the apartment. There, he would lovingly invent and machine parts and pieces for the yawl over the winter and put them aboard during outfitting for the summer. She had been furnished with a myriad of paraphernalia of his innovation. Everything aboard was "shipshape and Bristol fashion." The yacht had fitted bunk sheets and bedding, custom rail stanchions, handmade kerosene lanterns in the cabins, a complete tool cabinet in the engine room, every extra piece of gear one may need for the engine, including many spare parts, 12 bags of sails, everything labeled and categorized, a galley full of matching silver, crystal wine glasses, extra food of all kinds, and a locker full of foulweather gear. She even had a half dozen spare rolls of toilet paper.

Knowing Al Norton's reputation as an honest boatbuilder, I never looked at the vessel. I, on his word, gave him the check and made arrangements to pick up the yawl. When I got the key from the owner, he didn't even come down to watch her sail away, didn't introduce himself, shake hands, or say two words. Instead, he came out through the woods of his island mansion, grunted "Here!", slipped me the key, and turned around.

With two of my crew, I got aboard and taking one glance at this amazing piece of history, I knew she would sail like a witch. I set main, mizzen, and jibs, cast off the mooring without bothering to start the engine, grabbed the varnished tiller, and beat her smartly out of the harbor. We sailed *Cat's Paw* into Camden, tacked her in and out of the moored boats, curtsied by the yacht club to show her off, and hung her on a mooring so we could finish out the sailing season on the schooner.

That fall, as usual, I had so much to do on *Adventure* that I just could not do justice to a beautiful and delicate yacht. It was unfortunate, but, for the good of the vessel, I just had to sell her. This proved a blessing in disguise, though, as I was able to find a new owner down in Buzzards Bay where there was a collection of these old Herreshoff sailing boats and a club of men, all of them fanatical about preservation of the type. It was a perfect fit, so I sold *Cat's Paw* at a bargain price, hoping her new owner would keep her sailing forever. *Cat's Paw* proved to be just an hors d'oeuvre to the next incredible vessel that stole my heart.

Chapter 9

The Arctic Schooner *Bowdoin*

I t was spring 1969. I kept looking at the tidal slipway alongside my new wharf. Muddy and full of broken glass and dead rats, that slip was strewn with every manner of floating trash and yuck that the wind and tide could deposit. The slip was only about 50 feet across, but at the lower end was a good berth for a shoal-draft vessel. The old Frank Swift building, up on the street end of the wharf, used to be a lumber storage shed in the old days, but was now three floors of grand and imposing empty space. The idea of a small nautical museum kept creeping into my thoughts.

My head was full of dreams—models, ropework, anchors, parts and pieces of vessels, tools and rigging, a full-size working woodshop—everything historic, could be packed into this beautiful building. Then, my imagination graced that slip with the towering masts of a traditional schooner with her flags all a-flying, her mastheads etching an arc across the sky. Percolating with confidence about the instant success of a museum attraction, I was thoroughly convinced that every tourist who came to Camden would be just as crazy over these darned old schooners as I. It was easy to envision the public emerging from the museum to line up at a schooner's gangway, anxiously awaiting the chance to drop a handful of coin into the bucket.

Someone, I can't remember just who, mentioned the word *Bowdoin*. This was a world-famous little schooner designed by William Hand, only 88 feet long but as handsome and shapely as they come. Her hull was beautiful from any angle. I had seen her at Mystic Seaport Museum some years before, and remembered that she was getting in hard condition at that time. Admiral Donald MacMillan sailed this vessel on twenty six expeditions above the Arctic Circle, spending entire winters locked in the ice doing scientific studies. MacMillan had written many books, given many lectures, and had a host of exciting experiences too long for the telling. He had donated the *Bowdoin* to the museum some ten years previously and was now publicly addressing his dissatisfaction at the way they were treating her.

Mac had informed Mystic emphatically that if he could locate a new home for the *Bowdoin*, he would take his vessel back. 'Twas terrible publicity for the museum. But man, what a frontispiece that vessel would make for my own little museum! I called Captain Mac and told him about my property in Maine and the plans I had cooking. Since he had sailed from Wiscasset on many of his voyages and had named the vessel for his college in Maine, Mac was enthralled with the idea of having his beloved vessel returned to these waters. He explained that she needed some work, but wasn't sure how much. I assured him that we would take a long look at her condition and get her back sailing again if at all possible. If nothing else, we could block her up on a cement pedestal and keep her as a monument for the world to enjoy. Captain Mac suggested I go to Mystic. He would call the powers-that-be and arrange for me to take the schooner and tow her home.

The poor old thing! There she lay, ignored, paint falling off in sheets, tied to the wharf with ratty old rope, covered with a plastic shed full of holes and looking forlorn as a starving stray cur. The notice on the chain across the gangway said NO TRESPASSING. The masts had been removed, the mainmast broken off at the hounds (the lower part of the mastheads). Her engine was sitting on the beach with the sand blowing in its vitals. Most of the hardware and anything of value had been removed. She was obviously being prepared for her demise.

Captain Mac, by the skin of his nose, saved his vessel by publicizing her plight. We'll get her to Maine, I thought to myself, and give her a home and give her a new chance at life. Hoping it had sustained only minimal damage, I covered over the engine, then uncovered the schooner, made plans to reinstall the machinery, loaded the foremast on deck along with the broken main, and prepared her for a future tow to her new home.

I gathered all the blocks, rigging, hardware, parts, and pieces and loaded them into my trailer. It made for a heavy load. With the trailer groaning from the enormous weight, axles bending and wheels rubbing the wooden sides, I set out on the Connecticut Turnpike (now I-95) trying hard to stay under the speed limit. Twenty minutes later, a glance in the rearview mirror told me those tires rubbing on the wood of the trailer had kindled a beautiful fire! I didn't stop, but rolled off the highway and into a handy gas station. I ran in past the wide-eyed attendant shouting, "Get a hose! Get a hose, she's afire!" I grabbed the water can and, while he stood dumbfounded, sloshed it all over the tires and trailer, putting out the fire. With some emergency adjustments to the axles and wheels, an hour later, I was back on the road to Maine.

As I began planning the next stage of how best to deal with getting the boat to Maine, a development arose that came as total surprise. A group of men who had sailed north with Captain Mac formed an association—the Friends of the *Bowdoin*. They persuaded MacMillan that they should take ownership of the vessel. They convinced Mac, who was then in his nineties, that this arrangement would be for the best. While Captain Mac vacillated, his wife Miriam took their side, and Mac gave in. Even though I was ready to take her to Camden, the transfer of ownership of the vessel would go to the newly formed nonprofit Schooner *Bowdoin* Association. The Association could get a lot of publicity, but was unable do any of the work the vessel so desperately needed. So, the members decided to rent the vessel to me for one dollar per year. After initially shying away from the scheme, I eventually decided to support the cost of the rebuild myself. It seemed so wildly exciting to obtain such a wonderful schooner, so rich with history and fitting like a glove in my museum dreams.

Back in Mystic, my crew and I got to work, set the engine back in its bed, and nailed plywood over the holes and rents in the deck and hull. I got Ransom Kelly, a good friend from Boothbay, to tow us with his rugged party boat. Back in Camden, we laid her on the face of my dock, with

Adventure and the *Taber* outside her. With three vessels abreast, the fleet was expanding, and there was a multitude of projects in which to sink one's teeth.

Poor old *Bowdoin* had not been hauled for more than seven years. I had to shove her up in the slipway at high tide, lean her against the granite wall, run a six-part tackle to a nearby tree to keep her upright, and let the ten-foot tide fall away. Then we could scrape her barnacles, remove the well-rusted steel ice sheathing, and apply two coats of sorely needed fresh bottom paint. Working against time, we set up space heaters to dry the 88-foot hull before painting and then to help dry the new paint before the tide set in again. Because her deck had been leaking for so many years,

The Arctic schooner Bowdoin *bides time until spring and the stepping of her newly hewn mainmast. (author's collection)*

her timbers were spongy and soggy with fresh water. I had to dry her out somehow, so I took off the second plank below the sheerstrake on both sides of her hull and put a rain visor just above the opening, to encourage her to breathe fresh summer air. By the fall of 1969, we could see by her waterline that she had come up out of the water almost three inches—just from the weight of the water that had dried out of those soggy timbers. Then, we rolled up our sleeves and prepared to go to work!

There was a strange Volkswagen Beetle parked in an odd place immediately adjacent to my wharf. The inside was piled high with bags and bags of "stuff" and its occupant was obviously living in the cramped space left behind the wheel. He slept sitting up and ate from a brown bag. By the hour he would peer out of the dirty windows, face covered in a scraggly beard, and gaze over the harbor, hardly talking to anyone. I was so busy working on the vessels that I had no time to be civil to a drifter. Kind-hearted Orvil got him to open up and learned that his name was John Nugent. John seemed to be mulling over a heavy sea bag full of problems and just needed a quiet place to sort them out. Orvil offered to let him stay on the *Taber*, where he would have a bit more room than in his tiny car.

After awhile, when we got used to each other, John became the ship keeper on the *Taber*. He would stand in the hatchway over the kerosene heater trying to keep warm, alternately breathing fresh air from the slightly opened hatch and foul fumes from the oil heat source. Armed with the kerosene belching smoke pot, he sometimes would retreat to the tiny head, and sit for hours on the throne, reading and rubbing the frost from his fingers.

Eventually, we asked John to help with some special thing we were moving or doing and he got more and more into the activity with the vessels. The hard work became therapy for him. Soon, pitching in became natural, and we put him on the payroll. When we went sailing that next summer, John moved on to the *Bowdoin*, and this great old vessel became both a therapist and the love of his life.

I ordered a tree! I had to replace the *Bowdoin*'s mainmast. It takes a tall spruce to attain 12 inches of diameter up 75 feet at the top end. But the logging company from Aroostook County swore they could find just what I needed right in a tiny place that hardly justified a name. It was a dot on the map, deep in the Maine woods, called Donkey-Deadwater. They found what I needed, cut it, and delivered it that winter.

Cappy Quinn and I took that stick, three-and-a-half feet across the butt and, by the count of the annual rings, over 185 years old and, just as I had done with some of the *Adventure*'s spars, we fashioned that 12-inch-diameter mast the same old-fashioned way. Here we go again: first to square, then eight-side it, then drawshave to sixteen, plane to thirty-two, then sixty-four, and finally round. There was quite a pile of wood shavings under foot by the time we took the last lick with the plane. What fun!

We put winter covers over all the boats and went at it through all the bitter cold months. We tore the foredeck off the *Bowdoin*, took out the break beam, put in new top timbers, deck, covering boards, bulwark and rails, repaired the houses, redecked their tops, and then caulked everything. Drifting around the hull on a float, we put in new planking wherever necessary. I was able to open up the old Cummins engine that had taken Captain Mac to the Arctic, clean her, fuss over her, tune her, and get her running. Working against time, I had great hopes of taking the *Bowdoin* to Provincetown in the fall of 1969. I wanted to salute MacMillan, then ninety-five years of age, and show him that *Bowdoin* was back, proud, and sailing again.

That spring, before a crane was hired to install the *Bowdoin*'s new mainmast, we had some surgery to perform on the old foremast. She had deep ring-checks, spiral cracks, having twisted after being left in the sun while the vessel lay untended. That twist made the tenon—the wooden extension at the heel of the mast that notches into the keel—and the crosstrees out of line so the mast would set in crooked. I had to cut off the old tenon, cut in a mortise, and splice in a new tenon, at a proper angle. This enabled us to square up the crosstrees. This was a much more sensible solution than rebuilding the mastheads or replacing the mast.

With the last lick of the plane, a 185-year-old spruce tree turns to round and becomes the mast for the Bowdoin. *(author's collection)*

At winter's end and feeling quite a bit poorer, I hired a dredge to come and scoop out the slipway. *Bowdoin* was then in her new berth and, with her new paint job, she looked positively regal, a queen on her new throne. We rigged her up and opened the old girl as a museum for the summer. We had displays of artifacts aboard donated by Mac, and we pleaded that visitors drop a contribution in a handy box.

In October 1969, we bent on the *Bowdoin's* sails, fitted her out, and took her to salute Captain Donald MacMillan at Provincetown, Massachusetts. He was aching to see his beloved vessel again, and the press properly called our visit a "Sentimental Journey." I had to get there before anything happened to Captain Mac. I felt I couldn't wait another year to finish more projects on the vessel, so we took her with some things still wanting.

To knock a crew together, I gathered up a kaleidoscope of friends consisting of: a marine biologist friend named Spencer Apollonio; an artist named Imero Gobbato; my schooner cook, Jan Pomeroy; ship's carpenter, "Cappy" Quinn; my wife, Louise; and my number one son Topher (the name is the bitter end of Chris-topher, who was all of eight months old). You've got to start them young!

Passing through Casco Bay, we stopped in at Peaks Island for an overnight visit. My friend Spencer Apollonio knew a fisherman on the island who just happened to have a spare jawbone and three vertebrae of a right whale that he was desperate to give away. So why shouldn't we accommodate him? We improvised by propping up the jawbone on the vertebrae and created a whalebone bench on the main deck. We were now the only sailing Arctic research vessel in New England with a deckload of whalebone and a bench to sit on, to boot.

We stopped in Boston for fuel and crossed Massachusetts Bay in dungeon-thick fog with nothing in the navigation locker but a compass and lead line. Groping our way into P'town Harbor, blaring away on the noisy, old hand-operated foghorn, searching blindly for something to recognize, we finally found a buoy and squared away for MacMillan's house on the beach. The Lord blessed us because, just before our time ran out, the fog, like a curtain, rolled back and there was Captain Mac perched prominently on his porch blowing his horn back at us. We jibed her over, saluted him, and ran down the beach for the public dock where Mac came down to help us tie up.

Hundreds of people welcomed the *Bowdoin* on her "sentimental journey" to P'town that October 17, 1969, and they came pouring on board in droves to see this historic craft. Captain Mac, pleased as punch and proud as a peacock, was greeting people and telling stories of his trips north. Excitedly, my wife, new son, and I went to Mac's home to watch his movies of the vessel locked in the Greenland ice pack in the 1920s. Captain Mac cradled Topher in his massive arms while we looked at the memorabilia and Arctic treasures in his collection. It was indeed fortunate that we visited when we did. Admiral Donald B. MacMillan passed away only months after our sentimental journey to his home.

To me, the old *Bowdoin* was a great little vessel. You could count on her to always bring you home. John Nugent was my crew, and he and I could handle all the workings of that 88-footer by ourselves. Since she was so handy and the sail plan small enough, John and I would each take a halyard, throat and peak, and heave up every sail. She had an electric windlass to haul up the anchors and a powerful diesel to make her dance around the harbors.

When I first rebuilt *Bowdoin* and made her seaworthy again, we would vacation aboard her as a family. John and I would sail the schooner alone while my wife wrestled with the kids and the cooking. We would get quite a little nip in the air when the fall weather fronts would roar in from Canada, and I can remember shoveling snow off the deck in Gloucester one morning. Just to show off, I climbed into an authentic Eskimo outfit consisting of sealskin parka, polar bear pants, and seal boots, all part of the museum offerings we had for display over the summer. The sight of it drew a crowd of the curious on the Gloucester waterfront.

Among our most memorable trips was one we made to my old cruising grounds of *Malabar* days, the Chesapeake. We had spent idyllic days cruising the lower Chesapeake Bay when, in an unusual gust of wind, jibing into the Potomac River, the old gaff broke in half, right at a partly dry-rotted spot. The Piney Point AFL-CIO Trade Union School was just ahead and, as they say, any port in a storm. We, big as life and ignoring the five or six signs stating "Absolutely no trespassing under penalty of death!", tied contentedly to their dock. A plethora of security officers descended, insisting that we leave immediately, but we begged special dispensation, claiming disaster and pleading refuge because of our broken gaff.

The old *Bowdoin*, being such an interesting vessel, opened up many a door. "Okay, but ya gotta go see da big boss about dat," and they whisked us off to the boss's office. His size-fourteen shoes in the middle of the desk partially blocked the enormity of his Mediterranean proboscis from our view, but the five-dollar cigar he had clenched between yellow teeth stuck like a flagpole from the side of his head. A thick accent rolled out from the part of the mouth unoccupied by the rolled tobacco; we barely understood, "Watta you prrobllm Capin?"

I tried to explain our broken gaff and assured him that if we could beg two pieces of angle iron and some bolts with which to put it together, we would be quickly on our way. "Youa notta gotta goa so fast," he said and proceeded to ask me lots of questions about the vessel, her history, and where we had been cruising. We actually became quite chummy after shifting from one foot to the other for a half hour since we were not invited to partake of the office's numerous chairs. Anthony then summoned a subordinate by pressing a button at his fingertips. He instructed him, "Takea da gaffa to Peppy ina da machinea shopa. You tella Peppy, Tony say fixa heem!"

Leaving Tony's feet firmly planted on the desk, we were waltzed back to the *Bowdoin*. Five men appeared out of nowhere, came aboard the vessel, and shouldered the gaff. Things really moved fast then. We practically ran behind the porters to their enormous machine shop with a football-field-size room filled with every huge lathe, shaper, steel bending brake, and sophisticated industrial tool imaginable. Peppy was soon located. The chief machinist got his orders to fashion two stainless-steel, custom-bent angle irons with a handful of stainless bolts. The drill appeared and, in very short order, we had a repaired gaff.

Our five porters were standing around waiting for the return trip, and not only did they replace the gaff to the mast where it lived, but they helped us bend the mainsail back on, coil up, and make everything ship-shape. None of the porters and the curious security officers wanted to go back to the boredom of whatever it was they were doing before our invasion, so we gave them a tour and a little history lecture about the *Bowdoin*. They thought that was great, so they gave us a half-day tour of the school, its many buildings, boats, and facilities, and then gave us dinner. The best was the extensive tour of two 150-foot schooners they had as training vessels for the union students. They were fully rigged Canadian dory trawlers (fishing vessels), once part of the Zwicker fleet of Lunenburg, Nova Scotia, and were finished off to the nines without regard to expense. It was more than a little mind-boggling that these magnificent schooners were part of this union school to train kids to be oilers and wipers on a steel cargo ship in the U.S. merchant fleet.

The lower Chesapeake was probably the southernmost latitude that the *Bowdoin* had ever seen in her exploring career. Meanwhile, John Nugent and I sailed the little *Bowdoin* each year, spring and fall, mostly down east to Roque Island, Grand Manan, Bay of Fundy, and the Nova Scotia shore, including Lunenburg, Halifax, Shelburne, and many other Canadian towns. Captain Alan Talbot ran her in the summers carrying six passengers on regular weekly cruises and up to 10 people on special charters. He kept her beautifully clean, very much loved, and she looked so very proud and handsome with her gleaming white hull, and unusual, eye-catching ice barrel on the foremast. I could never have found a more capable, more conscientious, more affable, and experienced master than Alan Talbot though he, being twenty-one years old, was probably the youngest captain in the windjammer fleet.

The *Bowdoin* was a very special ship, and her passengers regarded sailing on her as a once-in-a-lifetime experience. We kept her busy by supplementing those passengers generated by her own fantastic reputation, with the overflow from the *Adventure* and *Taber*. The old *Bowdoin* turned heads everywhere she sailed on the coast.

Much to the consternation of Miriam MacMillan, widow of Captain Mac, I kept the vessel in seaworthy condition and sailed her on fall cruises. Miriam wanted to see poor old *Bowdoin* entombed in concrete as a permanent exhibit, and all the convincing in the world would not assure her that

Noble princess that she is, Bowdoin *sails stately off the town of Camden. (author's collection)*

a concrete casket would cause the vessel's demise quicker than anything else. Meanwhile, friction between me and the Schooner *Bowdoin* Association grew slowly but steadily. They felt they were in charge of the old vessel's destiny and in spite of our twenty-year lease arrangement, they often injected their noses where they chaffed my personal rigging. Our days together were always destined to be numbered, although I never could have foreseen the events that led to our parting.

By the middle 1970s, the poor old *Stephen Taber* was needy. Having been built in 1871, it was time to put her in the hands of a younger person with more energy and the courage to rebuild her from stem to stern. We thought Captain Mike Anderson would be that person. Mike had worked as deckhand and mate for me on the *Adventure* for several years back in the late 1960s, and, hoping the *Taber* would have the new beginning she so richly deserved, we sold her to him. We planned to have Captain Orvil Young shift over to the *Bowdoin*, as Captain Alan Talbot was planning to branch out on his own in a smaller power-driven passenger boat. One cannot hold these good young men down.

In the process of playing musical captains, Orvil went to reassign his license at the Coast Guard Office in Portland. The boys in blue said, "What vessel are you going in?"

Orvil answered proudly, "The *Bowdoin*, an 88-foot schooner carrying just six passengers."

"Not unless she is inspected," they said.

Now I always suspected inspection. I avoided looking up the regulation since you can almost always find a law inhibiting what you wish to do if you search long enough. I had gone about my thing and ignored the Guard, hoping they would ignore me. It was sort of the "Don't ask, don't tell" policy. It had worked for me for seven years.

Indeed, there it was—a something in the regulations to which the *Bowdoin* could not conform. A vessel of over 65 feet in length would not qualify under the Motor Boat Act, and could not carry even six people without full Coast Guard Certification, a requirement that would demand a total rebuilding and revamping of her physical features. I refused to change her historic character to accommodate such requirements. She was, after all, a national treasure. If we could no longer carry passengers to create a revenue source, the *Bowdoin* would have to find a new home. The *Bowdoin* promptly went over to the custody of the Schooner *Bowdoin* Association.

Chapter 10

A Sardine Carrier Comes to Sharp's Wharf

At some point in the midst of all my "doings" with the schooners, just for a change of pace, I bought a 60-foot ex-Nova Scotia sardine carrier and named it *Old Zeb* after my second son, Zebediah Peter. Zeb was launched into the world on May 17, 1971. *Old Zeb* was a double-ender and had been most recently used for biological research, dragging for shrimp all over the Gulf of Maine and its tributaries. Her name was, logically enough, *Draggin' Lady*. Going under the perilous premise of "a boat for every occasion," I intended to use *Old Zeb* for a tugboat, towing both the *Adventure* and *Taber* when necessary, and for any extra tuggin' work along the coast of Maine that I might find in the off-season.

Old Zeb was a fine little boat with a traditional pilothouse, fisherman's fo'c's'le, flopper-stoppers (paravane stabilizers) that hung from the mast, and good accommodations for six people. The only downside was that I had to rebuild her 4-71 GM diesel. Then, after a couple of years, I became restless. The long, cold winter must have been giving me the itch. It was the Great Circle that attracted me—that circle in the USA that went up the Hudson, through the Erie Canal, Great Lakes, Chicago Canal, down the Illinois River, Mississippi, and points south with the Intracoastal Waterway beckoning for the return. It would be altogether a tempting voyage of almost 7,000 miles. To help defray the expenses, I thought I would offer segments of the trip to passengers and put out a brochure to see how many I could attract. The paying people never materialized, but friends and family did, so my crew came and went.

After the '72 season, down the coast to New York City we steamed, *Old Zeb* thrashing into the afternoon sou'wester with Captain Orvil and his wife Andrea giving tiny Zeb a bath in the galley sink. We stayed overnight at the South Street Seaport Museum and steamed on up the Hudson River. I had to remove the mast to clear the bridges in the Erie Canal and figured to restep it on the Mississippi. That meant, however, doing without the stabilizers in the Great Lakes, and I had read horror stories about those lakes in the fall. There is a rumor that freshwater waves are rougher than salt. Well, I'll tell you, there's a lot of truth to it. The salinity in the ocean is dense and heavy, and the waves are longer and flatter. Freshwater waves in the same kind of breeze are so steep they seem to be wall-sided.

Old Zeb would punch into a wave, and the top of it would roll green down the entire foredeck and burst against everything in the way. The wave would have nothing but air on the other side. She would drop down into the trough and the wave would smash into the pilothouse, throwing spray right over the top and squeezing little trickles of water in the crack by the window.

I had read that almost all the shipwrecks and disasters involving the big lake ore boats occurred in November, and this trip graphically showed me why. The gales in the fall are killers, and they come roaring down from more than one quadrant because of the surrounding landmass. The *Edmund Fitzgerald* and many other ships fell victim to these November gales. In the Atlantic Ocean, the wind stays in one direction for quite some time before veering or backing. On the lakes it can come from three directions in as many hours. December ice frequently closes the lakes. The books warn that the ice sometimes closes the Chicago Canal by the first of December. I suspected I had to get through before that date or I might be trapped, frozen in, and have to spend the winter in the sub-zero north instead of basking in the sunny south. Nothing to do but push on! Okay, November gales, here comes *Old Zeb*!

The first gale was at Put-in-Bay, at the west end of Lake Erie where we holed up for a couple days while the wind roared through the windows. Our second was at Tawas City, and the third at Alpena with the snow building up on deck. We gave up counting the gales, slid into Presque Isle before a 40-knot nor'easter, then shoveled more snow off the deck in Mackinaw. Then, when we entered Lake Michigan, things really got crazy.

We coasted past Beaver Island, heading for Charlevoix with a northerly gale building, piling up the seas on our stern. Thank heaven she was an able little double-ender! It was blowing like stink right up our exhaust pipe when we spotted the double breakwater at the harbor entrance where we had to turn to port to enter between the two rocky fingers. With the gloom and spray in the air, and the tops of the waves breaking and blowing off to leeward, the only way we could identify the rocks was by the white surf where the waves burst into the air.

I surely didn't want to get the sea abeam of us. With those steep waves running at a dozen feet with their breaking tops, I was afraid we would roll over in a nanosecond, so I aimed her for the very end of the breakwater, figuring to just clear the tumbling surf and turn immediately into the protection of the rock structure. Needing steerage, I pushed the throttle open wide. She would get up on a wave and surf down, going "hell and delaripy" toward the rocks while I spun the wheel back and forth, trying to keep her from broaching and on course. It was a narrow breakwater, we turned just past the first set of rocks, and with the second finger of rocks perilously under our stem, we shot up between the two. I realized then, I had forgotten to breathe.

The wind was almost abeam now and pushing *Old Zeb* to leeward. I kept her nose to it, throttle wide open, crabbing the last mile toward the protection of the harbor. The sea would burst on the windward rock pile, and the heft of the wave would breach right up and over our pilothouse, at times almost obliterating all visibility, and then bespatter itself on the lee side rocks. It seemed we were inside a runaway washing machine on the rinse cycle.

Still pushing her hard, I saw the bridge that must open to get us inside, where shelter would finally end this insanity. I called the bridge on the radio. No answer. I started blowing the horn and called again. No answer. I was backing down trying to hold her in this breeze. "Stay, Jim," my thoughts were screaming, "in the middle between the rocks. Now forward. Now reverse. Forward again." All the while, we were getting doused with solid wave tops, one right after another. Where is that damn bridge tender? I called the Coast Guard. No answer. I continued unceasingly, calling and blasting the horn, and finally after about twenty minutes, which seemed like twenty hours, the bridge went up.

We entered the comparatively quiet harbor with a sigh of relief. Upon walking uptown, waiting for weather, I stopped in the bridge house to hear the intimate confessions of a bridge tender. Sheepishly, he confessed to taking a nap. "I really didn't expect there would be any damn fools out in this weather!" he blurted with conviction. I didn't say much, but I thought a great deal.

We licked our wounds, got supplies, and with a more-favorable forecast, set our course for the lighthouse across Grand Traverse Bay. It was a night run of maybe 30 miles, and then we had to clear a rocky point of land. We had gone only about 10 miles when it started to snow, and that snow came on harder and harder until we had a white-out. This wasn't in the forecast! The wind was blowing horizontally across the pilothouse windows and before we got to the point of land, steering by standard compass only, the compass card started to go around and around. I looked at the chart, and there was a note stamped on the front of the chart "local magnetic disturbances reported in this area."

Now that was a revolting development! I knew the direction of the wind, turned on the spotlight to illuminate the snow, and went to steering so the snow would stay at the same relative angle to the boat. Luck was with us. As we neared the point of land, the snow abated somewhat and we were able to pick out our lighthouse. We ran on down to—I think—Grand Haven and decided, after resting up, to press on from there, directly across Lake Michigan to Chicago. Our ice-free month would soon be running out. We had to get to the windy city forthwith!

There was a funny noise from the engine when I hit the starter button. She didn't start. I hit it again. She lit right off. I didn't think any more about it. With Chicago in our sights, we struck out for the middle of the

Old Zeb was named for my younger son. In her first life, she had carried herring (sardines) along the shores of Nova Scotia. (author's collection)

lake in the middle of the night, beginning our crossing of about 150 miles of open water. There was a moderate forecast with variable winds. Well, they were right about the variable part, anyway! First it breezed up from the south until we had quite a little chop abeam. We were rolling pretty hard when the wind came northeast and we had another sea running on the quarter. Then the damn wind started to blow from the west. We had seas coming from everywhere. The poor boat didn't know whether to pitch or roll. It was freeze-up cold and something was wrong with the heating system. I crawled into the engineroom to check the furnace boiler.

The old GM 4-71 was screaming happily and turning the propeller shaft round and round. I sat next to the warm boiler and noticed a puff of smoke wafting under the deckbeams drifting to the other side of the engine room. I watched it as it was sucked into the air intake of the engine. Then I traced it back to its origin. It seemed to be coming from my toolbox.

It was a wooden toolbox, an old-fashioned kind almost four feet long with a wooden handle full length on top. I slid over and touched the outside of the box where it had a funny dark color. It disintegrated under my finger. It was no longer a wooden toolbox. It still had the shape of one and the tools in it looked normal. But, the box was ash. It had smoldered for eight hours and, incredibly, it never broke into flame. The fire had consumed almost all of a four-foot toolbox! Then I realized what had happened.

When I first started the engine and heard that strange noise, a loose connection on the battery had produced a spark that must have flown into my toolbox, setting a small rag in it not afire but a-smolder. The second time I hit the switch, she started normally so I thought no more about it. To sum it up: we had been under way for eight hours, alone in the middle of Lake Michigan, blessed with a pitch-black night, a raging gale of wind, alternate snow, sleet and spray on the windows, the boat thrashing and crashing in the sea, "colder than a breeze off'n an Arctic glacier," on the tail end of the most dangerous season in the lakes, trying to make Chicago before it freezes up, with only God watching a contained fire in the engine room. What is more scary than a fire on a wooden vessel in the middle of a dark night! The Lord protects the dumb mariner. Thank you, Lord.

When we finally cleared the Chicago Sanitary Drainage Canal and entered the Illinois River, we found that the canal was so terribly polluted that it hadn't frozen in over twenty years—and we had ridden hard and fast to arrive before the deadline! I stopped in Joliet and went back to Maine for a couple of weeks to catch up on business and then continued heading on down the Mississippi. After a pleasant stop in St. Louis, we changed crew in Memphis, visited Elvis' digs, and happened on a construction site where we stepped our mast again under a monster of a crane with a hook the size of a Sherman tank. Looking at the crane operator, I kiddingly pointed to the mast and held up a fifth of Kentucky bourbon. He simply nodded and swung that huge hook over our heads. There was a four-foot smile on his face and a brown bag in his lap when we, with our mast tall and proud, steamed away for the big river.

The current was running hard. It had been raining a deluge and the run-off was coursing down the river at seven to eight knots. The gauge at the lock showed the river standing at 44 feet above pool. Water was over the levees, the farms were flooded, cars were under water, and we saw houses with water lapping against their living room windows. The tugs with their enormous 30- or 40-barge tows were having a gay ride downstream, but the ones coming up were looking at the same tree for half the day. The buoys marking the channel were all adrift, but it didn't matter because there was so much extra water, the shoals were completely covered. *Old Zeb* was making about 14 knots over the bottom as we steered the bends and yanks of that wild river, dodging the deadheads and sneaking up a creek or rivulet into the swamp to tie to a tree at night. Pleased at the progress we were making, we looked forward to New Orleans in about half a week's time. Then the fog set in. I was used to Maine fog, but this was bayou fog. Thick as alligator breath it was, and it smelled just that bad, too.

We waited impatiently while tied to a cypress tree hoping it would clear, but it had settled down to stay. For amusement, I was listening to the towboat men with their long Southern accents, engaged in discussions about the river, the fog, the current, and their most recent escapades with casual girlfriends. I heard one saying that he was approaching the creek where we were tied. A-ha, I said to myself, imagining his face glued to the radar, and I called him on the radio, explaining where we were and asking if he would give a little toot when he passed the mouth of this little river. "Sho-nuf!" he responded, and we dropped our lines and moved nearer to the main river.

By and by, we could feel the thump of his engine as he approached, then a toot came out of the fog, and we shot out into the swift river current mixing in with the whirlpools made by the turbulence of his wake. With *Old Zeb* following close enough to see the ghost-like outline of the towboat, we made good progress downstream and at our request he picked a good tributary for our evening cocktail hour and a quiet night. It was the same program for the next several days with different towboats, until we slid into the Dixieland city of New Orleans. The air here was thick, not with fog, but with river talk—a few days before our arrival, there had been a major towboat accident on the river right in the heart of the city.

Normally, the idle barges, when waiting for cargo, are tied by steel cables to the trees along the river bank. Now that the river was flooded 40 feet higher than pool, they were tied to the treetops instead of the fat part of the tree at the bottom. Several barges had gotten adrift and were swept by the current into other barges and, like dominos, 125 of these runaways came cascading down through the city of New Orleans, bouncing off the wharves, off bridges, and each other. A courageous but ill-fated towboat captain got underway to try to corral a barge or two and was overturned in a flash, and six men were drowned. The barges finally disgorged themselves through the delta, and only about half were eventually rounded up. The rest were never seen again.

Innocently, we cruised across St. Petersburg Bay. I say "innocently" as our route connected us to a curious event that we never suspected until we had gone through the Okeechobee waterway, cruised to the Keys, and chugged all the way up the East Coast. Two months later, we entered Georgetown, Maryland, off the Chesapeake Bay. Here we met friends and were just climbing into their car to go off to dinner when an unmarked vehicle pulled in behind us and blocked our exit. Three plain-clothes FBI men jumped out, with their hands on their holstered guns, and lined us up against our car.

It was obvious they were not going to stand for any funny business as they patted us down and started the volley of questions. "All right, which one of you owns the boat?" they demanded. I explained that it was my boat and where we had come from. "I know where you came from," quipped the officer in charge. "We have reason to believe you have contraband aboard that vessel!"

I laughed and said, "Well, if that's the only problem, let's go out there and give the old boat a good going over." When they discovered we were totally cooperative, they eased off the hard-core police attitude and explained that there was a big marijuana drop in St. Pete Bay that same day we went through and they had been tracking us ever since, hoping to catch us at the dealing. I guess they were running out of patience by this time and decided to pull an inspection. As they poked and prodded the cabinets and cubbyholes on *Old Zeb*, I suggested more and more places for them to check. When they stuck their heads in the bilge, they remarked it was too dark to see much down there so I lent them a flashlight. I remarked, "Fine bunch of cops you guys are without even a flashlight to find my stash of weed!" When I suggested they climb the mast to make sure the crosstrees were clean, they just laughed and called a halt to the foolishness.

Spring was almost on us. We pressed on toward Maine and ran into a great wall of spring fog. Welcome to New England! I snapped on a new-fangled gadget that *Old Zeb* had come equipped with, something called Loran A. It had an oscilloscope tube in the front like a little television and, since I was comfortable using a compass and lead line running the schooner around the rocks and ledges in Maine, the little squiggles and lines on the tube were a real mystery. Upon deciphering the instructions, I found the idea was to get them lined up, compare the numbers with a special chart, and presto, you knew just where in the fog you were floundering around.

I, of course, had doubts that a crooked line on a tube would show me anything but confusion. When the wizard told me we were under the Buzzards Bay tower and we couldn't see zilch, I said to my mate with great sarcasm, "I told you that damn electric gizmo was a fake." Then, I stuck my head out the window and of course couldn't see a thing but fog, until I looked up! Oh my God! "Back her down!" There was the tower, towering above us and we had run the boat right between the legs of the rig. I guess that contraption knew its stuff after all.

We kept her nose to it plowing northward and, finally, when we broke out of the Muscle Ridge Channel, passed Owls Head Light, and gazed again at the beauty of blue Penobscot Bay with the Camden Hills all humped up and stretching northward, the sight of it gave each of us a great lump in the throat and a bad case of the goose bumps. There is no place like home—no place like Maine.

Chapter 11

Someone to Watch Over Me

Captain Leo Hynes, the most famous master of *Adventure*, used to say in all modesty, "Oh, I was lost most of the time."

I felt that way, too, in the days when all we had was a compass, a lead line, and our eyes, nose, and ears for navigational tools. When the old fog would enshroud Camden and Curtis Island, we would frequently choose to head north. We had learned that, at the head of the bay, we would often find a "scale"—an area where the fog regularly thinned—and there would be visibility.

One Monday morning, both Orvil on the *Taber* and I on the *Adventure* ran towards Belfast looking desperately for that scale. We never found it. Instead, I felt my way into the harbor, poking through the wretched-thick fog, worrying myself bald over the rocks and ledges and hoping for a good place to anchor. Soundings, shouted from the leadsman at the bow, indicated shoaling and, with relief, I finally ordered the anchor dropped. After we settled in and cleaned up the running rigging, I called Orvil on the radio just to see where he ended up.

He said, "I'm in Belfast!"

I said, "No, I'm in Belfast, too!"

"Whereabouts?"

"I don't know!"

"Can't see anything!"

"Neither can I!"

When the fog finally cleared, there he was! We were anchored only a few hundred feet apart. We had sailed together all the way up the bay and into Belfast Harbor and until the next morning neither one of us had seen the other. Belfast was pretty polluted back in those days because of the chicken factory disgorging offal from packing the cluckers at the head of the cove. When we hove up our anchor, there was an old chicken foot on the fluke. From then on we dubbed it "Chicken Foot Harbor."

They call it "dead reckoning." You guess your speed, figure your time, and reckon your position. Dead reckoning navigation aboard the big *Adventure* with all her passengers in thick fog would scare me witless at times. If, when dead reckoning from buoy to buoy, you come too close to the mark and find yourself drifting over inside of it because of tidal current or wind, you may end up on the rock. If you are too far away and allow a wide margin of safety, you may miss the buoy entirely! Then, you've lost your position and don't know where the heck you are.

With *Adventure*'s enormous weight and no engine, there is no way to stop in time if you come unexpectedly upon a rock or an island. By the time you see an obstruction, it is too late! One time we were in Boothbay Harbor for Windjammer Days, and the weather came on dungeon thick—"thick as mud and twice as gooey," as the Maineiacs say. I waited for two days for the clearing and it didn't happen. Then Friday came and I just had to get back home, so I struggled through the fog around Pemaquid Point and into Muscongus Bay, a very dangerous thing to do. There was a big sea running and high surf all along the shore. No place to make a mistake! We had a boatload of sick people as we rolled our scuppers under with no wind, going around that foggy offshore point, our dependable little yawlboat bobbing up and down in the sea on a long hawser.

Then we had to feel our way through the vapor up through a myriad of islands. Muscongus Bay is like a graveyard of rocks and ledges. We anchored for the night, and Saturday morn, if you could believe it, the fog was even thicker. I gave in and called a friend with a radar-equipped boat to tow me home. Even that was a wild ride. Forty miles with the fog so thick, he had to turn his spotlight on us so my bow watch could follow where he was steering and signal to me at the wheel. There were times when the fog actually obliterated the light and we were following along by the direction of the towline disappearing into the mist. We could only see the towboat through the thick vapor occasionally and sometimes not at all, and all my eggs were in his basket! I just had to trust that he would dodge all hazards. I even had trouble seeing my crew on the bow. We were some relieved to arrive safely in Camden. Since we were so late, some of our passengers had to stay over on board. It made for a darned short weekend for us to turn that schooner around and refit, but that was the only time I was late getting home in twenty-five years of windjamming.

We were blessed, on occasion, with small miracles. I think of the time we were running from Mosquito Island, trying to thread our way into the Muscle Ridge Channel with the familiar fog thick, black, and dripping. White Head Light was dead ahead and I could hear the horn blasting away, loud enough even at that distance. Then we lost all our visibility. The channel entrance was strewn with islands, rocks, and ledges and the wind was aft pushing us toward the land. We had about six miles to run and had to judge the current and wind strength to determine our speed over the bottom in order to reckon just when we would arrive. When we were three miles closer, half the distance to the light, curiously, the foghorn ceased to blow!

Tension increased as we got closer and there was not the faintest groan from the foghorn at White Head Light. I hushed the passengers so we might hear breakers on the rocks ahead and sent more people forward, with a warning to keep a sharp lookout. Feeling the heavy responsibility of the forty-five people in my charge—wondering how many would drown if we were pinned on that lee shore of sharp rocks and surf, zero visibility and 50-degree water—I kept recalculating my estimated time to the unseen danger.

Still, no sound from the fog signal and, by and by, I decided my time had run out. Not knowing exactly where I was, but approaching a narrow passage bordered by a rocky beach of boulders sticking up like sharks' teeth, gave me no choice. I had to turn back. Where is that damn fog horn?

With the decision made, panic filled my heart. I was spinning the wheel as fast as I could, both physically and psychologically demanding that the vessel turn faster than she was capable, when the bow watch shouted, "Breakers ahead!"

Of course, if I had had an engine, I could have thrown her into reverse and stopped her dead in the water. As it was, in spite of my hopes, the old schooner took her normal quarter of a mile to turn slowly around. As she came across the wind, there, suddenly, was a great hole in the fog! It was a scale, a corridor about 50 feet wide, right up to that lighthouse! Now, too, the horn came blasting through, almost scaring us half to death. All too soon, once we re-entered the fog, the horn disappeared again, totally and completely muffled. By then, however, I had snatched a compass bearing on the lighthouse, and we were able to safely tack and jibe and run up the channel. That was luck. But you can't always count on luck to counter Mother Nature's tricks.

For example, consider the night some years later when we were anchored at Warren Island in the west bay with a very moderate forecast of light southerlies and clear visibility. I awoke at 4:30 hearing the wind picking up and the anchor chain rasping on the bottom. I poked my head out of the hatch to see that the wind had hauled into the nor'west and was piping up pretty fresh. Eternal vigilance is the price of safe seamanship, so there was no more sleep that morning for me. At five, I let out more chain to enhance the grip the anchor had on the bottom. At six, the harbor started to get rough. This anchorage was open to the bay and the wind was puffing up to 40 knots. So much for that moderate forecast!

Daylight had filtered in under a heavy cloud cover and I was able to see my neighbors, the *Roseway* to windward and the *Mattie* to leeward, both with crew up and checking anchors. By seven, wind increasing, I decided we had to get underway and escape this trap, but the wind had come on so hard, I wasn't sure my little yawlboat had power enough to move me. My mate, Peter, also known as the "skinny kid," jumped aboard *Hercules* and warmed her up. I called the *Roseway*, which had two big engines, and asked Captain Orvil—who was already warming his motors and heaving up his anchor—to stand by in case we had trouble.

We put the 65-horsepower yawlboat out ahead on a hawser, and I signaled Peter to see how hard she could pull before I hove up our anchor. When he started pulling at full throttle, the little boat began jumping up and down in the waves, ruining her efficiency, but the schooner did begin to move slowly ahead against the wind. By now, all the passengers were up and watching our endeavor. It was time to raise the anchor. I gave Big Bertha a little talking to and rolled her with the hand crank. She started right up and I signaled to Pete to slow down while we hove up the hook, and then slammed the clutch on the windlass to engage it. The chain started to come in, I signaled half-speed to Pete and happened to glance over at the *Mattie* in time to see her lose control and get blown off sideways. Her yawlboat was across the stern and useless in that position, and she was headed for disaster with the beach under her lee.

I was too busy to look at events there. Our anchor came off the bottom and I signaled to my mate to give the boots to the boat. Just then we got a hard gust of wind. The schooner started drifting backwards. Oh God! I could only stand there and watch, my stomach doing flips. The yawlboat was belching black smoke and pulling for all she was worth but mostly jumping up and down. On one of her jumps, the towing hawser got under the yawlboat's tiller and, to my horror, lifted the rudder right off of its brackets on the stern. This meant Pete was unable to steer and we would soon be joining the *Mattie* on the beach.

In a cold sweat, I watched the "skinny kid," calm as if he was sauntering down the boardwalk at Atlantic City, step back, retrieve the rudder, and in one motion return it to the pintles and gudgeons (brackets) on the stern where it belonged. The gust of wind went by, the boat's prop churned and churned, and the schooner started to move ahead—very slowly at first, but we finally broke the inertia and moved out of there.

The *Roseway* accompanied us out of the cove. The poor *Mattie* went ashore at high tide and pounded on the beach all day. There was nothing we could do to help. She had to go to the shipyard for a major rebuild, and they were lucky they didn't lose her altogether. We reanchored in a protected area, the wind soon went down, and we went back to help take the passengers and gear off the *Mattie*. It blew 55 knots nor'west that day. So much for forecasts. You just can't trust 'em.

Conventional wisdom suggests that, when you are running in fog, you just run your time out and when you hear the bell buoy, you adjust your dead reckoning. This is easy enough, until you are faced with inconsistencies like "full of the moon" tidal currents that race without logic in all directions imaginable. We had left Fisherman's Passage in the Muscle Ridges with a mid ebb tide, noting that all the pot buoys were properly streaming to the south just as neat as can be, and we struck out into the bay fog, thick and dirty, toward the White Islands off Vinalhaven. It was not a long run, but a nasty destination with lots of rocks and hazards on the other shore. When figuring my compass course, I naturally allowed an appropriate half or three-quarters of a point for the cross current.

My jaw fell right down with amazement when we happened on a well-defined, unmistakable line of froth and tidal swirls, right there in the middle of the bay. The tide line divided the current running smartly off to the south on one side—and to the north on the other. Yes sir, after carefully computing my course for the southerly set and after we sailed through the swirls, the damn tide was running to the north—just as fast and furiously—just as far as you could see in that fog.

How do you figure? The pot buoys don't lie. The change from ebb to flood current negated all my calculations and corrections. Had I an engine, I could have steamed into the current and gone to the safer entrance a little farther south where a large lighthouse and horn mark the channel. But the wind wasn't strong enough and was blowing in the wrong direction for that one. I had to hold on and give the hazards a sufficient guesstimate of clearance. It would be twenty more years until the global positioning system would be invented. But, after a decade of worrying this old vessel around these foggy bays, I was fortunate enough to purchase a low-powered radar and, just like having a magic wand, it took all the guesswork out of navigation. Even then, however, other forces were in play that helped protect us at key moments.

Jeff Thomas died on the deck of *Adventure* back in 1934. He was the original captain and owner of *Adventure* and, based on my research, I doubt whether there was a tougher, more hard-drinking, hard-fishing, hard-sailing, scaly, crusty old son of a sea cook fishing out of Gloucester. The dories were off tending their trawl, the wind nor'west, and it was cold. . . so bitterly cold. One day, ice began forming on the rigging, decks, and rails. If this continued, the old schooner would get heavy with the weight of the ice. The added weight would make her logy—unresponsive and possibly unstable, so Captain Jeff took a gob stick, the club for killing fish, and was vigorously pounding the encrustation from the rig when he suddenly felt his chest seize up, and he passed before the men came back with their catch. To this day, I'm convinced that Jeff's spirit is still with the *Adventure*. If you don't believe me. . . wait.

We had sailed through Stonington to pick up a deckload of lobster for a pleasant afternoon cookout and had poked the old schooner up behind Calderwood Island, let her range, sails all aflutter, bleeding off headway, till we fetched the anchorage. We then plopped the hook down and the chain roared out the hawse. Everyone jumped into the boats and rowed for the beach to gather firewood for an old-fashioned lobster bake. Making a mental note of our position and policing the below-decks, I was last to leave the ship. With the beach fire roaring, hors d'oeuvres a-flowing, the lobsters were soon beet-red and devoured ravenously, washed down with a little wine.

Since I had stared down into the eyes of hundreds of these ugly critters boiling in their caldron all summer long, I had my usual hot dog with peanut butter and made the coffee—fantastic schooner coffee! (The deed is done with a humongous pot of water on the open fire, into which is dumped the entire contents of a number 10 coffee can. Stir it zealously with an old driftwood stick and let it boil over three times. . . delicious!) Then, when the pies had been polished off, the hikers had returned, and the air turned cooler, everyone gradually retired to the vessel to enjoy a singsong in front of the fireplace in the main cabin or a game of cards in the mess room. At eleven p.m., the vessel quieted down and people turned in. I checked the weather and with a favorable forecast, I looked forward to a good snore.

Around three a.m., I woke up to the pinch of a strong grip, a hand on my shoulder, shaking it with gusto. I was instantly awake. The hair on the back of my neck was standing up, and I had a strange, overwhelming feeling of foreboding. Jumping up the companionway and poking my head out of the hatch, I felt the wind was of moderate velocity, still blowing from the same quadrant as earlier. Why then did I have this strange feeling? I jumped out on deck and peered over the stern, my eyes searching in the dark night. The ledges, I thought! The ledges are only an easy stone's throw behind us!

We had dragged our anchor. There was no time to examine the reason; we had to move immediately to get out of danger. I shook out my mate and deckhand, jumped into the yawlboat and got her started, traded places with the mate and grabbed a towline from the aft lazarette. Then we dragged the schooner, anchor and chain streaming behind, out to our original position where I dropped "King Kong," our 1,200-pound storm anchor. Now I was sure we would stay put the rest of the night and went back to my bunk.

Well, I got to thinking about why and how I was awakened, and I could still feel the pinch of the fingers on my right shoulder. As I lay awake in the quiet of the main cabin listening to the measured breathing of the rest of the crew, my eyes fell on our old rocking chair. More times than I can count on my fingers, I have returned from a lobster bake to the deserted schooner, only to find someone or something had tampered with that rocking chair. I would find it moved to a very obviously different position than where I had left it. A couple of times upon my return, it was pitched over on its side on the floor. I would always tidy up before going ashore and never left the main cabin in such obvious disarray. We always laid it to the spirit of old Captain Jeff Thomas!

Captain Jeff made his presence known on numerous occasions and even scared the living bejesus out of deckhand Doug. About midnight, when all was eerily quiet, Dougy was wetting the decks fore and aft, his last duty as night watchman before retiring. The next morning, still wide-eyed, he drew me aside and said in all seriousness, "Cap, I want to tell you something." He swore to me that Jeff followed him around as he, in record time, splashed the buckets of seawater from the forepeak to the fantail. Doug insisted he could hear the old fisherman's sea boots squeak and slosh on the deck right at his heels. "The hair was standing straight out on my neck," he explained breathlessly, "but no way was I going to turn around. I threw those buckets around and I practically ran back to my bunk!" From then on, Doug was careful to never be alone and to do the nighttime wash down only while there were still stargazing passengers sitting out enjoying the evening.

One time when Mike McHenry was mate, he had invited his wife, Lynn, to enjoy a week sailing on the schooner, but had neglected to mention anything to her about old Jeff. They were sleeping behind the curtains in the big double Pullman berth at the forward end of the main cabin. In the middle of a tranquil night, "Lindy Lou" awoke to the squeaking of the rocking chair as it rocked back and forth in its position in front of the fireplace. Now who in the devil could be rocking in that chair at this hour when we all want to sleep? she wondered. Her curiosity was insistent, so she boldly drew back the curtain, poked her head out and, to her horror, the chair, though slowly and steadily oscillating, was completely empty! She was so scared she closed the curtain and lay awake long after the old rocker had decided to quiet down. "Not only was it rocking," she explained excitedly next morning, "but its movement was deliberate, as if there was weight. . . the weight of a person or something in it!"

Old Captain Jeff visited us from time to time, and whenever anything strange or unexplainable happened along, we always laid it to his spirit. You can doubt if you wish. You can say that's a lot of prop-wash, but if you are there, sitting out on deck alone on a quiet moonless night with fog dripping a rat-tat-tat from the rigging, you just might hear behind your back the subtle squeak of rubber boots pacing rhythmically on the deserted deck. It wouldn't be the first time.

As for me, I don't believe in ghosts, but old Captain Jeff can come, pinch my shoulder, and wake me up anytime he wants.

Chapter 12

Reckless Abandon

As Captain Bob Douglas used to say, you should have not as many boats as you like, not as many as you can use, but as many as you can see! By 1974, there were lots of boats to see around Sharp's Wharf. The *Stephen Taber* was tied to the *Adventure*. *Old Zeb* was sandwiched in on a float just ahead of the *Adventure*. The *Bowdoin* was in the slipway, as were two Malcolm Brewer–designed dories intended for the *Adventure*. There was *Hercules*, my 16-foot yawlboat, and the 20-foot, shapely rowing seine boat *Spastic Spider*, a nameless fishing dory with a schooner rig in it, a flat-bottomed punt, a Sunfish, and a canoe. I had plenty to do to get all these vessels ready for the ensuing season. In fact, I was "maintenance mired." Certainly you can understand, however, that all these boats were not enough. I was thirsting for a tugboat.

I was not, however, utterly and entirely without reason. Before acquiring a new boat, the first thing was to sell *Old Zeb* to someone who could ignore the bad wood in her. She was built in Nova Scotia, as Orvil would say, of "rhubarb and burdock." I found a mariner enthralled with sardine carriers and I let him own it. Into the car and to the west I drove, escaping for a time the dismal depression of marital problems that my reckless abandon regarding all things having to do with boats had by now generated.

The first tug I came across was an interesting ex-Navy small yard tug named *Jaguar*. Owner Charlie Mitchell and I got to jawing, and I described my dream of the perfect personality of a small tug. He immediately responded, "You're talking about *Wrestler*!" He described at length a 50-foot

Staten Island Harbor tug with her original engine, pilothouse, hull, and all appurtenances from 1924. "If you go to Fairhaven Marine, you'll see her. They just bought her and intend to use her commercially and around the yard. She's not for sale, but you never know."

I high-tailed it for Fairhaven. When I jumped from the car, there approaching the wharf was the sauciest-looking little antique tug you ever saw, belching pie-size smoke rings from her stack and jigging up and down from the vibration of her engine just like an old Toonerville trolley car. She was just as sweet, lovable, and sexy as a high-school prom queen! Ten tires hung along her rails, each getting a little smaller as they strung out aft. There was a huge **W** on the stack, and the pièce de résistance—four multicolor, leaded stained-glass windows in the boot heel of the pilothouse. Coquettish? She stole my heart.

As soon as she hit the dock, before they had a chance to shut down, I begged aboard and ran down into the engineroom. There, lined up in front of me, were four cylinders of chug-chugging Cooper-Bessemer diesel. Where on earth would you ever find a sweeter sound? She was idling at about 50 turns a minute and you could count each fire-stroke. An enormous flywheel was spinning around at the forward end, and a host of pushrods, rockers, valves, oilers, pumps, and gizmos were all flying in different directions. It was a symphony orchestra. That engine was her first and only, and was installed in 1926. It had been faithfully turning that five-foot propeller ever since. Among the others like it that still survived, one was preserved in the Smithsonian.

I finally picked my tongue up off the floor and went into the office. "What are you going to do with that tug?" I asked the manager. "Take the engine out, replace it with a Waukesha, and work her," he responded.

"Oh, man," I pleaded, "don't do that. Take the steel tug you have in the back of the yard and repower her. I'll give you what you paid for *Wrestler* and you can buy an engine with that and, after all, the steel tug is more suitable for commercial work than an old wooden one. If you do away with the engine, the *Wrestler* won't be attractive to me or anyone else. That would be a crying shame. She is practically a museum piece!"

I pleaded like a two-bit lawyer in the box. There was no hope. They absolutely refused. I said, "Well, anyway, here is a check for ten thousand just to let you know where I stand. Call me if you change your mind." I didn't have that much money in the bank, but hoped it would help the psychology of the persuasion. I headed the old station wagon for Maine, emotions all a-jangle.

Life is so full of interesting and confounding turns. A week later, I heard the *Roseway* was in trouble. Her owners, who had bought her from the Boston Pilot Association, had tried to put her in the windjammer business but failed the Coast Guard inspection. They, for the summer season, spent almost $100,000 to fit her out for a swordfishing trip. Bragging loudly of catching those lucrative fish by the barrel and making a fortune, the owners figured to finance the conversion and pay a dividend to the investors in one fell swoop. It was a disaster. They caught one fish! It may have been the most expensive swordfish in history. The investors were mad as hatters. They wanted out and their money returned. The owners were between a rock and a hard place. For years I had had my eye on the old *Roseway* and I called Orvil, suggesting we go to Gloucester, where she was languishing, and have a long look at her. Yes, her hull, since the pilots had spent lots to keep her properly, was in beautiful condition. The engines were rebuilt, set in place but not hooked up, the hull was gutted, the steel watertight bulkheads, professionally designed, were in location, albeit improperly fitted.

The potential was there, however! She was 112 feet on deck, big and roomy, with open space for accommodation and heavily built in the Gloucester tradition. Capable of Cape Horn, she would last a lifetime on the coast of Maine. Orvil and I hotfooted it over to the owner's office. An unfriendly greeting awaited us in the richly decorated office of John D. Mahoney and Assoc. We found the heavy atmosphere was wound like a mainspring in a grandfather clock, and stress exuded from every corner of the room. When they told me what they needed to get out of their dilemma, I halved it twice and told them what it was worth in the present

Wrestler's engine—a four-cylinder powerhouse of Clydesdale horses.
(author's collection)

disarray of half-done projects, no Coast Guard certification, engines not running, and without an interior.

They laughed—most nervously. Earlier I had made a check out for $60,000 and slipped into my shirt pocket. With a very casual motion, I put it on the table and assured them there would be another like it if they wished to sign the agreements. They laughed again, but this time hollowly. We went back to Maine. As we were tooling along at 70 miles per, Orvil said something about leaving that check on the desk. "Oh, no, Orvie-babe, 'tis not a problem," I clarified. "I have only $400 in the account. That was for effect only."

Back home, a phone call was waiting for me. It was from Fairhaven Marine. They had decided to accept my offer on the tug *Wrestler*! I ran to the bank to make sure *that* check would clear. With gladdened heart, I got my gear together and went to acquire my latest treasure. My brain was still reverberating from a jumble of hasty instruction on how to run that fascinating engine when John Nugent and I backed *Wrestler* away from the dock and started for home through a freezing-cold January. We had barely entered the Cape Cod Canal when a call came through the marine radio from my secretary. There was an urgent call from Boston. The number matched the phone of the owners of *Roseway*. Blood racing, I returned the call. "Captain Sharp," said the voice on the other end, "we have decided to accept your offer for *Roseway* if you pay cash immediately." I agreed, and called the bank.

Oh my God! I bought two vessels in two weeks and I didn't have even a slim ounce of regret! What a hopeless addict is me! My growing marital problems had, if anything, *increased* my reckless abandon when it came to boats. For a fleeting moment, I thought of hooking on to the *Roseway* with *Wrestler* when we chugged past Gloucester to tow her to Maine. Coming to my senses, I gave up that foolish idea and we continued to Camden, arriving on the coldest day of the year with thick ice covering the rails and pilothouse of *Wrestler*.

Captain Orvil Young is a man with untold courage. I tried to forewarn him of the fine line separating courage from foolhardiness, but he, following my venturesome lead, ignored the dangers and jumped in, too. He agreed to go for a quarter-share of the *Roseway*, we shook on it, and he rolled up his sleeves and we went at it. I kinda felt as if I was getting high marks for reckless abandon.

There was no time to play with my latest towing treasure. So, making sure *Wrestler*'s bilge pumps were working efficiently, we set out overland for Gloucester. *Roseway* was soon hauled out of the water, her hull sandblasted and freshly painted. A mechanic temporarily hooked up the engines, putting the exhaust up and out on deck through a straight pipe, and with a supreme effort from both Orvil and me, by March 12, 1975, we were ready for the trip to Maine. The trip started auspiciously and we congratulated ourselves on our luck with the weather. Then, the wind came off nor'west, a screecher, and the temperature dropped unmercifully to nearer zero than freezing.

We were only three aboard, Orvil, our sometime crewman, a dairy farmer named Tom, and I, all taking alternate turns at the wheel. It was so cold we had to trade positions each 20 minutes; one in the engine room checking gauges and warming between the roaring hot engines, one in the galley freezing with cold and getting a snack to keep up the caloric intake, and one steering, stamping feet, beating breasts, freezing, standing just to leeward of the two unmuffled, raging exhaust pipes with the decibel level equaling the leeward end of a 747 on takeoff.

We suffered thus for 18 hours. I felt I was doing penance. Neither Orvil nor Tom deserved such atonement. Spray came over the rail, the wind blowing it halfway up the masts, where it froze into a solid sheet of saltwater ice. The entire deck was a sheet of ice and that, with the jumping of the vessel, made it suicidal to go forward. Rails, deckhouses, windlass, and helmsman soon became coated. We would pound our jackets to knock the ice off when our 20-minute watch at the wheel was thankfully over and then retire to the engine room for a little heat and to further encourage those two screaming GM 6-71s to destroy our eardrums.

We worried over those untried engines and, on one of our frequent engine room inspections, sure enough we discovered a serious oil leak in a fitting on the front of one diesel. I was afraid to disturb the fitting for fear it would worsen, so we took a broom handle, cut it just a smidge long, and braced it from the forward bulkhead to the fitting, putting pounds of pressure against the culprit. It cut the flow of oil to controllable ooze and we never even shut down. Inventive Orvil found some cotton in the medicine kit and stuffed it in his ears, claiming it cut down on some of the pain. Trouble was he couldn't hear when I gave the course or called him on watch.

For that entire trip, we suffered, swore, ranted, and raved, and finally, in the dark of night, we were coming up the channel into Camden's inner harbor. I was steering and turned to Orvil and said, "Is that the light of the yacht club just off our bow?"

He said, "What did you say?"

"Is that the yacht club on the bow?"

"What?"

"Orvil, take that damn cotton out of your ears!"

He answered, "I already have!" The poor guy was so deaf that we had to shout in his face to make contact. Later, when we had tied up alongside the *Adventure* and were heading homeward, Orvil got in his truck and was repeatedly grinding away at the starter motor, turning the key again and again and wondering why it wouldn't start when it was running all the time. After two weeks, most but not all of his hearing came back. We all lost a great parcel of acoustics on that one, and farmer Tom decided warm cows were preferable to cold schooners.

Man, what a crew we put together to get old *Roseway* ready for the coming season, and didn't the chips awesomely fly! Old Cappy Quinn with two hammers in his great paws, Chet Pooley, who always refused to take a coffee break and worked like a little beaver (but adamantly refused to work next to anyone with long hair), Grandfather Talbot with a sense of when to rough-hew and when to finish elegantly; all the finest kind of honest, down-to-earth, real-Maine stock, work-ethical boatbuilders. They went at it and built the floors, cabins, bunks, galley, cabinhouses, companionways, tables, benches, all manner of ice chests and boxes, shelves, and fittings. Orvil and I did our best to manage the process, revising plans and projects, installing piping and putting most-welcome mufflers on the machinery. We hooked up generators and windlasses and then confronted the knotty problem of where to put the galley stove.

Orvil's wife, Andrea, was the cooking guru of our fleet. She would be doing the cooking and she had to be satisfied. We struggled a big, black Shipmate wood-burning cookstove into the galley and set it up where we thought the most logical. Andrea came in and said, "Well, I don't know. It might look better over here." Five of us hooked on to that multi-hundred-pound iron monster and moved it three feet over, turned it around, and tried the other corner. "Well," she mused, "it would be more convenient over here!" The five of the hernia crew sweated and struggled it to the other corner. "No," she said, "that won't do, how about over there." We danced with it six times, did four pirouettes, and curtsied and, in the end, the stove was right back to the spot where we started. With bows all around, and resounding applause, we had a cook who was happy in her new home.

Right at the outset, we threw out the plans our predecessors had had professionally drafted. Orvil and I, with a gander at the Coast Guard–approved piping plan, saw immediately that the fire pump was hooked to the raw-water inlet. So when the fire pump was activated in an emergency, the generator would be starving for cooling and would burn itself to pieces. Rather than have to determine which fire to fight, I got out the old drafting table and we fashioned new plans. By the time we did the electrical, bilge arrangement, fire and safety, cabin and accommodation for 36 passengers and seven crew, sail and rigging plans, we had quite a folder-full to take to the Coast Guard for approval.

The *Roseway* had tanbark sails. They were dyed to look like the reddish color of the canvas preservative used in the olden days and were both distinctive and complementary to her name. But there must have been a vendetta against the former owner, because some creep had crept into the locker where they stored the sails and had taken a knife to the mainsail. It was hacked through several layers and unusable. We hadn't time to have a new one made, so we repaired it as best as possible with patches of material from a different bolt of cloth and a different shade of tanbark. The sail looked a little like that of a West Indian bumboat, but got us through the first season. The pilots had cut down her masts and we had a bit of rigging to do to make a proper schooner of her, so she sailed "bald headed" with only the four lowers that first season. The topmast and topsail would have to wait until next year.

There's nothing like a deadline to whet the edge. We, with luck and hard work, got Coast Guard approval and it all came together by the beginning of June 1975. In just two months, we had built the *Roseway* over so she was ready for passengers. What's more, the rejuvenated schooner soon proved so attractive that she generated repeat business for the following season. With all the devoted passengers Captain Orvil Young could woo over to the new schooner from the *Taber* days, and the excess reservations we could shift from the *Adventure*, things on Sharp's Wharf really started to hum. Between the two vessels, we were accommodating more than 70 people each week. But that was merely the core business. There was also my workshop, the wharf and its parking lot, a take-out restaurant, four rental apartments I had built in over the shop, and a leased retail outlet on Bayview Street. Of course, my attention was also needed for the exhausting separation difficulties with my wife, raising my two boys, and, let's not forget, tugging and towing with *Wrestler*.

I was stretched thin—thin enough, you would think! But no. Two years earlier, a nice little restaurant had opened up on Main Street, a pleasant "down home" kind of establishment where locals tended to gather, jaw, jabber, and spend too long a time warming the seats. It had come up for sale. What an opportunity! I called sister Chris, who was wintering in South Carolina.

"Teeny," I said, using a cutesy name Dad would use when he wanted to tickle her ire, "this little restaurant came on the market. It's the best location in Camden." Then I told her the price.

"Oh, that's too much for me! I would like to move up to something more permanent, but I don't think I can swing it," she expostulated.

"Okay," I said with emphasis, "but if you aren't going to buy it, I guess I will." After a very short pause, she blurted, "I'll buy it!" And then—"and you can help me get started!" Somehow, I knew that was coming.

Chris moved back to Maine, redecorated the place, called it Chris's Chowder House, and it became the schoonerman's hangout. I fixed the faucets, repaired the toilets, built benches, and I could eat for free! We schoonermen would have our business meetings there, right at the frontwindow table where we could look out and nod to people passing. In those days we knew most everyone in town. Chris had placemats on which the schooner fleet was depicted, and pictures of the vessels scattered around the walls for atmosphere. Captains Erland Quinn, Buds Hawkins, Orvil Young, Alan Talbot, and I would frequently be joined by others in the marine industry, including curious passing townsfolk, to sit and engage in coffee and banter about the schooner fleet and most anything else controversial that hooked our fancy. It was a great hangout. Chris was becoming quite a restaurateur. Yet, as events developed, this was just the beginning!

Chapter 13

Marry Me, El Capitano

What is it about the romance of the sea that drives people into marriage? The first couple that wished to be launched off the deep end of my schooner was Donna and Allen, a nice young pair from lower New England. They wanted to have El Capitano perform the ceremony dockside on Sunday and cruise aboard the following week. Of course, in those days, I'd do almost anything to land a paying passenger. So in preparation, I sent to the State of Maine for an application to solemnize marriages.

A short time later the application arrived and I sat down and carefully answered the questions, crossing out the part that said "You are an ordained minister of. . . You are a Justice of the Peace. . . You are a Notary Public." In the place of those words, I penned in, big as life, "A Master of Sailing Vessels." I enclosed the check for four dollars per instructions, and they sent me the license—good forever! No time limit.

Blissfully, I went about my business splicing up Donna and Allen in a pleasant ceremony with lots of flowers, formal wedding attire, and a large contingent of spectators, with champagne for the wedding party, including the other passengers cruising that week. The dock was crowded with the usual Sunday tourists, but that day they were rubbernecking and pushing to get a good view of the proceedings. I hauled my old blue blazer from the closet, dusted it off, and Donna and Allen were properly spliced and sailed off into the sunset with us for the next six days.

That ceremony seemed to launch a rash of marriages aboard, because it wasn't long before I got more calls. My blazer got quite a workout with some very formal weddings and some not so formal. I even did one with the wedding party in T-shirts and tattoos and the bride-to-be, judging by the stretch marks on the sweater into which she was poured, very much closer to delivery than conception, and she, all the while, making every attempt to appear casually composed.

For ten or twelve years I continued performing weddings, until suddenly I received an urgent notice from the State. It seemed some busybody in the State House found my application and was concerned about the "Master of Sailing Vessels" part. They insisted I cease and desist the performance of all marriages. They claimed my license was invalid and, to continue, I must become a Notary Public. I needed to pay seven dollars for two years, renewable.

I decided to delve not into the validity of those fifteen or so prior ceremonies and explore not where the participants now stood in the eyes of God and country. With my fancy new credentials, I have performed an equal number of notary marriages as I did under the guise of Master of Sailing Vessels. Their number included not only a generous handful of my crew, but my mate, one of my cooks, several friends, passengers of note, and some Camden townspeople. I dished out nuptials to Matthew Walker, author of a cocktail-table book of the interiors of famous vessels, including *Adventure* and *Roseway.* The long splice took place in Portsmouth on the *Roseway,* and to make the performance totally legal, we cast off from the wharf, steamed the vessel to the other side of the imaginary line in the middle of the Piscataqua River, firmly in the state of Maine, where the vows were valid and sworn.

It may come as no surprise that just as "a barber is the last to have his hair trimmed," he who splices landlubbers on schooners probably is unable to keep his own act together. Sadly, my own marriage, already troubled, now started to fall into serious disrepair. Along with the normal fit of depression experienced in the fall of 1975 when we had to lay up the schooners, a boatload of marital problems really set in. During the upheaval, Louise and I had the typical discussions and trial separations and we suffered through lengthy psychological summits. In the end, after we'd been dissected, analyzed, and disinfected by a plethora of experts and counselors, friends and foe, we found ourselves the recipients of lots of advice but no solutions.

Our efforts to find a solution were ultimately rendered even more complex by the lineup of lawyers ready to feather their nests. After wading through the last thick fog of the psychiatrists, we finalized our divorce in January 1976. It was my down time, big time! Since the State of Maine generally decreed that divorces were always and unequivocally the man's fault, custody of my two boys was granted to my wife. I had to battle for the least little visitation. Then, unexpectedly, because Louise had to deal with some medical problems, the boys came to live with me in an apartment I had built on the wharf.

It was a most precious time, and I was a happy old hermit with those two characters. Zeb was only partially housebroken and Toph was a preschooler. We worked on some great projects in the shop over that winter, and we grew together. We built a basket full of model boats. Those with sail were blown to kingdom come by puffed-up pink cheeks, and the rubber-band-driven paddleboats were wound so tightly that they would fan the air at their launching and endanger little fingers. Come the inevitable bath time, the boys and the whole basket of boats would all be crowded together in the tub—they had to be surrounded by each and every one, no exceptions—and the entire Spanish Armada would do battle with the soap.

I would get them dressed and ready for school, pull on their boots and mittens. Topher would take Zeb by the hand and walk him through the snow to nursery school. At home, we all ganged up together to do the chores. I did most of the cooking and, bad as it was, I would stand for "no complaints." If one whined, "I don't want any peas, Dad!" more peas would magically appear on the plate. The complainer soon learned not to say too much and, by the silence of the other diner, I knew the message had gotten through. I think to this day that they both hate peas.

Son, Topher, gives the captain a few pointers on how to trim the mainsail on a Gloucester fishing schooner. (author's collection)

It was a great joy working on projects and teaching them the use of and respect for tools. With supple minds, they learned so fast at that age that each new tidbit of knowledge was a wide-eyed wonder. They even built their own bunk beds. I sawed out the pieces and the boys hammered away, even hitting that elusive nail occasionally. Then they painted them to their own taste in color. Needless to say, the finished product was a bit rough and Zeb had paint all over himself, but we tossed the infected clothes out before the paint dried. They were pretty darn proud of that contraption they called a bunk.

At Christmas we lay down and blocked up a big sheet of plywood in their bedroom with two large holes cut through. Then we ran a train track in a figure eight around the holes so the boys could pop their heads up, one in each opening, and watch the cars coming by, right at their eye level. Topher, with fingers at the controls, would have his tongue sticking out with excitement and I was afraid Zeb would be permanently cross-eyed watching that train coming straight at his nose. We even built little houses and trees to make a village that looked like Camden, complete with harbor and lots and lots of boats.

I cut a hatch in the floor with a hinged cover and wrote "yucky stuff" on the front. Here they would toss their dirty clothes, and down the chute to the workshop below they went cascading directly into the open jaws of the washing machine. We all took turns washing up the dishes after dinner. Zeb would stand on a stool and mostly play in the water while I stood behind, reaching around him with the dishcloth, but he got the idea. I felt we were three small recluses, quiet, independent, solitary holdouts against the world. Those goons would prop me up when my courage faded, and I would dry the wonderful dirty tears on their cheeks when disaster struck a little finger or pink toe. Now that they were getting old enough to be safe, I was looking forward to a glorious season and sailing the summer away with my boys. When it was time for them to return to their mother, to clear my head, I decided to head for Florida in the little old tug with the big "W" on her stack.

That wonderful antique tugboat *Wrestler* was pulling at her lines and thirsting for a run to fetch a little warmth in her massive engine. So, after covering the *Adventure* and *Roseway* with their plastic winter houses and settling things for the long, cold season, my crew and I built accommodations into the little tug. We tucked a small quarter berth for crew on one side, and fashioned a large double berth forward, paneled a comfortable galley in between, and even "squoze" a head in the corner. From the pilot-house, it was just two steps down to the "boot heel," the small cabin with its charming settee on the after bulkhead and a black iron potbelly stove to kill the chill of sharp winter mornings. The gay kaleidoscope of colors from the stained-glass leaded windows and doors made rainbow patterns of light over the paneled walls. What a nice touch! Originally, when built in 1925, she'd been the baby of the fleet of Van Pelt towboats in Staten Island, New York. She was treated like the youngest child and given every amenity—yes, a spoiled brat of a tugboat. Thus, she had huge brass ports, a battery of horns, whistles and spotlights, wonderful rounded sections of hull form, and yacht-like varnished trim with fancy fittings throughout.

The settee in the cabin made for a comfortable bunk-seat with a bookshelf above. I took the back wall of the shelf out and replaced it with clear glass so that top of the old, red-painted, 150-horse Cooper-Bessemer engine was clearly visible and one could see the rockers of the valves and push rods all marching in cadence. We named the engine "Messy Bessie"—a play on her Bessemer heritage and a nod to the hand oiling she required. Then we named each of Messy Bessie's four cylinders. They were Herb, Harry, Fred, and Charlie. There were exhaust temperature gauges (pyrometers) that spied on the heat of each cylinder and would squeal on the guy who wasn't pulling his weight. We could then tinker with them and tune them so all would pull together. I would go for an engine room check, glance at the huge block of brass gauges, be sure we had the normal four pounds of engine oil pressure, two hundred pounds of compressed air in the tanks, and that the buzz box (automatic oiler) was full of oil and feeding the cylinder walls. Then I would take a wrench and tweak Harry or Fred or whoever was not in synch. I could take her pulse by hanging on to one of the push rods and make sure Bessie was clicking off her 225 rpms—her cruising speed.

Wrestler, with her sexy movie-star aura, always drew a crowd wherever she went. When I would start her, I first had to stand with all my weight on the bar inserted onto the enormous flywheel on the forward end of the engine in order to roll it up to the start position. Then, after pre-oiling and setting all to rights, I would reach up and pull the long air handle down, thus injecting pressure into each cylinder to start her rolling. The flywheel was so heavy that the centrifugal force of it, suddenly breaking inertia and turning, would rock the tug back and forth, giving the old boat the fluster of suddenly coming to life. Then the pie-size smoke rings would pop out of her able stack and soar skyward, and the sweet sound of her internal explosions would woo the crowd with the grandeur of a pipe band. She would sit there idling at about 50 turns a minute, little wavelets would emanate from the stout hull from the vibration, and onlookers with any sense of rhythm would inadvertently start an easy swaying at the hips. It was a big-band sound. Not much wonder I was in love.

Farmer Tom, patient fellow that he was, had by now recovered from his freezing and deafening *Roseway* experience. This dairy farmer's son proved to be a fine, sincere, even-tempered young man, and he returned to crew aboard *Wrestler*. Tom soon replaced his knowledge of a "cow hitch" with a "tugboat bowline" and all the other key splices and hitches needed aboard a vessel. Then he settled comfortably into the towboat world. After the 1975 schooner season ended, we took off with *Wrestler* on a lengthy cruise. We struck out for Gloucester, the New York South Street Seaport Museum, the Chesapeake Maritime Museum, and every interesting port of call on the Inland Waterway south. We gave tours, traded tours, had free dockage at almost every tugboat dock and commercial wharf from Maine to Florida, and were sincerely welcomed at many a private facility, too.

This saucy little tug, with her antique curved-glass, drop-type, rattle 'm-and-shake 'm pilothouse windows, engine thumping and jumping on its beds, every beam, every plank, and every rib reverberating like an old New York taxi on trolley tracks, had a sweet cadence that you would ac-

She's powerful, coquettish, and loveable—how could I possibly resist this tugboat. (author's collection)

tually miss at the end of the day. By comparison, when you shut down a screaming modern diesel after a day's run, you breathe a tremendous sigh of relief. The peace and quiet is always as welcome as a protected anchorage. When you shut off the old *Wrestler*, you would actually miss her music and keep on humming with Bessie's beat as if it was the theme of a popular musical show still going through your head. She would carry on in your subconscious long after you had collapsed in your bunk to work up a good "snore."

We chugged her through the Carolinas and the Golden Isles of Georgia, making friends along the way. Middy Ferguson, a good friend and grandson of Lucy Ferguson Carnegie, was so taken with the old tug that he gave us a fantastic tour of Cumberland Island. We were welcomed at Sapelo and traded a tour of *Wrestler* for a tour of the island and to see its rare and endangered animal species. After a cruise of the St. John River, at Sanford, we finally spun the wheel and turned her north.

Captain Jim Sharp conning from the port pilot house window. (photo: Steven Lang)

By this time we were tripping over a thousand-pound fisherman an-chor we had found on our travels and had draped over the walking space of the afterdeck—yet another "treasure" to fill up the dooryard at home. I had returned, off and on, to my office to catch up on business and the Camden hassles that were constantly plaguing me. But the experience of running that boat to the South is a memory I shall cherish forever.

Many years after that voyage with Tom on the *Wrestler*, in the early 1990s, I happened to be cruising once again down South and stopped for supplies in Fort Meyers, Florida. I boldly tied up to a glaringly private dock from which we could walk conveniently to a store for supplies. It was while I was puttering and fussing on *Dubbin' Around*, as we called the old cruising tub, that a man with a curious expression approached me. "You're from the state of Maine, huh?" he said, noticing our port of hail.

"Sure am," I responded.

He said, "I've been there. I got married in that state some years ago, and it was on one of them big schooners!"

"Is that right," I said. "What was the name of her?"

He said, "I can't remember. It was *Rose* something, I think."

"Oh," I said, "that was *Roseway*. I probably know the captain who performed the ceremony —was it Captain Young, or Captain Talbot?"

"No," he answered, "it was some guy named. . . Sharp!"

"That's me!" I exclaimed, just as amazed as he. "Well, now, how did it last?" I queried.

"Hey, man," he said, "I've been divorced for over five years now."

"There," I mused, "that shows you what kind of a splice I tied. . . musta been a slippery hitch!"

Chapter 14

The *Wannie* Comes to Town

Now, look out—my reckless abandon was flaring up again! It was the cold winter of 1976. Since the *Roseway* had sailed her first year and only needed a few little details like new mastheads, a large pulling boat for shore excursions, a work skiff, a dozen or more smaller projects, and since *Wrestler* was running as smoothly as a hundred-year-old grandfather clock, now a new idea popped into my head and started gnawing at my imagination. One little stop in Belfast—just one little short gander at the poor old *Clyde B. Holmes*, an enormous steam tugboat, laid up, out of commission, and looking horribly forlorn, got my gray matter completely out of control. Now, think of it—just think of what an incredible restaurant she would make!

Before tugboat purists jump all over me for turning a wonderful old steam tug into an eatery, consider my conversation with Clyde B., the owner. "Clyde, what will become of the old girl?" I inquired.

"Well, Captain Jim, I have tried to sell her, but not much luck there. Then I tried to give her away to a nonprofit foundation. She's been a hawser around my neck for a year now. . . costin' me money all the while, so I guess it's to the breakers for her."

"God, no, Clyde," I pleaded. "You wouldn't scrap her, would you? She has a history as long as your arm. . . She has an exciting story to tell the world!"

"Got no choice!" was the answer.

What was I to do? She was the last operational steam tugboat in the coastal U.S. She was a piece of history, a part of our past now too expensive to operate and too expensive to keep idle. "I'll buy her," I blurted out. "I'll give you the price of scrap. Will you tow her to Camden for me?"

"Yep, tomorrow," was the casual answer.

I headed back to Camden and went immediately to the code enforcement office. "What permitting is necessary for a floating structure in the harbor?" I tentatively asked.

"Well, if it is in the harbor, it's not in my bailiwick. You have to talk to the harbormaster," the official answered with all-knowing authority.

I went to the harbormaster and queried, "What permitting would I need to put a floating structure on the tidal flat up in my slipway beyond the harbor/wharf line?"

The answer was, "Beyond the wharf line is not in my jurisdiction."

I called the U.S. Coast Guard, inquiring about a floating structure permanently chained to the dock. If it was incapable of going to sea, it wasn't their problem. In the Office of Documentation, it was determined the vessel would remain in current documentation if she were "under repair" and with no time limit. I was sitting in a little niche the bureaucracy hadn't thought to regulate. . . yet.

The next hurdle was to convince sister Chris, who was happily running the Chowder House and living in Camden, to jump in to run the old tugboat as an elegant, expensive, and most unusual restaurant. She said, "You are nuts! How big is this thing?" I explained that the *Clyde* was about 140 feet long, quite burdensome, wide, had three decks and a towering stack. "Did you tell the town fathers that?" she demanded. I tried to explain that I didn't see the point in stirring up the pot before it boils. Who knows, it might not boil at all.

Well, it took some jolly moral 'suasion to bring Chris around, but around she came! After a while, her dear sweet brother, piling up the convincing arguments and raining them down on her common sense, soon had her launched into the project with gusto. As always with such projects of mine, this one commenced in the dead of the Maine winter with the temperature hovering around zero. The harbor had been frozen over and there were big blocks of ice in the slipway where the *Clyde* was expected to arrive on the high tide at 5:30 the next morning.

With a 10-foot pole in hand, I was drifting around in a work skiff, nosing these ice cakes out of the confines of the slip, in the dark of night, and of all people, Sam Manning, a local draftsman, artist, and a night owl, came roaming by about two a.m.. "Jim," he burped, "what in the devil are you doing at this hour in the ice cauldron of that slip, playin' polo with ice cakes?"

Avoiding eye contact, I answered, "Aw, well, I couldn't sleep, Sam, and had nothin' else to do." It was so cold, I was sure he wouldn't argue or prod for very long and, sure enough, he soon went off, muttering to himself.

Promptly at 4:45 a.m. the *Clyde B. Holmes* arrived, nosing through the sea smoke and into the harbor. The temperature was plus two Fahrenheit. With the tug *Mary Holmes* on the hip, propeller churning, the *Clyde* was shoved up the gravel slipway until she took the bottom and her starboard side lay gently against the granite wall. Leaving her charge, the *Mary* backed and filled and disappeared into the mist. Oh my God, didn't that old steam tugboat look positively colossal standing up high in the parking lot, her stack dominating the skyline of Camden Harbor! I turned to Chris and exclaimed, "I guess our town of Camden will buzz some good today!"

After we got her settled and ballasted so she would lie comfortably against the wall and put on chains to hold her, we started making plans for the conversion. Climbing aboard, Chris and I went through the cavernous interior, scratching our heads and wondering where to start. We had decided from the outset to change her name back to the original *John Wanamaker* and emphasize her history as a Philadelphia tugboat through pictures and décor. John Wanamaker is a name recognized in that city for he had been a very successful businessman, philanthropist, and a well-known citizen.

The *Wannie* had been built in 1925 to assist docking and ice breaking on the Delaware River and to provide convenient electric power from her capable steam generators when necessary for emergencies. No expense was spared in her construction. She had an enormous, 1,000-horse steam power plant resting in the bowels of the engine room, mostly covered with black, grimy oil, but, wow, what an exciting engine! Chris and I maneuvered around the huge brass handles that the engineer pulled to reverse the Stevenson link, and climbed down the steel ladder to view the enormity of that machine.

It was a two-cylinder, double-expansion behemoth fully 15 feet high and about 20 feet long. It had brass oilers everywhere, humongous bearing journals, brass gauges all over the bulkheads, little bells, big bells, and one huge brass signaling gong for enthusiasts to positively salivate over. We gazed at a plethora of small engines for pumping and transfer of fuel and other vital liquids. There were valves with nameplates everywhere and a fine film of grease, oil, soot, and grime covering all. The entire engine room was a mad maze of piping and valve handles, foot hazards, and head bashers. Poor Chris was horrified. I was ecstatic.

"Don't worry, Sis," I said, "someday we will have this so clean and polished, you will fancy taking your breakfast right here!"

Despite her look of disdain, we walked through the alleyway between the great square fuel tanks. "And see," I said looking at the fuel gauge, "here is our first pot of gold!" According to the gauges, the *Wannie* had 10,500 gallons of bunker C fuel left in the tanks. "We'll steam the fuel until liquid, pump it off, and sell it!"

"Sure you will," she grunted sarcastically.

We walked into the boiler room where a maze of steel, boilerplate, and rivets by the thousands greeted us. I slammed the firebox door open and stuck my head into the gloom and soot of the fire tubes. "Magnificent," I murmured reverently to Chris. It is best that I forgot what she answered. I banged the door shut. The sound echoed raucously from several directions. Our hands were already covered with black grease as we continued our tour.

The fo'c's'le, where the crew slept, would convert into the kitchen, the old galley would be an exclusive dining area, the fiddley (upper engine-room) would become the reception area. The after-house would become the bar area. Because the Philadelphia lawyers and politicians who built this tug wanted to have a vessel to entertain dignitaries on the Delaware River, they had paneled the rooms aft of the fiddley with imported mahogany. They did it up "round" with the taxpayers' money and included a vestibule with library, shelves, lounge chairs, and polished brass portholes. We would restore the woodwork, bringing out the warm patina of the fine, old texture and put in plush chairs with indirect lighting. I got my rule out and started measuring for scale drawings of everything.

That bunker C fuel was the first thing on my agenda. It was valuable. It was also thick, just black tar, and would not pump unless heated. I called the local tug company and hired their engineer to come and steam the old boiler for the last time to heat the fuel. Then I got a couple of tank trucks to load up that black gold and sold the fuel to the local hospital at the going rate.

Later that day, when I was driving home, I passed a used-car lot. Screeching to a stop, I jumped from the car. There above me was a complete Volkswagen with "Mainely Used Cars" painted on the side. The thing was advertising its message while dangling from a wire on a big Loraine crane, swinging back and forth like some kind of balloon. I approached the salesman and said, "How much for that?" pointing up to the 100-foot long boom on the crane reaching skyward. He said, "The Volks?"

"Naw," I answered, "the crane!"

We made a deal and he promised to deliver the crane to my wharf in the morning. Sure enough, bright and early, the old monstrosity came alternately squeaking, jumping, roaring, and squealing down the hill to my parking lot. It was 100-ton capacity and had two engines, one for the crane and one for the truck. There were two hoisting wires on winches, all controlled by eight levers and three pedals. I counted nine wheels, all with bald tires, only one with tread, and four hand-operated, backbreaking jack-up feet. When the boom was extended, it reached over 100 feet high, well above the highest part of the tug. It was ancient. It was dangerous. It was titanic and atrocious. But to me, it was a jewel, and I named it, with reverence, Ichabod.

Although most everyone in town thought me mad, I silently suspected many were secretly envious. Who else in town had a crane, named Ichabod, to play with? I begged the operator to help set up the thing and show me how all those levers worked. With a quick, cursory set of instructions, I put a chain around a piece of granite and, after making sure there were no little kids or Cadillacs in the lot, I picked up the granite, then carefully lowered it. I picked it up again, slowly moved a little, and lowered it. I went at it a little at a time until I was comfortable. "And now, Ichabod Crane," I said out loud, "'tis time for us to go to work!"

The *Wannie's* huge stack was the first thing to come off, opening a 15-foot hole in the deckhouse over the boiler. Gingerly, I laid the stack down next to my shop. I got a crew together, fired up the oxy-acetylene torches, and we started cutting the boiler to pieces. We had to get oxygen for the torches in the largest tanks from hospital suppliers as we were cutting through four-inch-thick boilerplate. It took weeks to carve that boiler into manageable pieces, hoisting them out the stack hole with the crane and piling them up in a mound of twisted iron that gradually rose higher than my shop. It sure looked a mess, but we knew it was only temporary. I had to separate the brass from the steel in order to sell it to the scrap dealers, but fortunately the price of soft metal was high. "What must the town think?" said sister Chris.

Next came the fuel tanks. I found a colorful local character named Don who was a self-proclaimed expert on fuel oil. He applied for the job of cleaning and burning out the bunker tanks. I gratefully accepted, as there was no way I was going down inside those tanks and strike a flame to a cutting torch. Now understand there was only one way to enter the tanks, and that was through a little, round, two-foot-diameter manhole down through the deck. Inside the 15-foot-deep tank, it was terribly dark, slippery, and cavernous. The cutting process had to start there on the inside, for if the torch cut through from the outside of the tank, the sparks would set all the leftover fuel on the tank bottom afire.

Before anything could happen, the tanks had to be cleaned. Don was built like a bait barrel so that when he entered the tanks to start the cleaning process, he had to assist his own entry by poking through the numerous rolls of his belly, working them down through the manhole a roll at a time, very much like half-filled balloons. Then his considerably smaller chest could follow. Once inside, he went down a 15-foot ladder to reach the tank's bottom. There was no way he would be able to exit in a hurry, unless perhaps he was blown out like a cork from a split of champagne.

Slopping around in, smelling, and sliding in all that oil until he was saturated and so much the color of bunker that his bulk was hard to distinguish in the gloom of the tank, our hero accomplished the washing and cleaning. Using light stove oil to thin the gooey, thick bunker C, Don scrubbed, cleaned, and pumped out the excess until he was happy with the result and was ready to cut. By then, Don was so oil-coated that when he got ready to strike the torch, I was sure the poor fellow would set himself on fire. I left. I wasn't going to be there if the old thing blew up. With one ear cocked for an explosion, I went uptown to Chris's Chowder House for coffee.

I've got to give credit where credit is due. Don, as planned, put the torch to it. He didn't blow himself up. The bilge was full of oil, too, so we had a man with an extinguisher on the other side of the tank to keep the sparks from setting the bilge afire. When he was ready, our expert casually struck the igniter to the nozzle, put the hot blue flame to the raw steel, and opened a great gaping hole in the starboard tank. He then walked out the opening and did the whole routine to the tank on the port side.

I screwed up my courage and watched when he burned the second tank out. We had many fires aboard, with the sparks going into old grease and oil, but only one fire got away to the point where we had to use the really big extinguisher. That was exciting. The flames shot up 20 feet as the fire heated up and the smoke billowed out the old stack hole till the phones were ringing merrily at the local volunteer fire company. We had it under control and all but out when they came screeching around the corner, sirens all a-singin' and horns a-honkin'. In the end, they thought it was a good exercise to massage their skills. I was able to sell the scrap at a fair price and pay the crew working on the renovation right up to the point where we laid the floor and started on the kitchen. Then, with empty pockets, I had to go to the bank and beg.

We cleaned, polished, and painted that old steam engine until it shone like a true museum piece. I had to get it running. Since it was direct drive—when the engine turned, the prop turned as well—I went down in the shaft alley, took a torch, and cut through the one-foot-diameter propeller shaft. This disconnected the prop and allowed me to rig a gear on the inboard end of the shaft. I then hooked the gear to an electric motor with a 64:1 reduction. If the electric motor, with its low gear ratio, would turn that engine slowly, quietly at dinner, it would be an incredible frontispiece! What restaurant in the world had a 1,000-horsepower steam engine rolling over in the middle of the dining room floor? This would most certainly be "a most unusual restaurant" and that phrase would become our logo.

Those enormous journals on the crankshaft were at 90 degrees opposed, so she wouldn't stick on center and then be impossible to start. Since they built this huge engine without counterweights, it took an incredible amount of power to simply make the shaft rotate. My electric motor just wouldn't lift the pistons, rods, crossheads, and a zillion nuts and bolts, so I decided to take the heads off and remove the pistons from inside the cylinders.

We started with the smaller, high-pressure cylinder. We removed half a hundred bolts to release the head and, using an overhead traveling crane and a chain fall, we lifted it aside so we could attack the piston. It took four of us hanging on to a six-foot pipe wrench (to which we'd added a length of pipe to further increase our leverage) with all our strength on the bitter end to dislodge the king nut on the piston rod shaft. Then, hooking the chain falls to the piston and taking up quite a strain, we squirted on a good slather of penetrating oil and gave the shaft a heck of a licking with a 20-pound maul. The piston, with a bang, finally jumped off the tapered end of the connecting rod.

The low-pressure cylinder, at eight feet across, was a different matter entirely. Even using the biggest wrench we had with a long pipe extension on it, we had to put heat on the nut and then use a chain fall on the wrench to get that king nut to turn. This piston was about six inches thick, was made of solid steel, and had been on that tapered shaft since 1925. The darn thing sure seemed to be happiest where it was. We took three chain falls to an overhead I beam, bolted their hauling parts in three places to the piston, swung that 20-pound maul up over our heads, and with every bit of fire we could muster, came down on the top of the protruding piston connecting rod shaft. The old shaft paid no attention to our efforts. As we continued with the internal destruction, I told the crew that every time they went by this stubborn piston shaft, to give it a squirt of penetrating oil, jerk a little more pressure on the chain falls, and "pound the darn thing with the maul 'til you're winded." Then, go back to whatever they were doing!

It took six days! For six days, each time we passed that mulish, obstinate piston rod, which happened at least fifteen or twenty times a day, we pounded the living hell out of the top of the shaft until our heart rate went through the roof. We continually pulled with a gut-wrenching strain on those three chain falls and continually slobbered on quarts of penetrating oil until she finally succumbed! Miraculously, and as luck would have it, I was the one on the business end of that maul when she popped! Hallelujah!

We wrestled that huge piston out of there and on to Ichabod's big hook and swung it ashore. It had occurred to me that working on this old steam engine might be viewed as an accident waiting to happen, but the first accident came, as they always do, quite unexpectedly. When reinstalling the head, my glove caught on one of the scores of head bolts, and that steel cylinder head came down right on my little finger and took the tip right off. I could see the bone sticking out of the end. I wanted to go ahead and try to turn her but they argued me into the car and off to the hospital for half a dozen stitches. The injury was incidental, but the result a bit of a nuisance. The little finger healed about a quarter inch shorter than before the accident. Now I had a bum finger to match my bum leg, and when I would sit down to play the guitar, I had to reprogram that finger to reach certain chords.

As soon as I returned from the hospital, I, with great excitement, tried the electric motor. The engine still wouldn't turn. Dejectedly, I went back to the drawing board. The only solution was to create a counterweight. I could do it way back in the shaft alley where no one would see it from the dining room. Taking some scrap steel, I welded up a box eight feet long and tacked it to the shaft opposite where the weight of the journals came. Then I filled the box with rails and scrap iron, poured cement in the crevices, welded a cover to the box, and pushed the button. Hallelujah—she turned, and I was some excited! Without giving the matter much thought, I jumped up on the side of the engine to oil some of the shafting and foolishly put my hand around a jackshaft that had never turned before. Now, however, the engine was turning, and the jackshaft was, too. It crushed my hand, exploding the fleshy part between wrist and thumb to the tune of over a dozen stitches. That was my second penance, but she turned!

It was really a wonder that we didn't have more accidents, considering the magnitude of the project and the kind of work we had to do. All in all, we really got off easy. I seemed to be the only one who was accident-prone, and probably that was 'cause I was always in a hurry. Had to get finished like I was in a race or something. Time was money! I can still see the horror of what happened next in my mind's eye.

It was a steel bulkhead we were cutting. I was on a ladder, severing the last of a fitting to release a heavy steel plate about 10 by 15 feet and weighing in at hundreds of pounds. After severing the steel connection, I jumped from the ladder. With a sledgehammer, I hit that steel as hard as I could. It refused to budge. Yet, there was no apparent connection. I had cleanly cut the entire piece, but it seemed to be held there by habit only. We put pressure on it and pried, jacked, and pounded it to make the damn thing move. No luck. I went behind it to see what was holding the cussed thing and, to my surprise when it fell, it came the wrong way! Although tipped away from me, the bulkhead came toward me, not away.

What happened to the laws of gravity? By the grace of God, there was a small bracket left in the center of the plate. It was the only little bump left on the steel plate and it caught on the ladder for only a half second, just as the plate was teetering and ready to crash down on my head. This afforded me just enough time to jump aside, and the ladder collapsed under the steel and was instantly crushed and splintered to matchwood. I suddenly became a believer.

We encased that beautiful engine in glass. We polished every fitting until they gleamed and installed indirect lighting that dramatized the engine's motion. Then we moved on to complete the rest of the restaurant's décor. I had saved the front crown of the boiler, truly an engineering masterpiece. As we needed a little ballast on the port side, I painted that boiler crown beautifully and chained it to the bulkhead in the lower dining area. Many of the small steam auxiliary engines and pump engines were fascinating works of art in themselves, so these were restored and displayed on miscellaneous shelves around the lower decks. Then, we hung a large collection of huge, historic photographs of the old tug steaming along, docking ships and towing up river. These were framed and hung to hide any unfinished remnants of our cutting and welding, to screen the "no-want-to-see-'em" areas, and to lend a true tugboat atmosphere.

Our carpenters crafted natural wood paneling, beautiful mahogany trim, sweeping, curved rails and stairways, all highly varnished to perfection. When the thick carpet was finally laid, we had three dining rooms with seating for 125 persons, plus twenty-five more in the fiddley for cocktails. Then we arranged the top deck for a lunch area accommodating seventy-five more. The tablecloths were rich Scottish plaid. There were wonderful, soft linen napkins, sterling utensils, and wine glasses that rang in anticipation of the truly fine French product to be served.

My sister hired a pianist and harpist to entertain at the dinner hour and, by August, dressed in royal evening garb, Chris and I were celebrating our grand opening. When the musicians took a break from their musical interlude, they would push the button and start that colossal engine rolling slowly over. The highly polished brass and steel rods and journals would flash in the spotlights, and our dining guests would excitedly jump from their chairs to see the grand sight of that magnificent machine showing off. Old engineers and steam men were positively enthralled. They would point out the various parts: the Stevenson link, the valves, the oiler, the journals, the knuckle of the connecting rod, the main shaft, the levers, the bells, the gauges, the engineer's log, and the main steam line. I loved standing in the shadows, just listening.

It was an expensive restaurant. I confess that, although I owned the joint and didn't have to pay the tab, the tip alone tempered my dining habits. Walter Cronkite became a regular, and John Wanamaker himself presented Chris with congratulations and a family heirloom to display in the foyer. In fact, the restaurant proved such an attraction, it drew in a wide variety of famous guests. Chris made sure the food was excellent, the atmosphere spectacular, and with twenty-one employees running all over the ship, the service was impeccable.

With an unequaled view of Camden Harbor, the *Wannie* was a humming place. We needed a sign up on the street. It had to be something elegant to attract attention. I drew up plans for a sign with a full model of a tug in the middle of an eight-foot oval of wood with rolled steel scrolls on the perimeter, a hawser in the oval, and gold-leafed carved words, "SS John Wanamaker, A Most Unusual Restaurant." My crew and I made the sign and the tug model in the shop and I went to a tin knocker to have the steel rolled for the scrolls. He had the stock for three weeks before he whined and complained that he couldn't do it. I got angry, grabbed the steel strips, built a jig of wood in my own shop, rolled the steel, made all the scrolls, and bolted them on. It was a splendid sign.

In all, it took us six months to convert the old tug to an elegant restaurant. At the same time, I had to outfit the old *Adventure* that season and sail her over the summer. Yes, there were some fun times with the *Wannie* and some rough times as well. I remember one roaring sou'easter we had in the fall when she unexpectedly floated on a high run of tide and started to roll back and forth in her berth. Chris about died when the chandelier over the upper dining area started to swing precariously and some diners started to complain about being seasick.

I had to get the old boat up higher in her berth so she wouldn't float even on the highest tide. With the next storm tide, I hooked on to her stem head with the crane and, with Ichabod puffing and blowing, I lifted the *Wannie's* bow. Then I pulled her ahead with my straining station wagon, using the poor old buggy like some kind of a bulldozer. I was only partly successful in drawing her ahead into shoal water, but was completely successful in annihilating my poor suffering transmission!

Of course, we had to have a large, nasty holding tank for sewerage down in the bowels of the ship. There was a cussed complicated pump that pumped the indescribable effluent congregating in that tank to the sewer ashore, and that pump was always giving us trouble. The worst happened when the pump clogged one Saturday evening with a dinning room full of elegantly dressed, hungry diners looking for a very perfect, very expensive, sumptuous repast. I was on hand trying to fix the problem and sent for Wayne, my mate on the schooner, to come over and bring the largest pipe wrench he could find in the shop. He arrived looking like the typical schooner bum, pants ripped, shirt dirty and torn, and needing a shower as we had just come in from the week at sea. He'd been busy cleaning up *Adventure* and had no time to clean himself.

Wayne had an eight-foot wrench over his shoulder and marched along in cadence, rather evocative of the changing of the Buckingham Palace guard—Queen in attendance. He entered the storeroom with a huge smirk on his face, bubbling over with all the gory details of his march through the formal dining room packed with astonished patrons. Then he rolled up his sleeves, and we turned to and took the cranky sewage pump apart. Ah, the cans of deodorizer used to quell the tragedies behind the scenes!

Thanks to her experience at the Chowder House, Chris understood the delicate balance of restaurant economics. One day, when checking stock, she discovered that wine was mysteriously disappearing from the wine locker. Even though the very expensive bottles were locked and guarded, the pilfering was going on right under our noses. My sister suspected the cleanup boy, who was helper and gofer for the supplies stored in my shop across the parking lot. I said, "Sis, you send him over for some weird supply tonight when it is pitch dark in the shop, and I'll confront him."

The only way to turn a light on in my shop was by a string in the middle of the room reachable only by dancing around and through boxes of stuff, wood, tools, and small boats that were always scattered around. At the appointed hour, I stood behind the door in the shadows and waited. The gofer arrived and let himself into the darkened shop. He carefully shut the door and I grabbed him from behind. I was pretty strong in those days from working on the schooner, and I locked him up with one arm encircling his limbs and torso in a death grip and taking my flashlight in the other hand, putting it full in his face, I bellowed, "All right, I want a complete confession."

"A-a-about what?" he mumbled in fright.

"The disappearance of the wine!" I shouted in his ear. Poor fellow was so afraid he went limp in my arms. He did confess, however, and we learned he was taking the wine from the locker when the waiters needed a bottle and had temporarily turned their backs. Then, hiding it on the shelf by the porthole in the utility locker and leaving that port slightly ajar, he would return to retrieve his hooch at night after closing. He had been enjoying some very good French wine for some time, thanks to Chris's trusting nature.

Live and learn in the restaurant business while the balance sheet turns red! That fall, four days before closing for the season, there was a purchase of a large box of steaks and chops that our cook had ordered before he went to his new job. They never made it into the freezer, and we didn't even discover it until we had time to total out the invoices and go over the purchases.

We owned and ran the *Wannie* for four years. The first year, opening late in the season, we lost money. The next year we broke about even, and following two years we were so busy that Chris was exhausted. With employee problems, four decks to run up and down, cook problems, and Chris so conscientious and worrying over everything, she finally broke down. I came back from a week on the schooner and found her on Saturday, about noon, dissolved in tears on the front steps. The cook had broken his leg; the salad chef had quit due to family problems; the cleanup boy hadn't shown up for work; and the holding tank was overflowing again! I said, "Sister dear, we don't need all this to make a living. Let's get rid of the monster and lease it out." She reluctantly agreed, so I started casting around to find a site for her in some other neighborhood.

Strangely, in 1979, restaurateurs surfaced who wanted to lease the vessel and tie her up in Boston at the Children's Museum, and it looked like a fitting opportunity. I tightened her up, pulled her out of her slip on a high tide, backed two cement trucks to the side of her, and dumped their full load into the bottom of the bilge through a hole we cut through the floor of the main dining room. This, I figured, would partially replace the tons and tons of weight of the removed boiler and tanks, giving her ballast enough to remain upright for the tow to Beantown. I found a tug headed that way, and we sent her off—relieved but with a tear in the eye—to her new fate. After the dust settled, we thought we were in clover! We had the income and not the responsibility. What a glorious release! Someone else had all the employees, bookkeeping, taxes, liability, ordering, and maintenance, and they even took that damn sewage tank! Two years later they went bust and could no longer pay the rent.

Now we had a tug in Boston that was threatening to cost us bigtime in both bucks and aggravation. Do we keep her there or bring her home? The whole thing could easily turn into an overwhelming financial disaster, not only short term, but if she sat abandoned for a long period, she would soon start to deteriorate and could easily end up a derelict like so many other dream vessel projects in the world. We were scratching our heads to determine how we could collect the rent or what disposition we could make of the old thing when a friend gave me an article from the *Cape Cod Times* about a consortium of men preparing to purchase an old and

A most unusual restaurant—the converted steam tug John Wanamaker.
(photo: Neal Parent)

decrepit wooden tug named *Pegasus*. They were intending to convert it to—of all things—a restaurant!

It didn't take me long to dial their number. "That old wooden vessel you're considering will bury you with maintenance," I exploded, "and since she is older than sin and in very poor condition, just to clean her up will cost you months of hard labor and expense. Look," I explained, "I have an iron tug just around the corner, all converted and operating there right in the heart of Boston. All you have to do is tow it to your site"—which was Quincy, south of Boston—"and plug her in to the shore!"

They bit down hard and we let them own it with a 10-year mortgage at 12 percent! Their new name, shamefully, was *Edmund Fitzgerald* and they painted her a disgusting light blue color. A light blue tugboat! But what a piece of luck for us! Interest rates fell, but ours was fixed and, fortunately, it took them over nine years to go bankrupt. Then the vessel lay empty, but since we were sure we were sitting pretty with the first mortgage, we applied a little pressure, telling them to come up with the balance or else!

Then, by chance, we found to our amazement that, through incompetence and negligence by our fast-talking attorney, our mortgage had never been recorded. We actually had nothing backing the note but friendly persuasion. Fortunately, however, the owners hadn't discovered our precarious position, and we soft-pedaled our complaints until they were able to sell the ship and pay us. They never suspected the legal error and were sure that they needed our wholehearted cooperation to effect the sale. We were just marshmallow landlords all throughout the process. We got paid. Phew!

Chapter 15

Hollywood Comes to Camden

"We are the vessel *We're Here* and bound for Glow-chess-tar."

"No, Karl, it's Gloucester, pronounced Gloss-ter!"

I was trying to get Karl Malden to sound nautical and proper for the 1977 movie version of *Captains Courageous* in which Rosemont Productions was, to my mind, floundering around in an effort to do a remake of this famous classic. Poor Rudyard Kipling would turn over with a groan if he were forced to endure the eventual video. Ricardo Montalban took diction lessons to enhance his Portuguese accent for the fishing dialogue, but they neglected to teach Malden how to pronounce his home port.

The 1930s version of this movie, with Spencer Tracy, Freddy Bartholomew, and Lionel Barrymore, was wonderful. That film had used the *Oretha Spinney*—sister ship to the *Adventure*—as the novel's famous *We're Here*. The producers of this modern version for the Bell Telephone Hour were looking for vessels and a backdrop. Where, now, could they find authentic Gloucester fishing schooners for the fishing scenes except on the coast of Maine, and where other than at Sharp's Wharf? I guess they had no choice. They had to charter me!

The film crews thundered into my dooryard in March 1977, with trucks, trailers, buses, and camper rigs. There was a team of artists, carpenters, and research men. The object was to age and antique the vessels as they would have looked when fishing, restore the fo'c's'le as the fishermens' living quarters, and to collect dories and fishing gear that would have been used on the Grand Banks. All of this had to be done in advance of the arrival of the production crew and cast. They were good guys to work with. I could show them pictures of how the gear should look and just how dirty and disheveled a Gloucester fishing schooner would be when doing her thing. I agreed to have them paint my beautiful white hull a dirty black with streaks of rust and gurry running down all over it, but I would paint it white again before the summer season. They put new nameboards that read *We're Here* over *Adventure*'s name. They artfully made everything look weather-worn and authentic.

In changing our mess room back into the original fisherman's fo'c's'le, the set crew agreed not to use any nails on our pretty varnished paneling. Instead, they would prop up all bunks and tables using wedges. Their carpenters were clever and, when finished, *Adventure* looked just like a Grand Banker down below, even to the oil skins (foulweather clothes), underwear, and dirty socks hanging around. The rails, waterways, and decks were painted a faded gray and had fish guts, gurry galore, blood stains, and streaks of dirt and filth. A potato sack was thrown over the radar dome, and fish hatches were knocked together to replace my varnished skylights. In the meantime, the dories, fishing tackle, trawl tubs, baskets, and a goodly supply of wiggleable rubber fish were piling up all over the wharf.

Both *Adventure* and *Roseway* had been chartered, so Orvil and I were out straight putting on sails and rigging and preparing the vessels for sea. We were two months early, but had to get this movie made and then reserve enough time to get re-outfitted for summer. In the middle of this frenetic activity, no one noticed a man with blue pants, a blue matching tie, and black, polished shoes standing on the wharf. If you add a fine mustache to that garb, you have a Coast Guard inspector every time. He quietly asked for me, stood too close for my comfort, and said, "The penalty for an illegal or unregistered name change is confiscation of the vessel, a fine, and possible incarceration!"

When I picked up my jaw, I explained that it was only for two weeks and just for the movie. None of this impressed him, but he did give me twenty-four hours since our real name was still on the bow of the vessel under the painted *We're Here* name board. He admitted quietly that, had he not seen the picture in the paper, and an article describing the film, he wouldn't have had a clue. I burned up the roadway to Portland's Office of Documentation to fill out the applications for a formal name change, but we decided to leave the *Roseway*'s name alone.

All the rest of this frenzied preparation went "finest kind" until the filming really started. Then the quality and emphasis on authenticity slowly went downhill. I got the feeling that the cost amounted to more than they had budgeted, so they started to cut down. I was fierce to see a quality movie out of this, and started to offer some things to help, such as the use of my crane, harbor floats, and small boats to move their gear to facilitate the logistics of setting up some of the shots.

For the sake of convenience and budget, we sailed from Rockland, where we could fetch open water more quickly than in Camden. What's more, the cast, who was housed at the Samoset Resort, could sleep a little later. Except for the fog scenes, we would be filming offshore with no sign of land in the background. The director hoped that filming would be done with a little—but not too much—sea running. They had a hell of a time with their equipment when the wind blew. The big, heavy light stands and reflective umbrellas used for lighting balance would get carried away by most any little breeze, or fall over with the rolling of the vessel. This could not only damage the equipment, but also threatened to put great ugly scars in my deck! Of course, we had a huge 4,000-pound generator thumping on the foredeck to power all the equipment.

The funniest part for us extras was the crew of actors. They were all dressed up and did look like fishermen, but they turned immediately green around the gills when we had a little weather. They complained that they were used to working in a studio on solid ground where they could pop out and pick up a pizza anytime. This business of actually sailing on a real vessel proved to be a terrible hardship.

As things developed, the crew's biggest problem turned out to be, of all things, the ship's head, the toilet. Flushing required manual labor—pumping—and this impressed the actors as incredibly primitive.

In wardrobe, the courageous captains—Jim Sharp, Karl Malden, Leo Hynes.
(author's collection)

They refused to flush after use. At my wit's end one day, I called a captain's conference and lined them all up, put on my master's voice, and read the riot act to them. There was Karl Malden, Ricardo Montalban, Fred Gwynne ("The Munsters"), Jeff Corey (*Butch Cassidy and the Sundance Kid*), Stan Haze ("Roots"), Neville Brand (with the perpetual cigar), Charles Dierkop ("Policewomen" on TV), Jonathan Kahn and John Doran (both 15 years old and playing Harvey and the captain's son, respectively), the director, producer, sound and light crew, and a host of grip-and-gripe Hollywoodites.

I cleared my throat and exploded with a wrath that came very close to unbecoming language. I explained in no uncertain terms that if they wouldn't act like a housebroken collection of educated dogs instead of barbarians and savages, we would call this whole damn thing off. "I will not hold your hands, and I will not flush your toilets for you. That is final!"

They all looked like little school kids under the dean's whip. Things began to shape up after that.

Actually, with time, they learned to accept the vessel, and soon the old *Adventure* cast her magic spell over most of them and brought them into her fold. They came around to act the parts with more proficiency because it was the real "schooner thing," not a studio with a union-approved lounge with fresh coffee and flush toilets. One day, we had a delivery of 400 pounds of real fish. The pile of slimy fish and the flies that accompanied them were in a heap on deck for four days (sans ice), contributing further to the ambiance and aromatic atmosphere.

The numerous jokes while the cast handled the slippery fish seemed to put everyone at ease, and a whole lot more feeling went into the production. My crew put the old fish on the hooks of the trawl and had a big laugh when Ricardo, hauling in the line, a fish on each hook, went to unhook the catch. He tried to do so without getting the fish too close. His arms were stretched at length, slimy fish extended as far away as possible! Of course, the cameras caught just about every embarrassing spasm. Meanwhile, the fish, basking in the sun on deck, had become mealy and tough. The director instructed Ricardo to "wiggle the fish when you put them into the boat so they look more alive!"

Finally, on the fifth day of filming, a professional gang of real Rockland fishermen was sent in to split and gut the catch. The lights and cameras started to hum. "Quiet on the set," spat from the director. "Rolling. Take one." Knives flashed and, anxious to show their expertise, the old pros went at those torpid scales with verve. The quiet on the set was, not surprisingly, interrupted occasionally with a rash of profane utterances as the fishermen had a terrible time cutting into the rubbery, days-old flesh of those old scaly *poissons*.

The biggest scene coming up was to be the race to market. Everyone was abuzz about it. We were praying for a suitable "breeze o' wind" so the *Adventure* and *Roseway* could do their stuff, and a helicopter had been chartered in anticipation of a great shoot. The day came with 25 knots of wind, but the director had scheduled a mundane deck scene and turned a deaf ear to both the weather forecast and to my entreaties. We pitched and rolled the morning away, picking up overturned lights and feeding Dramamine to the cast. I kept telling them that this is the day for the race and they may not get another. Finally, in mid-afternoon, to everyone's relief, they gave up the deck shots and we got the chance to let the vessels romp. They couldn't contact the heliport, so they settled for a fast powerboat to take one of the two big cameras aboard and go out in front of us.

The seas were tumbling and old *Adventure*, leaving *Roseway* behind, took off reaching at 13 or 14 knots. Spray and spume crashed aboard forward as we raced up the bay, and actors and crew alike were electrified with the scene and with sudden passion for the sea. It was the first time they really allowed themselves to be captivated by the panorama around us and the excitement of sailing such a vessel. We spent a couple of hours doing pirouettes with the *Roseway* in the lower bay, reveling in the great sailing, while the camera boat struggled to stay ahead and the cinematographer dug his nails into a none-too-steady platform for the takes. They got some footage until the boat took a sea, lurched, and threw the $100,000 movie machine to the deck and broke it. That ended the shooting for that day.

Then, with the wind moderating, we started for home, everyone aboard higher than a kite. I was getting chilly standing at the wheel, so Fred Gwynne, with a wry smile, lent me his coat. It was huge, of course, big enough for a Munster. In fact, it was so big that one of my crew who was standing beside me joined me! We both fit easily inside, my right arm out of one sleeve and his left from the other. We looked like a two-headed helmsman. Returning the coat, I then went below for a mug-up and met Ricardo humming to himself. I started to sing with him in harmony. Others gathered around, and for an hour we all sang at the top of our voices, cast and crew alike, and darned if we didn't sound pretty good. They insisted it was the most exciting day they ever had on the water, and from that day on, not one of them ever mentioned feeling seasick, took Dramamine, or complained about pumping the head.

We were a week at sea. In and out each day, down the bay to Matinicus and back each night. We were all in wardrobe and had to grow beards for the costume. I grew one that looked like an old whitewashing broom, and Captain Orvil had a beautiful "Abe Lincoln" face. Most everyone had horrible stubble, and the makeup artists would come with a toothbrush before the shooting and comb out the whiskers in a futile effort to try to make them behave. I tried to tell the director that, of the hundreds of photos I have of Gloucester fishermen at work, not one had a beard.

The only actor with a clean-shaven face was Stan Haze. He was a huge black man with a completely bald head, polished and ebony all over. He wore a derby of the same dark color, and I used to kid him, saying, "Stan, I like your lid. . . I want that lid! After all, you don't need anything more than the brim. The top of that hat already looks like your own head." He was a great guy, and we joked back and forth about his head and his suntan until, at the end of the filming, he gave me the hat. I still have it.

The two fifteen-year-old kids were miscast. Jonathan Kahn was a very polite, refined English boy that everyone liked. In the film, he played the spoiled little rich kid who was picked up by the *We're Here* and who tried very hard to be disliked. John Doran was an American and a typical teenager, with smart answers and a know-it-all from the get-go. He played the captain's son, a hardworking good boy trying to help the rich kid get adjusted to shipboard life. He should have looked at himself and taken a lesson from Kipling. Karl Malden was a polite and modest man. When he took his place at the wheel, expounding the entire nautical dictionary to the cameras, I would be behind him quietly saying, "Three spokes to the right, Karl. . . two left. . . steady now."

We were a few more days shooting up in the bay and in the fog. The Maine coast fog didn't cooperate, but they had several fog machines that burned vegetable oil and laid a great smoke screen over the whole bay. We worked the dories alongside and even the old *Bowdoin* joined us for a Grand Banks fleet shot. (What a historic Arctic schooner would be doing on the grand banks was my concern, apparently, not the director's.) Captain Orvil got a speaking part, a one-liner, and came sailing past shouting some garbled phrases. Of course, no one could hear him above the din of the sailing, the ocean, and shouting by the crew. But they filmed it anyway. Then we moved into the inner harbor for the storm scenes.

When the original version of *Captains Courageous* was filmed in the 1930s, the moviemakers hung around Cape Ann with the schooner *Oretha Spinney* and a good crew of the "finest kind" of Gloucester men, waiting for a good "rouser" (a strong wind) to come along. It never came and the production crew decided they had to return to Hollywood. They sent the vessel off to sail to California, and the remainder of the production was to be created in a West Coast studio.

My very good friend, the late Captain Jack Crowell, was part of the complement of professionals and fishermen aboard. On the trip south they got their rouser, when off Cape Hatteras it came on to blow up a storm. They had to stow the mainsail "to hell and quick," as the vessel was working and straining under that huge piece of canvas. Now they had a crew of real experienced "Newfie" (Newfoundland) fishermen aboard, and each man knew exactly what to do.

Captain Jack had detailed the process for me back in the 1970s when I sailed *Adventure* into Isle au Haut Harbor and visited him at his home on Kimball Island. He leaned back in his favorite chair while his wife, Alice, served coffee and scrumptious apple pie. He said, "Captain Jim, did I ever tell you of the time we jibed the *Spinney* to furl the mainsail in 50 knots of breeze?" He went on. "We were running off to ease that big sail as much as possible when the skipper said to drop it. I wondered what would happen to that sail if we let the halyards go, but that is what we did. The sail fell into the water alongside the schooner, half of it sinking in the sea. There was nothing to hold it on deck, no lazy jacks, and the boom was way out on the single topping lift, Gloucester fashion.

"We secured that boom into the crutch and fastened it down, lashed the gaff with the sail still overboard, and jibed the vessel before the wind. Now, that wind was blowing at near 50 knots on the quarter right where that sail was overboard, and they took a long boat hook and picked up the second reef cringle at the leech, to get the wind under it. That sail came up, streaming water all over the decks, dumping a solid deluge on all the gang lined up there and over the deckhouse until it was a half-a-foot deep all over the quarterdeck. The great mainsail was lifted by the wind right up onto the house top and dropped itself, a sodden mass, right at the feet of the crew.

"All we had to do then was pile it on the boom and put gaskets around it. It was the neatest trick I ever saw and could only be done by a bunch of really experienced fishermen." Captain Jack leaned back in his chair and puffed a couple of times at his pipe. "Guess they aren't doin' it that way with Malden or Montalban, are they?"

"No, Jack," I answered, "not with my mainsail. No way!"

And, how the wind did howl! How the wind did blow! If more wind was needed, turn the propellers faster. More rain? Turn up the torrent from the fire hoses. The storm scene was underway! Two huge airplane pro-pellers hooked to automobile engines turning up 9,000 rpm mounted on trailers provided the wind; two big fire pumps with four-inch hoses and fire nozzles spraying into the props provided the rain. It was effective! A deluge of wind-driven water beat against *Adventure*'s mast, rigging, and deck.

Was anyone fooled? I doubt it. The schooner had no sail up, was not heeling, not rolling or pitching, but remained perfectly still as if tied to the dock. And that's what she was, tied securely to the dock and valiantly fighting a whole gale of wind. The director wanted to see the vessel heel. Basking in the insane excitement of this kind of a project, I agreed to hook my crane to the masts and draw her down against two of my 1,200-pound storm anchors set out in the harbor, bow and stern. We could then hoist the mainsail and give the illusion of sailing. It was an interesting experi-ment in heeling moment. I put two nylon straps around the mastheads, backed old Ichabod to the center of the yard, and cranked her up.

With not the foggiest idea of how much strain would be needed to obtain a little heel, I dropped the brake and shoved the grunting, antique crane into gear. There was quite a strain on things as she started over to, maybe, ten degrees. I pulled the levers, drawing in more wire, and screwing up my courage pulled the levers again. Poor old Ichabod was complaining and grinding until I suddenly noticed the old girl was crawling! Her wheels were locked, her feet were down, yet she was underway. The whole crane, shuddering, squeaking, and groaning, was dragging herself, making deep furrows in the gravel driveway, pulling herself by her own bootstraps toward the vessel. It finally came to me that with all that strain on the anchors, if something let go, *Adventure* would come crashing into the wharf. My wharf! Replacing my reckless abandon with a conservative judgment I don't often possess, I abandoned that foolishness and went to help construct the dump tanks.

The special-effects crew brought two colossal tanks by tractor-trailer and set up a framework on the float next to the schooner. Ichabod deftly picked up each tank and mounted it nimbly on its built-up perch. Each held about 1,000 gallons of water pumped into the container from the harbor. They were round tanks, open on top and mounted on an axle so they could be rolled and dumped, the water coming down a ramp in one rushing, splashing, great undulation to the deck of the schooner. When they had them all set and the wind and water effects ready, we had a dry (hardly dry!) run to test everything. The actors were in their places, the director gave the signal, the crew pulled the tripping chain, and the great wave cascaded down the ramp. Crashing and bursting on the break beam of the deck, it exploding against the deckhouse, a three-foot wave that washed the actors off their feet, and they slid across the deck into the scuppers. "Just like a rogue wave, huh, Karl?" I remarked to Malden. I guess he was glad his stand-in was in his place at the wheel. Next time, they dumped the tanks a little more slowly.

They brought a professional stuntman all the way from Hollywood. The script called for a fisherman to go insane and leap from the masthead at the height of the storm. He would have to dive into the water between the vessel and the wharf, a space only about 20 feet wide. His aim had better be flawless. The arrangement with the producer involved a set fee. If the jump was not a photographic "take" the first time, he had to do it all again at his own cost until it was perfect. When he got up the mast, he realized the masthead was too high to safely jump and decided to do it from only halfway. Good thinking! Just before the cameras started rolling, he shouted down to the cameramen, "Don't forget to take the lens covers off! I'm only going to do this once!" Dressed in oilskins, boots, and sou'wester and right on cue, he screamed, jumped off, arms clawing the air, and rolled into a little ball just as he hit the water. It was a "take."

Our Hollywoodites beat up the vessel, scuffed great gashes into the varnishwork with their lighting stands, drove holes in the deck and house top with their tripods, used my crane and small boats, and took advantage of my car and other equipment, all of which, of course, they agreed to pay for without question. Oh, but that was before! Once the shooting ended, they packed up in a flurry of activity, loaded their cinemobiles and trailers with the generator and other equipment (using my crane), and I, like a fool, let them skedaddle over the hill and out of sight still owing me about $4,000.

I tried to have my small-town lawyer ring their bell, and they responded with three big-time, big-city lawyers. They squashed me flat. Working with the movie people was trying and the product disappointing, but all in all, it was a great experience. I only wish they could have stuck more closely to reality.

Our local lobsterman Phil Raynes managed to sum up much of the movie-making experience. "With all the jeezly weather we git here," he said, "you wouldn't suppose they would need to come in here with all that machinery ter make a little rain and a little breeze!"

After the Hollywoodites were over the hill, the 1977 season descended like an express train and the pressure of outfitting was upon us. We had only about three weeks to put both vessels to rights, to repaint, refinish, and replenish. It seems I was always trying to squeeze a size 10 foot into a size 6 shoe with a size 15 shoehorn. Well, there are only so many heartbeats in a lifetime, and one must get all the goodness out of each and every one. With that thought firmly in mind, on June 4, 1977, I took time to go to

New York State and, after a whirlwind courtship, I married Pat Smith, a girl too young but with a quick, warm smile. She had been my galley girl in 1976, and she swept me off my feet with her captivating singing voice that everyone, including my passengers, enjoyed.

My two boys were spending more time with me and they, like me, needed a little mothering. Pat willingly turned to and brought stability to our home. In '74, I had purchased the "ranch," which was a little "summa cottage" on the Megunticook River only a mile from town. It was a little Garden of Eden, a haven from the craziness of the business, town bureaucrats, the occasional moviemaking, and the general hubbub of Camden in the summer. I soon winterized the cottage, built indoor facilities in "lieu of the loo," and a kitchen so we could enjoy a year-round home. To my great delight and wonder, my number one son, Topher, wanted to join us and live at the ranch so he could attend Camden High. We built quarters for him, first in the loft and then in the playroom under the new living room, where he could practice and play his trombone and listen to some unusual music. It would be a few more years before my second great joy, number two son Zeb, came into the fold and we built him a room in the expanding cottage. When Pat joined us, it felt like we had the makings of a new and stable family.

Chapter 16

Passengers

When it came to vacationing aboard an old schooner, most of our passengers had many adjustments to make. They were taken right raw out of the city and placed aboard this old museum piece of a vessel. There was an enormous and traumatic psychological adjustment to make with the first glance at their cabin. Here was a space of about eight feet square, probably smaller than the broom closet they had at home. Then we would drop the bomb—they would be sharing the space with three other people. The bunks themselves were two feet wide and six feet long. There were two on the bottom, under which to store baggage, and two on top. These were reached by a small ladder and lacked head-room enough to sit upright.

Our guests were barely over the indignation of seeing their bunk when we would escort them down the passageway to show off our heavenly heads. Enclosed in a space smaller than a telephone booth, those commodes were not only lovable, but, of course, had a long, hand-operated lever, and a sign that instructed: TO PUMP IS TO FLUSH.

There were no showers, and the only aid for the *salle de bain* was a face pan, with washcloth and towel, that had to be lugged to the cold-water barrels on deck. Washing was accomplished by leaning far out over the rail, and when totally refreshed, the dregs were dumped into the sea. When the glamour-conscious girls, coming aboard with high heels and short skirts, inquired about washing their hair, I would explain how salt water and a simple squirt of liquid Joy would enhance the sheen and luster of those precious locks. The bucket with a piece of line that they could

Adventure Accommodations Plan

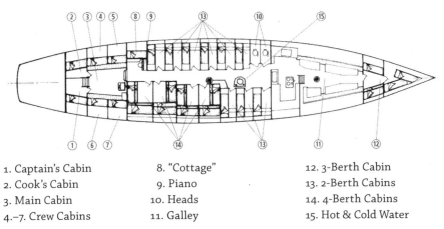

1. Captain's Cabin	8. "Cottage"	12. 3-Berth Cabin
2. Cook's Cabin	9. Piano	13. 2-Berth Cabins
3. Main Cabin	10. Heads	14. 4-Berth Cabins
4.–7. Crew Cabins	11. Galley	15. Hot & Cold Water

lower into the salty sea to wash and rinse was always handy. Then I would assure them that they would love it because the temperature of the water was near 80 degrees. (The temp was more likely about 56.) When they finished screaming at the cold water, most were pleasantly surprised to find the golden strands squeaked pleasantly after the deed was done.

It was fortunate that we had so many passengers returning year after year, and those repeaters were anxious to take the green landlubbers under their wing. They urged the newcomers to just "hang on" and assured them that, once settled in, they would surely have the time of their lives. After all, we're talking about old schooner stuff! It is called roughing it with ease!

In keeping with *Adventure*'s original role, I had two small dories built for the passengers' use. Good exercise, I used to tell them. These boats were nested on deck, one inside the other like a sandwich, so the names *PB* and *J* were painted on the transoms in deference to the crew's favorite snack. Now, a regular dory, with half a ton of fish aboard, is an able, stable little craft. Fishermen have survived in them for days and sailed hundreds of sea miles. However, with two tourists aboard, these little, tender, tipsy boats assumed a mind of their own. Although warned to sit in the middle, one passenger would always lean over to look in the water at heaven-only knows what, and the dory, as if out of spite, would roll her rail to the water's edge, sometimes spilling the occupants clean out of the boat. The dory would then dance upright again, shipping hardly a cupful of water, and seem to grin tauntingly as it skidded off, rocking gently next to the embarrassed and struggling bather. When finally getting the hang of rowing the critter, passengers would pull off to enjoy the evening sunset, sometimes too far from the schooner, only to be recalled by shouts and gestures from the watchful mate.

I was fortunate in buying an original seine boat—a very shapely open boat that used to work the seine net in the herring fishery—from an old fisherman, Captain Clarence Howard of Marshall Island. He had hauled thousands of pounds of "scales" from the coves around the islands in this beautiful 20-footer and sent them off to Stonington for packaging as "Maine Sardines."

A "bad hair day" on Adventure's *foredeck. (photo: William MacDonald)*

I said, "Hey, Clarence, wanna sell me that boat? You don't get much use out of her anymore."

"Want to?" he says, "Hell no! But I guess I got to, the way things is."

The herring just weren't running anymore, and I sympathized with him, massaging his pain. At an appropriate lull in the conversation I asked, "How much do you want for her?" Clarence replied in his thick Down East accent, "Whatdillya give?"

"Well, what do you want?" We went round and round with this for too long, and finally I said, "Clarence, I don't want to pay too much, but I don't want to cheat you, either. I'll take a poll of the guys you went fishing with and see what they think it's worth and average it out. Do you think that's fair?"

"That'll do nicely," he said. So I got her! She was 20 feet of double-ended beauty, quite full-bodied and stable. She stowed in *Adventure*'s waist right on the main deck between the fore halyards and the break beam as slick as a smelt. She would row easily with a crowd of 16 people, their life jackets, oars for eight rowing positions, a steering oar, two crewmen, and she would consistently ferry everyone on the schooner ashore in three trips. One of the crew would steer and shout encouragement to the rowers, while the other crewman would handle docking lines. The passengers would do their own rowing.

Landlubbers from the city who had never seen an oar would have an incredible experience. The process of learning how to pull while laughing their heads off—how to move the oar in unison, to row without hitting the next rower in the back, without suffering the embarrassment of catching a crab (getting the oar caught in the sea), and staying in the confines of the boat—was something they all found greatly appealing. That little boat, in spite of the rowers' disabilities, would always make it ashore and back without a hitch. It was a howl sometimes, but the boat seemed to know what was expected of it and always came through. The very first time we watched it row away from the schooner, with the oars all flying up and down to different tunes, not one synchronized with another, some pulling, some pushing, some splashing, and some getting stuck, an obvious name for the boat came to me. We named her the *Spastic Spider*.

We had many memorable characters over the course of my 25 years as captain of the old vessels, and many of these addicted characters would return year after year for more windjammer experiences. One woman sailed with me on 54 trips! Helen Hawkins got the gold star for several reasons. Not only did she love sailing on *Adventure*, but also she was a talented artist and woodcarver. She did some beautiful carvings on our hatches and nameboards. Helen would come for two weeks each season and would always ask for a project to keep her busy. I accommodated with a fresh, dry pine board and a project of one kind or other. We transferred tracings of *Adventure* and, with the passengers grabbing knife or sandpaper, we would all gather around and start to carve the image. We did stars, lettering and decoration, gold leafing, and painting of many a rich-looking sign for Sharp's Wharf and the schooner.

One beautiful sunny day we were sailing blissfully across Penobscot Bay. I was by the wheel, pacing back and forth, while my crew was up doing something on the foredeck. Among the gang of people stretched out on the main cabin top were two sun-drenched, shapely gals in bathing suits dozing in the warm sun. I went to the rail as is my habit to look at the set of the sails, and, while my back was turned, I felt a drop of water on the back of my neck. Funny, I thought, there isn't a cloud, nor a seagull anywhere aloft.

A few minutes later, continuing my pacing, I felt the same thing again. This time, in the corner of my eye, I caught a movement from the gals presumably asleep. I spun around and both were motionless as carved stone. I thought I could see just a faint little smile on the face of the skinny one and decided to take a chance. We always kept a 10-quart pail under the rail aft for deck washing, so I quickly, quietly dropped it overboard and scooped up a load of cold seawater. In one motion and, before they knew what hit 'em, I swept the water over both of the bathing beauties from head to toe.

"All ashore that's going"—with oars all aflying, Spastic Spider makes for a deserted island. (author's collection)

Of course they screamed bloody murder and jumped halfway up the rigging and, what do you know, there was nothing left on the cabin top but their two wet towels and a loaded water pistol. The skinny one was just full of beans. I named her Filthedelphia, her hometown, which was, of course, not far from the Upper Darby of my youth. She came year after year and was always stirring the pot, playing tricks, and dreaming up all manner of entertaining fun. Her husband was a weightlifter and built like a Brahma bull. I used to threaten to pitch him from here into Kingdom Come and beat the living tar out of him and, all the while I ejaculated these threats, he was picking me up over his head with one hand, holding me suspended over the deep sea.

Since I was so bad at remembering names, I had the habit of naming people by their hometown or some characteristic trait. There were lots of Brooklyns, Bayonnes, Cincinnatis, Georgias, and New Jerseys. There was Goldie Locks, Curly, Freckles, Bubbles, and Queenie. There was even "The Dear Old Thing." Passengers loved the names. It individualized them and gave them a different kind of attention they normally didn't enjoy.

This habit of mine did, however, did get me in trouble now and then when a voice on the telephone said, "Captain, this is 'Brooklyn.' I want to make a reservation for next year. Remember?"

I would always answer in the affirmative even though there may have been six or eight "Brooklyns" from the year before.

These old schooners attracted people who were game for the outdoors, who liked the unusual, and weren't afraid of a little inconvenience. Many were very talented. Our advertising suggested they bring an instrument even if they were not professional musicians, and the instruments came. One guy bought and paid for an extra berth so he could lug his stand-up string bass aboard. We had harmonicas to balalaikas and hordes of folksingers. We started the "theme" cruises with a local folk artist. When we advertised a folk-music cruise, passengers came in droves—expert and amateur. The music was incredible all week.

We eventually traded *Adventure*'s squeaky old pump organ for a 66-key melody grand piano, rearranging a cabin space to accommodate it.

Our artist, Helen, found it and brought it to us in the back of her Volkswagen. The piano was hard to keep in tune but was a great addition to our music department. We even had a passenger who was a professional classical pianist. He sailed the week and was a great entertainer to boot. I invited him to host a classical music cruise the next year with his two colleagues, a violinist and cellist, and I would not only pay them to come but I would also have the piano professionally tuned. There is nothing quite like sailing quietly up Blue Hill Bay, the sunset over the hills to the west and a full moon rising over Cadillac Mountain, accompanied by all three movements of the *Moonlight Sonata*.

We added a naturalist for another week, and every year people could take their choice of a particular type of vacation. Of course, I played the guitar and sang songs of the sea almost every night aboard. The layout of the old *Adventure* was perfect for music, games, and socializing. The "main cabin" back aft, filled with atmosphere, was the music room with the piano, fireplace, kerosene lamps, nautical photographs and artifacts. It connected by a central passageway to the mess room where we took our meals, and the evenings always saw a card game going on, a puzzle, trick show, extravaganza, or a lively conversation. Our cook always had a tray of extra desserts begging for a taker at one table or the other.

In 25 years I had to put only five people ashore. I think that is a pretty good record. It was always for excessive drinking, and they were all warned. Mostly they had a serious problem but, problem or no, I wasn't going to baby-sit a drunk. Most of the time we had wonderful people, and each group became one big family by week's end. When we docked at Camden on Saturday, there would be tears and hugs all over the deck. One high-powered businessman I will always remember remarked, "Captain, I am an executive from Wall Street. I get up at four or so each morning so I can get to work and get something done in the office before the place opens. I come home late and never see much of my family. I came on this schooner for some peace and quiet so I could face and solve two overwhelming, monumental problems in my life. One affects my personal home life and one my future business career, and you know, after a week on this schooner, I can't remember what they were."

The Dear Old Thing was a short, plump, bespectacled, white-haired, rosy-cheeked, sweet lady who had a wonderful attitude about life and living. She would drape herself in the royal seat in the seine boat on deck and demand of all the men around her their total attention and service. She would get it, too! She had a twinkle that made the most crotchety curmudgeon her immediate slave. On a calm night in a quiet anchorage with a host of stars and a big moon smiling down, she would gather a crowd and convince them all to "howl at the moon." They did it, too. Looking at each other in absolute disdain and disbelief, our passengers—doctors, lawyers, executives, teachers, nurses, scientists, ditch-diggers, and you name it—would, with gusto, open their mouths and follow the example of The Dear Old Thing, sounding off like a pack of hungry Alaskan wolves.

Aboard the schooner, people were all reduced to one wonderful plateau. We had good, benign, clean fun. Nothing at all X-rated here—not even R-rated. Radios were only allowed with a private earphone. No TV, telephone, or distractions other than wind, wave, and seagulls. There was no "getting away" with anything as there were 45 people packed on the vessel, and there was always someone around. There was no prejudice, profanity, profiteering, or privacy. The captain would allow and engage in only harmless shenanigans. Many of our passengers suggested world peace could be attained if everyone took a windjammer cruise, and I endorsed that. The focus of fascination was, of course, *Adventure*, a living, sailing museum piece of history. She was a dominating personality loved by all. But it was the passengers who inspired the fun.

One beautiful night, we were anchored in Gilkeys Harbor. The moon was out and the northern lights swept in bars to the horizon. We were on deck, I with the guitar, and we were reverently singing the "moldy oldies." Our kerosene deck lamps cast a flickering, soft glow on mast and rigging. The world was hushed and tranquil. About 9:30, a sloop of around 30 feet with four young men aboard came up and anchored much too close to us. They proceeded to drink and get loud. By and by, they began catcalling to the female passengers in our singing group. We tried to ignore them, but it was hard. Eleven o'clock is "quiet hour" when we shut the schooner down for the night and insist on quiet for those who wish to retire (a rule that was strictly enforced). So we broke up the "singy-songy" about 10:45 with several choruses of "Good Night Irene." The foursome continued, bent on their bender, until about 11:30, when I could endure it no longer.

My mate, standing night watch on deck, knew I was fuming so when I motioned him into the yawlboat he was ready for action. I ran the boat flat out, popping out from beneath the stern of the *Adventure* and roaring over to the sloop, heading for her anchor line under her bow. The beer boys welcomed us, offering us some of their cheer until they saw me, all in one motion, swoop under their anchor line, jerk the anchor off the bottom, take a turn with their anchor line on our towing bitt, and put the boots to the boat's big propeller. The little sloop lurched so smartly that they all fell down on their beer cans in the cockpit. Their boat reared up, and we took off into the night at eight knots towing them with their own anchor line. Eventually, they came to. Then they started to holler about being hijacked and all the things they would do to us. We paid no attention and didn't even look back, but towed them a half mile away and reanchored them where they could make all the damn noise they wished. We felt pretty smug.

Two weeks later, back in Camden, a well-dressed man with a briefcase asked for me. He proceeded to explain that he was a lawyer retained by the owner of the sloop we hijacked over in Gilkeys Harbor. He went on saying how his client wished to bring an action against me. "Oh, I didn't think my client had much of a case," he said, "because he is a bit of a boozer, but since it was such an interesting happening and since I was coming through Maine on vacation, I thought I would stop to meet the hijacker and congratulate him in person!"

It takes all kinds of really strange folks to make up this beautiful world. We had one weirdo who came alone and looked rather benign at first glance. She settled in with several cabin mates, but after about 24 hours she started to complain. She complained moderately at the outset, but her efforts multiplied as the week wore on. The more she settled in, the more the complaints came until it was like an open torrent. Many of our old regulars tried to dissuade and disarm her, to no avail. It was nothing specific. She just hated everything. The sailing, the food, the entertainment, the people, the facilities, the weather, the scenery—all were objects of her criticism. It was some relief to watch her go ashore on Saturday morning, and I immediately called my secretary and put her on the top of the black list.

Imagine our shock when this same passenger called the very next day to make a reservation for a week later in that same season. My gal told her we were full. She tried for an alternate week and again we were full. In fact, we were full for the rest of the season. Then she tried for next season with the same result. At this, she shouted into the telephone: "I know what you are up to and you won't get away with it."

Darned if she didn't call a lawyer, who called me with her complaint. I couldn't believe she would actually go through legal action to enable her to enjoy another week of constant complaining. The lawyer realized there was no case and probably knew her personality. At any rate, he didn't pursue it. Fortunately, her type was extremely rare aboard the old schooner.

Among the more memorable of our guests was a blind guy who came with a friend. It was a pleasure to watch him. His friend took him around, and, with a quick perusal, he knew by heart where the dangers were, how many steps were on the companionway, and just when to step up for the break in the deck. He needed only one tour around the decks to know the rigging, from halyards to sheets, and he always jumped in and helped when setting sail or with anything else he was able to accomplish by feel.

My crew and I would try to describe the set of the sails and he, with a hand on the straining halyard, could feel the power of the wind in the rigging, the strain on the lines, and the hum of the breeze aloft. What really astounded us was that he came back again two years later by himself. A new crewman on duty showed him to his cabin and delivered to him the prepared safety orientation speech. Our blind passenger patiently listened to all instructions and tossed his duffel on the bunk. Upon returning to the deck and hearing of this man's condition, the crewman was flabbergasted. Throughout the entire tour of accommodations, heads, hazards, and layout of galley, main cabin, and decks, my crew never suspected that he was blind! After two years, he still knew exactly where all the risky places were and remembered just how many measured footsteps to take when approaching another hazard. He had a memory that didn't need sight.

Running a big passenger schooner isn't all good times and glamour, of course. Consider the story of the *Adventure*'s sewage holding tank, for example. The bureaucracy, in order to preserve our waters, came out with an edict that we all must have holding tanks for our wastewater. What a howl that set up in the schooner fleet. Most of the vessels didn't have room for a big tank, and none of the marinas had facilities for pump-out. Even if they had a pump-out station, none of the treatment plants could accept waste more than two days old, and no way mixed with salt water. There was no place to dump: the law preceded the practical. I presented this predicament to the Coast Guard inspector, who replied, "Just go out beyond the three-mile limit and dump. No problem."

"But sir," I retorted, "our certificate promulgates no more than three miles from land." With impatience he barked, "Go to the line and put your discharge pipe on the offshore side. That should take care of the problem."

Most of the smaller coasters almost never get that far offshore, and the weather would many times inhibit that kind of a passage, so the windjammer fleet pleaded hardship and they all got waivers. What luck. I happened to have a tank left over from the renovation of the *Wannie* and I, feeling very smug with a rare good-citizen cooperative air oozing from every pore, installed it in the old *Adventure*. I waived the waiver and decorated the heads with instructions, "Flush nothing you haven't eaten first (except single-ply toilet paper)." Of course, some people simply refuse to read.

We were anchored in Southwest Harbor one night, and right around dinnertime the discharge pump failed. The tank was plugged. There was something buried deep in its foul, squalid interior blocking the pipe. Gosh, what to do? I absolutely could not take the floor up just then and open the tank, thereby releasing the captive odiferousness to permeate the entire below-decks when everyone was topped off with consummate table fare. I had opened that tank in the past and, believe me, it was not pleasant. It was something I couldn't face after a great day's sail and a grand supper. The decision was made to wait until morning, hoping that the tank was large enough to accept the night's activities and the morning's crush.

The next morning, right at breakfast, the heads backed up.

Taking my mate aside, I said, "Rig the *Spastic Spider* as quick as you can, get it overboard and set up lots of brouhaha to draw everyone on deck. Leave me the two crewmen and insist everyone leave the ship. Quickly, now!" Then, quietly, sheepishly, I hung the sign: "out of order" on each head door. To see the pained expression on the faces of our imploring passengers tore at my sympathies.

Once the vessel was about empty, I led my crew with mop, bucket, and bailer, and we marched into battle. Up came the floor, out came the wrenches, off came the manhole cover, thereby releasing waves of fumes, toxic enough to gag a host of maggots. The galley crew, busily engaged in drying the breakfast dishes at a distance of about eight feet from where we worked, went about their travail sans the usual carefree song and banter. Meanwhile, the crew bailed the commodes, mopped the overflow from the over-full tank, and transported the indescribable contents I was dipping from the tank by ladle into the bucket. Then it was up the companionway, across the deck, and over the leeward rail, fortunately the side away from the watchful eyes at the Coast Guard Station.

The tank was about three feet deep, four wide, and six long. When she was bailed down about half way, with my eyes tearing and throat gagging, I could reach to the bottom of the tank by half entering the manhole and immersing my arm through the depths to the discharge pipe. It had to be done. There was no other way. I held my breath and plunged.

Yes, there it was! The culprit was a washcloth wadded up into a tight obstruction in the pipe. Once cleared, all worked as before, and I went on deck for my personal disinfection processes. By this time the vessel smelled like the local sewage treatment plant on a rainy day, wind to the east'ard. We went at the cleanup with buckets of Lysol and air freshener. We scrubbed and sprayed like an automatic car wash until all was presentable, and I was some proud of the way my able and willing crew had pitched right in without hesitation. Looking very relieved, the passengers returned, laughing uproariously at how they waited in a queue, eyes crossed, legs crossed, suffering outside of the only public restroom on the wharf. There, all thirty-five of them had pleaded, coaxed, and begged the embarrassed and confused officer at the desk of the Southwest Harbor Group of United States Coast Guard to please, please, PLEASE unlock the door.

Chapter 17

A Second Career

It didn't take me long to call Clyde Holmes, the Belfast man from whom, two years earlier in 1975, I'd bought the steam tug *Clyde B. Holmes* ex-*John Wanamaker*. I had heard that his tug fleet's captains and engineers struck because they wanted a union. Clyde said no, but that, if they wanted anything specific, anything at all that he could afford and justify, then, okay, they could have it. Clyde was no wealthy operator. He doubtless wondered whether, if the union moved in, what would the crews demand next?

The shipping, of course, was unstoppable. The tankers would continue to come up the bay to the oil terminal and be docked, and the union be damned. While neither Moran, nor any other high-powered national tugboat conglomerate, was beating down the doors to take over the shipping in the fair city of Belfast, Maine, some risk existed. Some tugboat crew could, no doubt, come from Boston and possibly take over the whole port. I felt that we should try to keep the business in Maine, so I called Clyde.

"Clyde, I have a Coast Guard towboat license and would be happy to run one of the tugs docking the tankers at the oil terminal for you." I told him that I could only work in the winter because of the schooner, but that he should give a call if he needed me. Five days later, Clyde called.

"Go to the Rockland Shipyard where the *Thomas St. Phillip* is tied up and bring her home. I'll send the engineer over early to warm her up. Leave the dock at two a.m. and be on station at Searsport at five. Oh, by the way, with the strike and all, you probably will want to leave without showing any lights until you are well away from the shipyard."

I had never run a big tug like the *Thomas* before and was all puffed up with the thought of being a part of the commercial tugboat scene. The tug had an engine that produced about 1,200 horsepower—a lot more than I was accustomed to—but she was equipped with straightforward controls and was an easy boat to operate. Even with a half-century of service, she was the newest of the Holmes fleet and a nice vessel. With the dawn growing in the eastern sky, a huge tanker, well loaded down with crude oil and straight from Saudi Arabia, came lumbering up Penobscot Bay. I knew the docking pilot, Captain Gil Hall, a Camden man. At his instruction, I hooked up to half speed, chased the ship, and ranged along her starboard side under the monstrous bow anchor to get my head line up through the hawse hole.

I had just shouldered in alongside and fastened my line—the ship was towing me at this point—when I noticed a raggedy-looking sort of a tug named *Ellen F.* going under the stern. "The Boston crew has arrived!" I said to myself.

The pilot blurted on the radio, "*Thomas*, one bell straight on!" I clutched in, thinking "straight on" must mean just as we are, shaped up and parallel to the ship. I jumped when, 30 seconds later, a loud, rather insistent voice on the other radio said, "Left rudder on the *Thomas*!" I thought, that isn't the pilot from whom I am getting my orders. Who in hell then belongs to this raucous voice telling me what I should do?

"LEFT RUDDER ON THE *THOMAS*!" It came again, unrelenting and rasping on my nerves. I decided I'd better look into the matter and inquire if I was in error. I called the pilot. "Gil, do you mean straight with the ship, or 90 degrees to the keel?"

"Oh, 90 to the ship, Jim!"

Well, I felt a little dumb but applied the left to the rudder and shaped up, now pushing the bow. With a few more helpful hints from the pilot, we managed to get the ship safely in her berth, and then I discovered the Boston man in the other tug was my new boss. Arthur Fournier had just bought the entire tugboat fleet, wharf, and business from Clyde B. Holmes, all on the QT, and the striking gang didn't even know it!

Arthur was the owner of three of the Holmes tugs—the *Pauline Holmes,* of about 600 horsepower, the *Mary Holmes,* 1,200 horsepower, and the *Thomas St. Phillip,* plus the *Ellen F.,* of some 1,600 horsepower, that he brought from Boston. I was his first employee. Having "blown in the pilothouse windows"—the term used for captains who do not first spend an apprenticeship on deck—I was thrilled at this great opportunity. Of course, I was also a scab—a dirty strikebreaker. I never really thought about it until we went back to the dock, tied up the tugs, and got in the vehicles to go home.

We were met by a belligerent crowd forming a continuous, impassable human chain across the drive into the wharf. I saw many a familiar face among the group, guys I had ridden with and sailed with and had seen when I bought the *Clyde B. Holmes* from this same wharf. They were in no social mood. As the human chain opened up to let us pass, some spat at the car and pounded on the fenders. As we sped away, I realized that, were it not for the presence of the police across the street, we would possibly have had a more serious confrontation.

I felt badly, but rationalized that I would only be there until things were settled, and would soon be back on the schooner for the summer. A few days later, as I entered the drive to the wharf, I saw Sandy, captain of the *Mary Holmes.* I stopped to speak with him. That was a mistake. He was in no mood to be civil to a Camden windjammer kind of scab, even though it was better than a Boston scab. I tried to explain that I hoped I was only protecting his job by filling in temporarily and he would surely be back once things settled out. Such naiveté harvested out my innocence. He spat on my windshield and cursed me roundly.

Determined, I drove on in, jumped aboard the tug, swung her off, and followed the *Ellen F.* to sail the departing tanker. We did the same maneuver as in docking, but in reverse order and with fewer mistakes. Little did I realize I would be working for Pen Bay Towing (the new name) off-season for about eight years, running twelve very different tugs in a variety of most unusual circumstances. Arthur, frequently and with prolific profanity, tossed many a worker out on his ear during my tenure, but, curiously, I would be the one employee who lasted.

I tried to be a conscientious captain for Arthur Fournier. I was never late, was very careful, and I tried hard to follow orders and use good judgment. I never complained, although that was rather challenging at times. The first time I ran the little *Pauline Holmes* was very much a tribulation. We had to meet a ship in the middle of the night—they usually came at odd hours—and Arthur was late getting out of bed, as was his custom. He came running across the dock, pulling his pants up as he came, and shouting orders at me in his own habitual, explosive style. I ran to board the *Pauline*, climbed the ladder to the pilothouse, and, since this was my first gander at this boat, hunted for a flashlight, hoping for a quick look around to locate the controls, etc. There was one flashlight. It didn't work and had no batteries. This was typical.

Arthur fired up the *Ellen F.*, and we started out of Belfast Harbor still tied together and him towing the *Pauline* alongside. She had insufficient air in her tanks to roll the engine so Arthur dragged her at eight knots with the sea smashing between the two boats until he had the prop turning in good shape, then ran down into *Pauline*'s engine room and slammed the clutch closed, belted what compressed air there was to her, and at the same time the engineer sprayed great gulps of ether into the cylinder intakes. I had never heard of jump-starting a boat before, but I was to learn lots of oddities working in Fournier's Navy. As soon as *Pauline* was firing, he jumped back on the *Ellen F.*, took the helm, and told me to cast off and follow him. My engineer-deckhand, the only other person aboard, cast off and I sheered away from the boss's tug.

The next thing I knew, I was steaming in circles. The rudder was jammed to port, and I was hollering to the engineer to do something. Arthur got on the radio, wondering what in the very devil I was doing, all of this punctuated with a volley of profanity enough to make the wires melt. Arthur had a problem with the King's English. He had a self-inflicted speech impediment of which he remains very proud. On good days, he would consciously inject the most vile cuss words in about 50 percent of a common paragraph. But when things went a little wrong, which was more frequent than not, one was forced to listen most intently to separate the profane from the sprinkling of words that would describe the thrust of the text. So, when he took a breath and I could interject, I explained our predicament. I stopped the tug, the boss came back alongside in a god-awful flurry, tied up, and pretty soon there came a raucous pounding from the engine room, well besprinkled with the vernacular of the tugboat society. Miraculously, the steering started to work again.

I straightened out and started towing the *Ellen F.* toward the ship that needed docking. Arthur poked his head out of the engine room, saw we were en route to the job, disappeared back below, and there was more banging, crashing, and pounding like the hammering of a thousand devils of hell down there. By and by, he came up and, in a continuing blood-pressure panic, returned to the *Ellen F.*, and we went to our positions on the ship.

This tanker had a flaring stern, and the little *Pauline* was just right to sneak under the counter. I put her into that dangerous little spot almost like I knew what I was about, and got a head line up. As we eased the tanker into her berth, I had to give a push on 45 degrees aft, which put my pilothouse under the overhang of the stern. The rail around the catwalk forward of the pilothouse came in contact with the ship and bent back in a big "S." I felt so bad at bending that rail that I came the next day with my toolbox and went to work straightening the damage. Arthur didn't see me until I was almost finished.

"What in the livin' hell are you up to?" he said, although he didn't quite use such mild language. Well, he never forgot. He was so impressed that I would fix that rail on my own time, that he often referred to it, to impress his errant captains. Years later, one of the gang bent the wheel on one of the other tugs and no one would 'fess up to the deed. The boss expostulated, "I know Sharp didn't do it. He would have been here with his own damn wrenches the next day trying to fix it!"

Fuel was less expensive in Boston than in Maine. The engineer was instructed to sound the tanks; "15 feet of air" was the answer. (Somehow that information was ignored, even though the tanks were only about 16 feet deep.) Arthur had called me to take the *Thomas* to Boston. He claimed she was all fueled, provisioned, watered, and ready. "Be here at midnight. The weather, although plenty cold, looks good for the offshore passage."

I arrived on time and we, the engineer and I, struck out for Beantown with a box of Twinkies, a jar of peanut butter, and a fresh new box of Ritz crackers—Arthur's idea of a fully stocked galley. About three a.m., we were going down the Muscle Ridge Channel, a place fraught with rocks and ledges, when the main engine started to hesitate. She died a quick death just north of the vicious Yellow Ledges, with an ebb tide and southerly swell setting us down directly for the white, tumbling breakers on the Yellow.

I was sure we were out of fuel and told the engineer to give her a start and, if she didn't respond, to get back on deck, quick as a flash, so we could do something about an anchor. Our generator, fortunately, continued to run so we had lights and radio, and as I played the spotlight on the rocks of the Yellow Ledge Bank, I called the Coast Guard. They responded with typical procedural questioning: "What is the color of the hull? How many people aboard?" Etc.

I broke in and explained that we had about fifteen minutes until whatever was to happen would have happened, and asked them to please call a lobsterboat from Spruce Head Harbor (closest place) to come out and give us a hand. I signed off and ran down to the afterdeck to hunt for an anchor. There was nothing but a 20-pound Danforth, which would have been a lunch hook for a skiff, not a big, heavy tug. We had no anchor line and not another blessed thing to anchor with except a three-inch frozen hawser and a quarter-inch heaving line stone-stiff with blue ice.

Well, I took the heaving line, knocked the ice off, and used it to lash the anchor to the hawser, going round and round its three-inch girth with a constrictor knot. Then I told the engineer to be ready to drop the thing overboard when I sang out. I ran back up to the pilothouse. Our spotlight illuminated the peaks of ragged rocks on the top of the ledges, and our poor disabled tug was rolling helplessly in the swell, pitching herself steadily toward the danger. If we were to come down on the ledge, she would be holed and probably sink right there. I was imagining the two of us holding on to the ledge's day beacon—a steel pole now sheathed with ice—for the rest of the night, half-drowned in salt water and mostly frozen. I couldn't anchor now. We were much too close to the frozen rocks. The tide, doing its thing, would set us right on top of disaster. The news would read, "Tug fetches on Yellow Ledges. Total loss. No survivors!" All I could do was wait, hair standing up in horror, and watch.

With the spotlight pitched down, illuminating the ledges right under our bow, I could almost feel the rocks splitting up through the steel plate of the hull. I was looking almost straight down at the boulders and knife-like ledges, and could clearly see the barnacles attached to the crevasses and rifts in the rocks. Why she didn't smash herself to pieces was a mystery. There must have been a counter-current around that ledge that kept us off, but we providentially drifted around the rock pile without striking and were able to attain deeper water downstream. This gave us just enough space to anchor before the next ledge came up under our stern. I shouted to the engineer to let go the hook and put out 100 feet of hawser, hoping that little anchor would catch on something substantial enough to hold us against the tide. Luck was with us. She caught. But we spent the rest of the night worrying, trying to stay warm and alive, and waiting for a tow back up to the Rockland Shipyard.

With great satisfaction, I called Arthur and got him out of bed. His one concern was that we tell the Coast Guard only that our fuel pump must have failed (they usually do when pumping air) and not to even give a hint that we were out of fuel. If they had known, it would be a case of negligence, and the Guard would have to be reimbursed for the tow. We took on fuel enough to get to Boston, and I did finally complete the trip. Cope—that was the norm in Fournier's Navy. Then I had a wreck of a barge to bring back to Maine.

The barge was tied up at Pier 50. It was an ancient-looking work barge with both bows stove in and looking like a pile of rust. Arthur said, "Jim, tow it home." So that is what we did. We hooked a couple of chains from the barge to bridle off our hawser, crossed Massachusetts Bay, and waited for weather at Gloucester. Things looked good for a night run, and we set off. Come the middle of the night, the forecast being more favorable than the reality, the sea rose mightily about the time we passed Thatcher's twin lighthouses. Seawater in copious amounts started flooding down into the hull of the old barge through the gaping holes in both her bows, and it was apparent by the way she was diving and cavorting that we would be in trouble if we continued up the shore toward Maine.

So, with choices limited, we ducked into the lee and semi-protection of the breakwater at Rockport, Massachusetts. I, vacating the warm, snug pilothouse, switched to the after steering station, and ran to the rear of the deckhouse where those controls were perched, unprotected in the wind and freezing weather. We got our spotlights working and shortened up the tow until the raked bow of the barge was heaving, lifting and falling in the swell, right over the drying rack on the stern of the tug. I had to hold the *Thomas* with just enough strain on the hawser to stay ahead of the barge and steady the distance between so we could get a ladder up and put the first man aboard.

The dark, the shadows, the raging wind, spray, and the glaring lights painted a horrific picture, and I felt heavy responsibility for those guys working on the slippery deck below my controls. They would have to climb 15 feet up the rake of that barge to her deck while the sea was heaving that deck sometimes four to six feet up and down. Our timing had to be perfect. Like a monkey, my crewman, at just the right moment, sprang to the rungs of the ladder and started climbing as two others leaned it against the rusty steel barge. The fleet-footed crewman raced up and, in one motion, jumped on deck to steady the ladder for the next man. With the second man on the barge, we then wrestled a four-inch gasoline pump aboard, primed it, started it, and got pumping. For the best part of an hour, a healthy four-inch stream of dirty water poured from the barge. We were all wet and cold by the time the pump sucked dry, and quite relieved to return to the heat of the pilothouse. Fortunately, the wind and sea had moderated while all this was going on and gave us a "chance along" to steam her down east to Maine.

It was just like tapping your head while rubbing your belly. The *Mary Holmes* was the most complicated boat I ever attempted. She was about 1,000 or 1,200 horses and had an old-time, slow-turning, direct-reversing engine. With no reverse gear in the boat's transmission, the engine had to be stopped and, after the camshaft was repositioned, restarted backwards. All this was controlled from the pilothouse. Arthur wanted nothing to do with the *Mary*, but, man, did I love that tug. She was all original from the '20s with lots of brass controls in her varnished wheelhouse. The *Mary* was narrow, had a high center of gravity, and leaned in the turns when going

Running the Mary Holmes *was more fun than a barrel of monkeys.*
(photo: Steven Lang)

around a ship or doing tight maneuvers. Running her, especially docking ships, kept a fellow some old busy!

There was a large, round, brass-and-mahogany engine-operating plaque on the bulkhead to starboard with a large brass handle and pointer. The top was marked "Stop," the 10:00 and 2:00 positions were marked "Run," and the 8:00 and 4:00 positions "Start." To the left of the center was "Ahead" and to the right "Astern." That big handle with the pointer was connected to the engine with a complicated system of cables, and, to convince the engine to do your bidding, you had to haul the pointer first to "Start"—either "Ahead" or "Astern"—which injected air into the engine to get it rolling.

At the same time that you injected the starting air, you tweaked the throttle, a lever on the bridge deck by the wheel, so she would pick up rpm. Then once she was responding in the desired direction and as soon as you heard her "take" (start), you had to yank the handle to "Run." Now, quickly, you'd set the throttle a little higher to keep her "to it" and, of course, by now the prop is turning and she is answering her helm, so you'd have to correct it by the immediate spinning of the wheel to get going in the right direction. If you were working straight on into a ship, you'd now have to stop and back before crashing into the side. At the same time, you must pull the peanut whistle to answer the pilot's instruction, take an easy strain on the head line until in position and up against the ship, and then come "on her" hooked up. About this time, the pilot would give backing instructions and you'd have to start the whole process again in reverse.

I was constantly doing a jitterbug around that pilothouse and was busy as a one-armed paperhanger. The first time I brought her home from a ship-docking and waltzed up to her berth, Arthur had two frowning critical eyes watching how she landed against the pier. The *Mary Holmes* was good to me and, in spite of my inexperience, she stopped at just the right place with an easy shoulder against the wharf. From then on, I was nominated skipper of the *Mary*, and for all the jobs for the rest of the winter she was my baby, right up until I went back aboard the *Adventure* for the summer season. Arthur never liked the old girl and, to my chagrin, the *Mary* was soon ostracized from Fournier's Navy. When I returned to duty that next fall, I found she was replaced by the more powerful, bell-controlled tug *Cape Fear*.

Chapter 18

Fear Rings My Bell

"A bell boat! Horrors! No self-respecting towboat man would operate a bell boat. Not in this day and age. That thing is archaic! A leftover from the age of steam! You wouldn't get me out on that thing!" That's what a tug-boating friend of mine spouted when I told him I would soon be running the *Cape Fear* for Pen Bay Towing. She was the latest addition, a new tug for Arthur Fournier's Navy, but that was the only new thing about her. She had been a true steamboat most of her career, but was converted to diesel with the installation of an 18-cylinder Fairbanks opposed-piston engine. I was flabbergasted to find that she retained the same engine-room controls with which she was built.

Cape Fear was a true bell boat. The pilothouse had no controls—no throttle, no gear shifter. She had a wheel, compass, and two little levers called "bell pulls" on the starboard side with cables disappearing through the floor, a brass speaking tube to the engine room, and, other than the horn pull and radios, she was clean. The two handles on the bell pulls were shaped a little differently so you knew instantly which you had in your hand at night or without looking. One pull rang a big gong in the engine-room and the other blasted a whistle. Both were necessarily loud so the engineer could hear over the roar of that mammoth engine. It was inevitable that I would love running such a vessel!

Tugs always have to be at the ready. If you happen to be docking a big ship and the pilot gives an order, the tug must respond and do it efficiently with due regard for the responsibility involved. If you are running an electric boat (diesel-electric), clutching is easy. You can go from full ahead to astern without a care and do it without hesitation. The world gets much more complex in a bell-operated tugboat, especially a heavy-displacement, deep-draft boat with a direct-reversing engine and a lot of power. Say you're lying by with a slack hawser and the pilot comes on the radio with, "*Cape Fear*, two bells (reverse) hooked up (full)." First you ring the gong twice to the engineer. You acknowledge the order to the pilot on the tug's whistle, and the engine starts in reverse. Then you give the engineer two engine-room whistles to hook up and get the boat backing.

As soon as she is moving back in good shape, you ring off. You've got an incredibly heavy pull coming up on a line affixed to a gargantuan tanker loaded down and as solid as a cement pier! If the tug keeps at it, she'll come up "all standing." Then that line may part off, might even wipe out crewmen standing on the foredeck with its viciously whipping, snapping end. Even if no one is injured, such an event could, at the very least, spoil your day with embarrassment. If you are backing too fast, you must hit one gong to stop, then one gong to start ahead with one whistle to break the backing inertia. Then ring off while she is still moving back slowly, followed by two gongs again to bring the strain gently on the line. As the line comes tight, one long (dead slow), one short whistle (slow), followed by two (half), three (full), and four (flank) until the old tug is hooked up and pulling for all she is worth.

About that time, the pilot changes his mind or finds a necessity to push instead of pull. He gives you a "*Cape Fear*, stop," followed by, "*Cape Fear*, one bell, half." You drop a single gong to the engineer to stop the engine, and acknowledge to the pilot with the ship's whistle. The weight of the tug hanging on the line up to the tanker and backing hard has the bow of the boat hanging half out of the water. This and the stretch in the hawser combine to send the tug zinging toward the side of the ship, threatening to bounce off or, worse, crash and dent the ship. So, quickly and at the precise moment, you must drop two gongs for reverse and one whistle to kill the headway but, just before she stops completely, drop one bell to stop the engine, allowing the tug to continue slowly until her "puddin'"—the rubber or rope mat protection over the stem—comes in contact with the ship. Now, you are set to signal one bell for forward and two whistles for half speed to keep her from bouncing away.

All this can be done fairly quickly with a good engineer. I had a good one. Leo Mazzerol was top-notch. We had a great rapport, a necessary ingredient! Arthur used to say, "With a good engineer on the *Fear*, you could pound nails into the wharf." Leo was passionately attentive. He would have his eyes glued to the wire connected to the gong and, when the slightest movement would come from my hand on the pull, he would jump to the engine controls.

I enjoyed giving him fits, just to hear him chafe and cuss. Occasionally, I would slip him a "soft bell." I would grab the bell pull and yank it up as if in a panic and hold it open, hammer ready to fall. I could almost hear him steaming, waiting for that gong to ring, one hand clutched to the cam shifter and the other on the air valve. I would, after a half a minute, lower it slowly and, making no sound, the hammer would come to rest. Then Leo would come to and realize what I was up to. Oh, the bad language and wrenches that would be flying around that engine room. I would stuff a rag in the speaking tube to muffle the tirade erupting into the quiet pilothouse. I couldn't let my guard down for a minute as, sooner or later, he would always find a way to retaliate.

The old *Cape Fear* and I docked many a ship at the Searsport Terminal and in the sweeping river current at Bucksport. Every maneuver with this old girl was a kick in the head. She was thin as a razor from years of rust, her hull full of Bondo from temporary repairs, especially back aft under the quarters, and we had to be extremely careful working in the ice. The Penobscot River's fresh water created some very dense ice floes that would come sweeping down with the current, and the threat of punching a hole in the old boat was ever-present.

She was a powerhouse of thrust in spite of her rust, and bringing her in to a dock at seven or eight knots was eerie. I would ring off as we shot for the wharf, and the boat would shut down. All was weirdly quiet as we closed the pilings on the wharf at eight knots. When near to our berth, I would ring two on the gong and four whistles and the engine would start in reverse. With the first revolution, nothing seemed to happen. With the second, the foam and froth would come boiling up around both bows and she seemed to stand on her head. This is all fine and fun when you have plenty of blunder room, but all that power is a problem when you have only a small space in which to back and fill.

Captain Gil Hall, the pilot, was leaving an anchored ship, coming down a 70-foot Jacob's rope ladder, looking for me to pick him up with the tug. Gil was a friend from Camden, an extremely good, well-respected pilot, and one for whom I had great admiration. He was hanging on the ladder about 10 feet above the water as I approached with the tug. I didn't dare go alongside the ship and slide up to the ladder for fear of striking him or the rig he was dangling from. With a pilothouse-controlled tug, especially when underway, you could run alongside the ship and make your tires stick and stop just before the ladder where the pilot could board over the bow.

I was afraid to try skidding since the *Fear* had so much power and I was either in gear and making knots or stopped. Instead, I ran up to the ship alongside the ladder, planning to land the puddin' against the ship and hold her there while he boarded. My problem was being too conservative. So as not to hit Gil or his ladder, I was too far away when I landed. But, I sure didn't want to trap Gil's legs against the ship. Consequently, I had to back off for another try.

I could tell Gil was tiring, hanging on to that ladder. Ringing gongs and whistles to Leo, I stopped and, when the tug drifted away a little, I came ahead with a little rudder to land closer. I had to do it twice and Gil was finally able to get a foot on top of the puddin' and get aboard. He was winded when he came into the pilothouse, but never said a word. I apologized, and his only answer was, "All in a day's work, Jim."

Another memorable "day's work" soon presented itself.

It was to be a gravity launch, probably the last gravity launch of such a big commercial ship in the U.S. The *Maui* was a 1,000-foot container ship, the biggest ship ever built in the state of Maine, and the Bath shipyard was planning a spectacular event. To the great consternation of Winslow, the tug company normally on station, Arthur Fournier had talked his way into the operations at the yard and we had been doing a number of moves of the guided-missile frigates under construction. A few short years before, at their last gravity launching, a new ship came roaring down the launching ways, tripped the hawser tug, and drowned two men. Arthur, with his favorite expression, said to the powers that be, "You guys need horsepower in the pilothouse! That's what you need." The *Cape Fear* was chosen to be hawser tug for the biggest gravity-launching.

What a challenge for this old windjammer captain! Arthur would ride the ship and be docking pilot, I would catch the ship with the hawser, turn her, and then, when the other four tugs moved in, I would move to the bow position to help dock her. The launch was set for slack low water—a time critical to the last minute. The Kennebec River is a millrace of current, and the slack only lasts about fifteen minutes. There would be speeches by politicians and dignitaries, the bottle of champagne would be broken on the bow of the ship, and large steel plates would be cut through with torches, allowing her to be severed from the land and start her trip to the briny. Everything hinged on the time of that slack.

I moved the *Cape Fear* out into the stream with slow deliberation and picked up the hawser from the assist tug, the little *Kennebec*. I was forewarned, in no uncertain terms, that there should be no strain—zero strain—on the hawser until the launch. We couldn't have a premature launch and leave a politician with his speech half-delivered! There were also warnings about being overhauled by the ship, having her yank on the towline and trip the tug, creating another disaster as happened at the last launch.

Arthur warned, "STAY IN FRONT OF THE SHIP, JIM, and don't let the hawser go too slack and foul on the barn doors [a wall of wooden plank across the stern of the ship to help slow her down during the launch] because a fouling hawser could conceivably shorten the line and trip the tug. As soon as the plates are cut through, and there is a launch, you will receive notice on the radio. Remember, the ship, in a gravity-launch situation, will accelerate to 14 knots as she enters the water. The barn doors and blocking will slow her quickly as she plows into the river, coming off the ways."

"Oh yeah, thanks a lot," I complained, "the *Fear* will only do 12 at flank speed!"

"Just stay in front," was the answer. "Your hawser will be long enough."

Carefully, I stretched out the towing hawser without putting any strain on it. There was still quite a lot of ebb tide, and we were only about a half hour until launch time when I gathered my crew for a conference. "Two deckhands aft watching the hawser," I instructed, "and take the fire axes down from their racks. Have them handy by or, better yet, in your hands. Stand away from the stern, stay in the alley for the protection of the house in case we part off, and if I start screaming bloody murder from the pilothouse and the ship is passing us, come down with the axes on that hawser with all you've got!" Leo, my faithful engineer, was at the controls. By prior arrangement, the little assist tug *Kennebec* came on my downstream side to push gently and hold me against the press of the ebb tide. While we waited, the anxiety mounted. And we waited. And waited.

The tension increased like the mainspring of a hard-wound watch. The tide slacked off, the speeches wound down, and zero hour approached. The crew on the *Kennebec* was terrified, looking at the immense stern of the ship right on course to waltz down on them, to pursue them across the river. They were only a little yard tug and would have to get out of the path taken by that gargantuan. I could see the captain strutting like a chicken, nervously peering out of one window and then another. Finally he could stand it no more. He put her in reverse and backed away. "Hey," I roared, "you can't leave me yet, I can't clutch in yet! Hey, come back!" He never looked back. He was gone.

With the last of the ebb still running, I was forced to cheat, turning hard to port and giving Leo one slow—dead-slow bell, easing ahead until the tug used up the natural slack in the hawser. Then, I stopped her before the strain came on and waited until the tide drifted her downstream, where I had to repeat the cheat. We spent what seemed an interminable amount of time at this, waiting anxiously for the launch. There was a lot of chatter on the radio, and with ears tuned, I listened intently, waiting for four little words, "We have a launch." Finally, after cheating ahead and drifting back over and over again, those words came blasting through the speakers and, of course, they came when we were shaped up and cheating, bow heading upstream, tug out of alignment.

I dropped one gong to Leo to get the engine turning, and glanced through the back window. The ship, looming larger than before, was starting to move toward the water. I spun the wheel to the right and pulled four whistles for all full ahead. Leo was right there. She jumped ahead immediately. But, the old *Fear* had electric steering, and she responded slowly. Her wheel was hard over to port for the cheat, and it would take her some precious seconds to straighten out. She, however, immediately felt the left rudder still on her from the cheat and sheered off to port. Oh God, I thought, I won't be lined up, and I again spun the wheel hard right. Adrenaline running and panic pushing me, I oversteered to the right. Then, as we sped up, I was soon oversteering to correct the left. I steered a perfect S in front of that ship like a rabbit running before a speeding car.

Oh Lord, the humiliation! The radio blared its raucous voice: "*Cape Fear*, what is wrong? *Cape Fear*, are you having trouble?" As I came out of the second turn and straightened the course, finally under control, I glanced out the back window. The image has been cast indelibly on my retina. That huge stern, covered with a wall of plank, plunging deep into the water, the 1,000-foot ship tobogganing down the ways, smoke pouring from the skids pushing a veritable tidal wave, water cresting, curling high, cascading down all white with froth and breaking like some unrestrained rogue wave of a North Atlantic perfect storm. Yikes!

I grabbed the radio mike hanging on its wire and said, in a voice as calmly, slowly, and in control as I could muster, "She's steering a little slow, Cap, but we've got her now," and jumped back to my wheel. One more glance aft told me we were up to speed and the ship was slowing down. I blasted two whistles at Leo and heard the engine immediately slow. The hawser was picking up fast now, the other tugs moving in, I rang stop and two for reverse. We killed our headway just as that hawser stretched in the air, shaking, trembling, and wringing itself out like an old wet dog.

The *Maui* was all afloat now, still moving across the river, dragging all the wooden timbers and blocking with her. I rang slow ahead and sheered off to starboard, brought up a strain, and spun the ship around while the other tugs made up on both sides. When she was turned 90 degrees, we pulled her downriver until just off her berth, and got the order to drop off and move to our position at the bow. As we got our headline up, Leo called on the speaking tube. "The generator died, Jim. I can't get it going again, and you have only one tank of air." (The air pressure rolled the engine to start, whether it is forward or reverse, and the generator built up the necessary air.)

"Jeez, Leo," I said, "I've got to push and pull until we get her tied up!"

"How many times?" he asked.

"Dun'no," I grunted, "I guess that depends on the pilot."

"Well," he said casually, "use as few starts as possible. When you're out, you're out."

I cheated as much as I could. When the pilot said stop, I would go down to easy, taking the chance that he might want another push and I wouldn't have to restart. I got away with it several times. After awhile, Leo called and said, "I think you have about one more start." Knowing we were almost finished, I ignored the last order to push easy, and we were finally dismissed. Desperately avoiding the shame of calling a rival tug to tow us back to the dock, I let the *Fear* drift until the current caught her. She rolled, bouncing away from the ship, and we gained maneuvering room. Leo hit our last start, and dead slow we headed to our berth. As we approached, I rang "Stop," she bled off her momentum, we bounced off the piling, but, quick as a wink, we had a line on the wharf and secured the old *Fear* like nothing had happened. I don't think anybody noticed. The pilots didn't know it. No one on the dock knew it, and I don't think that Arthur even knew it. But we knew it—and I'll never forget it!

Chapter 19

A Fascinating Freighter

Life is too short to own an ugly boat! That was my motto, and I adhered to it with almost religious devotion. The next boat I was destined to drag into Camden Harbor was one handsome vessel and, as a powerboat goes, she was the closest thing to an object of worship that I ever owned. She was called the *Record* (or *Reckord* in old Norwegian), and she was more than attractive in a thousand different ways. She had history, intrigue, humor, challenge, personality, and humility all trunneled together into one magnificent hull. Just a look at this old girl and I was instantly hooked.

Now, to add yet another boat was truly ridiculous! In the year 1979, in Camden Harbor, already lying at Sharp's Wharf were damn near 500 linear feet of Sharp-owned vessels. They went on for a country mile! The colossal steam tugboat restaurant, then being prepared for a move to Boston, would leave a large gaping hole on a dock already crowded with a real New York working tug, an original Grand Banks Gloucester fishing schooner, a beautiful, graceful pilot schooner, the yawlboat, two rowing seine boats, a couple of dories, a couple of Whitehall pulling/sailing boats, three or four skiffs, and a pastureful of floats, ramps, anchors, and buoys. Talk about maintenance! You would think that enough was enough. But that open dock space was burning fantasies in my brain. All I needed was one more damn boat to test my sanity. But a freight boat! Just the thought of it sent me soaring.

The ad was buried deep among the classifieds in *Boats & Harbors*, commonly known to all within the world of commercial vessels and equipment as the "Yellow Pages." I should never have taken my copy into Fitzpatrick's Deli to peruse the "Boats for Sale" listings over my coffee. It was just a small picture and really fuzzy, but it snapped the hair-trigger on my snooping addiction. The caption read, "1914 Norwegian inter-fjord freight and passenger boat." That in itself is enough to grab your attention! It went on, "Repowered 1934—two-cylinder Brunvoll semi-diesel, variable-pitch prop, came from Norway on its own bottom, now fishing in USVI" (U.S. Virgin Islands). I thought to myself, "My good friend Haddie, Captain Buds Hawkins' son, is there on a boat in the harbor. I could fly down and stay with him and look this thing over." Did it make any sense at all? No—but this boat had the air of a once-in-a-lifetime. I ran to the telephone to call for more details.

Flaps down and engines roaring, the big jet squealed to a stop on St. Thomas' short runway. From the window I had seen the boat at anchor in the harbor before we touched down. She was far more striking than her picture. With heart pounding, I grabbed my duffel and ran for the first taxi in line. Young Haddie Hawkins welcomed me at the harbor. With hardly a "hello and thank you" to my friend, I prevailed upon him to lend me mask and flippers, a screwdriver, flashlight, and a skiff to get to the *Record*. I lit out for the old vessel like a scalded cat.

Elmer Bouchelle, the owner, welcomed me and let me roam through every nook and cranny. And many a cranny she had! Made of heavy Scandinavian pine and built the old-fashioned way with double-sawn frames closely spaced, thick planking, and thicker ceiling (inner planking), the vessel appeared to be in good condition, strong and able. Although there were but spartan accommodations below and a minimal galley, I fancied I could fix all that when (not if) I got her to Maine. The important thing was the condition of her bottom, as the worms in the tropics are voracious and love to chew labyrinths of tunnels in old wooden boats. I dove into the gin-clear Caribbean waters and inspected every inch of the underwater planking, deadwood, rudder, and shoe. It was not bad. There was some worming, but nothing that would be a structural problem, and those worms would soon die in our cold Maine water. I think I knew I would buy this boat before even stepping aboard. Then I asked Elmer about the engine.

"It was installed in 1934," he drawled in a Chesapeake waterman's accent. "That was the year she was lengthened out the first time. . ." He, seeing the quizzical look on my face, started in on *Record*'s history. "You see, when first built in 1914 she was 42 feet long. She ran from Alesund to the islands in the fjords of the west coast of Norway and brought back milk from the farms. When the business grew and passengers started traveling, they cut her in half in the middle and gave her another three meters of length, installed this engine, and ran her until she was again too small. Then in the 1950s, they cut her again, and with another three meters of rebuilding she is now just over 60 feet." I gasped at all this news.

He then went to explain that he went to Norway and bought her from the ferry service in 1972. "Knowing she had a zillion hours on the engine, I went to old Otto Brunvoll, the manufacturer, and asked him to do a total rebuild. In a thick Norwegian accent, scratching his head, he looked at me saying, 'Vy do you vish to do dish?' I tried to explain the trip to America and dependability and with all the hours she has run. . . but he waved me silent, saying, 'Ze ole boot *Rekord* has run 50 year here in Norvey. She vill take you to Amerika and back if you vish and she vill still be running for your szon und his szon. You yust keep ze oil to it und she vill run.'

"'Well,'" Elmer said, "okay, but I want to purchase from you enough spares to repair anything that may go wrong." Otto's answer was: 'Keep ze oil to her, und nozing vill go 'rong.' "I was finally convinced," Elmer stated, "but I bought the spare parts, packed them in oil, and started out. My wife and I, only the two of us, ran 26 days across the pond, day and night, and she never missed a beat. When we arrived here in the Virgin Islands, that engine, turning at 260 revs, sounded and acted just as when we left Europe and, after seven years of running these islands, the spares are still in their crates, packed in oil."

Now in 1979, with the "old boot," as Brunvoll called her, running like a Swiss watch, I sat in the engine room contemplating that two-cylinder semi-diesel—all painted white and flashing its brass fittings in my eyes. These two huge 15-inch pistons rolling up and emitting a dull thump with each hit, swapping with the other jug, rolling slowly over to the first, back again to the other, and to the first, boom-boom-boom, back and forth, were keeping that big heavy flywheel spinning in everlasting slow and seemingly determined perpetual motion. What a rhythm! A symphony in two cylinders! Most of the noise and all of the smoke and fire seemed to go up the stack, where it was sculpted into 10-inch smoke rings, ejected with each belch up to about 15 feet into the calm air. That old engine would run forward or backward with equal efficiency, and it seemed to be totally oblivious to the engineering diagrams.

I was completely charmed. This was a great old boat imbued with endless character, able, interesting, and challenging. I could just visualize her on the Maine coast—her powerful plumb stem, the sweep of the open foredeck, the tiny pilothouse two decks up with bridge wings port and starboard, the long upper deck with my Maine peapod on the davits, and a huge staff 12 feet long where Old Glory could flutter majestically in the breeze—a real little ship! I couldn't resist it. I was her new owner.

Now came the problem of learning to run the old thing. Being a foreign ship, all the *Record*'s labels were in a language strange to me, and there were many mysteries of Norwegian marine protocol waiting to be solved. The variable-pitch prop had two blades, which were controlled from the tiny pilothouse two decks up. The throttle was on the port side and was turned left with the right hand. The wheel controlling the variable-pitch prop was on the starboard side and was turned to the right with the left hand. Running, maneuvering, and remembering that cross-over was a real challenge. It almost got me in trouble more than once.

Captain Orvil and his wife joined us for the maiden cruise, and as soon as Orvil had shed his long winter underwear in the 90-degree heat of the men's room at the airport, we went aboard and got down to work. Armed with Elmer's cursory instructions, we confronted the Brunvoll, the gray matter of our two heads against the knobs and levers of those two mammoth cylinders. The first time I belted the starting air to her, she started backwards. The second time, she just rocked. We finally got her purring, and we headed to our first "perfect paradise Virgin Islands" anchorage. We were chugging along confidently, jiggity-jig, and as the anchorage opened up in front of me, I saw our dreams of a secluded cove quickly but surely evaporating. It was beautiful all right, tranquil and lined with palms, but there must have been 50 boats snuggled in there for the night.

We squeezed our heavy 60-foot freighter through the fleet of little 30-foot yachts that were all anchored too close to each other. I rolled the pitch out of the prop, carefully turning the crank the proper direction, and cut back on the throttle, opposite direction, other side. . . but oops. . . a little too much, she's dying. . . catch it before she stalls. That was a close one! She is still running. But the vessel was stopping. . . I checked; yes, the pitch was still cranked in forward.... I gave her a little more just to keep her moving. But, whoa. . . the vessel started backing up!

Geezz! With anchored boats all around us, we were losing steerageway. Then it occurred to me! The engine had almost stalled—could

The Norwegian-built freighter Record *awaits weather on a typical Maine black, foggy day. (author's collection)*

she possibly have stopped, rolled backward, and restarted herself in the other direction? It seemed inconceivable. Quickly I rolled reverse pitch in. . . yes, she started ahead. . . so there was the solution. She had taken it upon herself to pause and restart backward, just to be ornery. Okay, Brunvoll, since it makes no difference to you, we'll then use forward for reverse and vice versa. We anchored without further incident. Then and forever more I would remember—there is no stop on the throttle. Cut her back too far and she will die. And, since there is no start button on the dashboard, the only way to restart is a panic trip two decks down and five minutes of prep time.

Almost every harbor or cove in "paradise" was overcrowded. We love the open space in Maine, where you can anchor without 50 neighbors with their blaring radios, screaming kids, and barking dogs. After five weeks, I decided "paradise" here, as in the Bahamas of my memory, is a misnomer. I swore that would be the last time I cruised the U.S. Virgin Islands, where the anchorages are too much like living in a tenement.

On our first night, we discovered the old boat's cockroaches. These uninvited bedfellows suddenly appeared by the thousands, traveling their nocturnal route over near-naked bodies perspiring in the hot bunks. I flipped on the light and observed an army of bugs in full dress marching up and down the walls. "Now hear this! When the Maine winter sets in, me boys, all you guys will be history!" I saluted to the hordes and shut out the light.

After our month's cruise, I arranged for Elmer to enter the *Record* into the U.S. to get a duty-free document. The vessel's use was listed as "fishing," but there was a hint, only a rumor, mind you, of trading "flowers" to the Lesser Antilles. A clear title was a condition of the purchase and, recognizing the ability of the seller to pull strings and do things in the islands that frequently raise inquiring eyes, I insisted on delivery to U.S. waters.

Home in Camden, the *Record* nestled into Sharp's Wharf, where we rafted her outside the *Adventure* and *Roseway*, and my crew and I went to work on her as well as all the rest of the flotilla tied there. I found five curved-glass tugboat windows at Witte's salvage yard in Staten Island and built them into the new curved saloon on *Record*'s main deck, installed a new center-island galley with a tiled counter, and paneled a new luxurious master's stateroom. Then we hewed and stepped a mast with a working boom on the foredeck and got the winch rigged for hoisting heavy loads.

The middle of the 1970s had ushered in the fuel crunch. The costs of fuel went through the roof, and the offshore fishermen of Monhegan, Matinicus, and Isle au Haut were switching to less expensive coal for their houses, enabling them to save some extra bucks for the fuel for their fish boats. Here was an opportunity to give the old *Record* some wintertime work. I rigged that hand-hewn mast to handle 55-gallon drums filled with pea-coal and to do it all with just one man—me. I could throw a turn on the winch and whisk them up, swing them ashore, and land them in a lobsterman's pickup truck, all from standing on deck. He would then zoom home, dump them into his coal bin, and return the empty to me.

The *Record* shone at this occupation. Working alone, I could easily load 25 barrels of coal on the foredeck and, with her autopilot steering for me, chug to the islands in about four hours, land at the wharf, and with the old Brunvoll ticking over and holding *Record* on a spring line, I would swing off the barrels. Buying my cargo and reselling same to the fishermen circumvented the marine freighting laws and kept it simple.

Old *Record* and I became good friends, and the engine, just as old Otto Brunvoll had preached, sounded as if it would go on forever. The old boat was a positive joy to run and own. She turned heads all over the bay. One cold, cold day we shouldered through the sea smoke and delivered a half load of coal to the wharf at Isle au Haut, and deposited the remaining coal at Matinicus on the high tide.

Anxious to get home before the breeze came up, I swung off to the nor'ard. Ice was already forming on the deck hardware from the dollops of spray spattering aboard. With the autopilot, Iron Mike, at the controls, I was brewing a pot of java one deck down in the galley and keeping a weather eye out the forward port when I noticed what looked like a large log off the port hand. Making a mental note that we would pass clear of the hazard, I returned to the wheelhouse. As we got closer, I could see what looked like a shag (cormorant) or two on the log flapping their wings. But hold on, that log is going up current. Now, that was curious!

I hauled the old boat over to investigate, and lo and behold, the log was no log at all. It was a bull moose swimming along almost three miles from the mainland. The birds weren't shags at all, but his ears flapping back and forth, and what looked like branches were his rack. I said, "Mr. Moose, you are lost," and I twice slowed the boat to try to head him off towards shore. Mr. Moose would have none of it. He twice turned around, swam under my stern, and with great determination continued on his course. A later discussion with the game warden cleared up the puzzle. He said, "That old moose had a cow out on one of the islands and he was goin' a-courting." Such incentive can create a real hazard to navigation!

The *Record* was a honey of a vessel and a near-perfect freight boat, but I was still leaning more towards towing. Towboating, with the obvious exception of sailing a large engineless windjammer, is the most challenging kind of maritime work. Sadly, I put the *Record* up for sale. I just couldn't keep them all. In '83 she went to a man from the Great Lakes who really didn't understand her wonderful old engine. Even with lengthy explanation, plans, and diagrams, he just could not seem to get the hang of running it. We sent him off with hopes and prayers, accompanying him down the bay with the *Port Assist* (my newest tug acquisition), and I watched sadly as she chugged off to the south, puffing pretty little smoke rings out of her stack. Little did I know how many wonderful times that beloved vessel would return to my charge.

That very summer was the first. Near the end of the schooner season, I got a call from a boatyard in Albany. "Hey," said the voice, "do you know anything about this foreign-looking weird boat called *Record*? The old thing is illegally tied to some piling here in the middle of the river and has been abandoned for over three months. We are trying to find out something about it, so we went aboard and found your name in one of the drawers. There is food aboard, clothing, and all, but no papers of owner-ship!" I was not exactly enamored with this news, since I had taken a large deposit from the new owner and held a note for the balance. I called him forthwith.

A long dissertation ensued about how he had trouble with the engine while steaming up the Hudson, and his wife was at him, nagging and claw-ing like an angry Siamese cat. They had gotten as far as Albany and she had hit him with the ultimatum, "It's either me or this damn boat, and, Baby, I'm leaving!" It seems Mr. Milk Toast had slunk off with Mrs. Henpecker, saying nothing to anyone, and left the poor old boat to its own defenses, made fast to some unused piling in the middle of the river.

When the schooner season closed, Pat and I went to retrieve the old boat. I jumped aboard, fired up the old engine, tuned it, and spent three weeks gaily cruising the Champlain Canal, Lake Champlain, return-ing down the Hudson, visiting the sights of New York and cruising out Long Island Sound. That old engine ran just like the Swiss watch that Otto Brunvoll had bragged about back in Norway before Elmer steamed the *Record* across the Atlantic to the U.S. of A.

While exploring our way along the North Shore of Long Island, the marine operator called on the ship-to-shore radio with traffic for motor-ship *Record*. "Hey, Captain Jim, do you still have that boat for sale? Over."

"*Record* back, yes, curiously enough, and as a matter of fact, I do. Over."

The new owner met me in New London with a brown paper bag stuffed full of $100 bills, and my wife and I went back to Maine in a rental car while the *Record* steamed on to her new home in Newport, Rhode Is-land. Little did I suspect she would reenter my life with a vengeance. It was 1995 when, ironically, the *Record* was dropped back in my lap. By this time, the poor old gem had been sold to a wealthy Brit who had lost in-terest in converting her to his style of luxury, and she was loaned to the Museum of the Treasure Coast in Stuart, Florida.

The museum's curator happened to be a former passenger of mine, and since I was one of three people in the U.S. who knew how to run the

Record's engine, I was asked to deliver the vessel from Rhode Island to the museum's facility on the St. Lucie River. I was thrilled to run her again. My wife was not quite as enthusiastic but, being a good sport and a good mate, went along with the project. We visited lots of museums along the way south, and drawing over eight feet in that shoal water, flags-a-flyin', horns-a-blowin', we made a grand entrance into Florida. I happily ran the *Record* winters for museum cruises on the St. Lucie River until 1999 when the operation changed hands. My wife and I, then, at the owner's request, cruised the old boat back to Maine, and I became her unofficial caretaker for several more years, until she was sold again. I still keep track of that grand old freighter and worry about her future care and keep.

Chapter 20

Hammering Out Retirement

'd been slaving away on various projects on Sharp's Wharf ever since I bought the property in 1967, starting initially by rebuilding the broken dock, laying new planking on the wharf area itself, and, of course, sneaking in fill when possible. Still, there was always the gnawing feeling that this valuable land on which I was paying all these high taxes should be better utilized, especially if I intended to retire someday!

At the time I made the big purchase of the lot and slipway, I built my woodworking shop in the basement of the three-story, white painted lumber storage shed that everyone on Bay View Street called "the old Swift building." However, this building was 200 feet from the wharf itself. With my bum leg, that was some long walk when carrying heavy tools and timbers. What's more, the building was vulnerable to flooding when the tidal surge coursed in up the slip on a winter gale. Using sandbagging and pumps, we put up with this for many years.

Sculpturing great, heavy oak planking and frames for rebuilding the vessels soon demanded a building dedicated to their fabrication. Inspired by this critical need, we all grabbed hammers, and one bright sunny autumn morning, we set up sills for the new structure next to the slipway. Soon there were five of us banging away and nailing on that building, and all you could hear was the *wham-bam* of the pounding. We had most of the framing up by the time we broke for lunch. It was while I was munching a sandwich that I began thinking about where we had located the structure and, by the time I was finished munching, I had decided our partly completed building needed to be moved.

Immediately after lunch, we all gathered around and moved the entire frame, sills, rafters, and all, in one fell swoop, across the parking lot to the opposite side of the property. Then we continued on with the construction as if nothing had happened. As we worked, we were critically observed by another group of men laboring on a project next door at the public landing. Just before quitting time, they came over and one, with a puzzled look on his face, queried, "Am I crazy, or did you start that over on the other side?" Orvil, with his typical dry wit, denied every word, insisting they must be hallucinating. The men went off scratching their heads in disbelief.

When it came time to do the roof, I said to Erland Quinn, "Cappy, I love the old Maine buildings with the sway-back in the ridge. Let's put a few inches in this one."

"Not by a damn sight," he said, "I'll build no building unless it is straight and true. I've looked at enough of that old decrepit stuff over on the island."

The hammering continued—*wham, bam, wham, bam*—for three days straight out and, when completed, the building was square and true. Then someone, probably Orvil, wrote in big letters on the siding, "Wham Bam Building." The name stuck.

Cappy, because of his stove-up legs, worked from nine to four. He was supposed to take it easy as his poor hips must have been very painful. He often stood his crutch in the corner and went off without it, only to cuss it and wonder where in hell he left it. As soon as he'd finished his day's work on our new building, Cappy disappeared to immerse himself in the real joy of his life, the repairing of old skiffs. Friends would lug in some old, abandoned wreck of a boat to Cappy, and he would fix it up with loving care, removing the old, broken, rotted frames, and steaming new ones, thus strengthening the hull. Then, with new caulking and a fresh coat of white paint that covered over a multitude of sins, he would put them up for sale.

He almost always had one of these basket cases taking up space in the shop and at quitting time, four o'clock, when he should have gone home and rested, he would start to work on a skiff for an hour or two. Once, after a hard day's work at the wharf, I caught him pounding on the stem of one of these wrecks. He had a hammer in his left hand and a hammer in his right, and his mouth full of nails. I said, "Cappy, for God's sake, it's after four, and there you are with a hammer in each hand." He, with a wry smile and an insufferable twinkle in the eye, replied, "Yeah, but this is my own time now and I ain't goin' to waste it."

The addition of the infamous Wham Bam Building to house my ship's bandsaw and lag bed planer did nothing to solve the problem of our distant woodshop and lumber storage. Our timber still had to be lugged all the way from the Swift Building. Then, sometime in the early '70s my next-door neighbor decided to be rid of his grandfather's beautiful "Sunday team" stable and I, on impulse, bought it. The hope was for a more convenient shop, locating this building on the wharf next to the schooners. My crew, thinking me bonkers, braced themselves for the move.

Resembling a fair-size house more than a stable, my new purchase had two stories, windows, doors, chimney, a bale of hay or two, and a few little piles of manure in the corners. From my neighbor's, the route would be through a snowbank, over a four-foot gully, a squeeze between the Swift Building and the slipway, and altogether maybe 400 feet of gravel lot to the north side of the wharf. Built with heavy, hand-hewn timbers, that beast weighed some tonnage. I rented two long, steel I-beams, jacked the building up, and slid them under. I put pipe rollers on planks under the sills and, with the winch on my Dodge Power Wagon hooked to the hauling part of a nine-part block-and-tackle, we hauled the building up over the gully. There, we jacked it up a second time, slid the beams ahead, drew the building onto the parking lot, and then jacked her down off the beams. With the stable poised on its own sills for the final move, we flooded the parking lot with water and let nature take its course.

The 10-degree winter weather in Maine soon froze that water glassy-smooth and slick as a smelt. I put a chain to a piling on the wharf, hooked up the nine-part fall, and dragged the building bit by bit to the edge of the harbor. We broke not a window nor lost a brick. At last I could move my woodshop into the old stable—saws and machinery, paint and brushes, dirt and sawdust, and gobs of schooner hardware. Finally we had our shop in a spot that was only a few steps from the vessels!

Now, I had to renovate the space in the bottom of the Swift Building that had been previously occupied by my shop. That space couldn't sit unoccupied. We built in a restaurant facility, rented it, prepared commercial rental space on the second floor, and then built three apartments on the third. I was fast becoming a landlord.

As the 1970s passed and our need for more space pressed, I hooked the Wham Bam Building to the stable-shop, then added an 80-foot spar and boatbuilding shed, a garage, and a separate wharfinger's house, all on the north side of the lot, and a five-bay antique car shed to the south.

In 1980, I sold my crane, Ichabod. I loved that crane. It was my first and biggest. However, now that the tugboat restaurant *John Wanamaker* was gone, I only needed a smaller model. Besides, Ichabod's 100-ton bulk, 100-foot boom, and complex machinery added up to a gob of maintenance to keep running. She could pick up anything in sight as long as I could keep both engines running, and do it as offhandedly as any new, modern, fancy, OSHA-approved crane. She was just too fat. I sold her to Joe Sawyer, a man from Camden who wanted to use her to build a dam and generating plant on the Megunticook River just below my house. I can see her there to this day.

To replace Ichabod, I bought an old Michigan shovel for $200. She was a six-wheeler with only one engine to keep running, and I converted her to a crane with a 60-foot boom, and, after naming her Lula Belle, painted a set of red lips on the door. She was worn-out and had almost no compression, but she surely could do a day's work. I was drop-dead amazed every time she faithfully started, even in the brutal cold of winter, and although she would lay a smokescreen all over the waterfront, Lula Belle was for me, indispensable for the development of Sharp's Wharf and the slipway.

Lula Belle's first big project was the remodeling of the stable to include an upstairs office. I took a chainsaw to the sides of the stable's loft.

Then I called on Lula Belle, reached over the building with the crane, and hooked onto the rafters through a hole we'd made in the roof. We put a long timber inside beneath the rafters and then, with one yank of the old crane, we had the makings of an instant dormer that ran the length of the roof. Soon, the dormer was outfitted with studs, walls, and lots of windows, for I had this lovely vision of my shop and office overlooking the schooners below, where I would sit in my tower paying my taxes.

In the early days, permits for construction were nonexistent. As time went on, however, anything to do with the wharf, slipway, or waterfront became a nightmare of paperwork. Although I found that slipway handy for grounding small vessels for maintenance, the schooners were too large for the tide range. After the *John Wanamaker* went to Boston and I sold Ichabod, I applied for permits to fill the upper portion of the tidal beach. Eighteen months later, after meetings, applications, and fifteen town, state, and federal permits, I was able to start the reconstruction of the slipway. I dug up the granite wall, moved it to retain the new fill that would extend the parking lot, dredged the lower end, and created a beautiful basin for a couple of tugs, freight boats, or who knows what.

Our local restaurateur ensconced in the Swift Building had named the place Fitzpatrick's. "Fitzy's" was soon the local on-site coffee-and-hash house. One day, as the dump trucks were moving in and out, bringing load after load of expensive rock fill for the construction of the new slipway, I found myself sitting in Fitzy's drinking coffee with Captain Alan Talbot. Out of the blue, I was overwhelmed by another one of my fits of reckless abandon.

I turned to him and said, "Hey, Al, what would you think if we moved the stable-shop to the south side of the lot where the slipway is being filled, pour a cement slab on the site the shop had vacated, move the big spar shed over that slab and jack it into the air, and build another story of retail space underneath?"

It was a mouthful and I guess I shocked him, because it was a long time before he answered me, saying, "You must be kidding or you are truly out to lunch. You, a few short years ago, moved the shop in there."

"But," I retorted, "that spar building has a perfectly good roof, it has a lot of volume, it's too good to throw away, and that will allow me to bridge to the next new building on the north side for more retail space."

Alan shook his head in disbelief. But, six months later, in 1982, I was applying for more permits for the next phase of my retirement scheme. The town officials got pretty tired of seeing me at the zoning board of appeals. I got pretty tired of applying over and over. We, severing the spar shed from the complex, moved the shop and Wham Bam Building together to the south side of the lot. Of course, we moved it with all its tools, paint, and sawdust. Then we poured the new slab where the shop had been, dragged the spar shed over it, and, after jacking it up, built a complete new first floor underneath it.

I might add here that my controversial dealings with the town, often the subject of articles in the local paper, weren't always received by the town fathers in the spirit intended. In an effort to gloss-over touchy and delicate disputes, I tried to dream up new projects to improve both our image and our credibility. If we found a few new passengers at the same time, well, that was all right, too. I cooked up a run each spring to a different island for a benefit beach cleanup. I felt that since we used the Maine islands for our lobster cookouts, we would be better received if we groomed some of the uninhabited islands, cleaning up the debris blown ashore from the winter gales.

We would pick out a different island each year and knock together a party of about twenty local volunteers to gather the trash. They loved the experience and came back to the vessel proudly displaying bags and bags of plastic and paper. There were always several old tires, lobster buoys, and fishing nets. It put us in the news every spring, and some of the townsfolk who usually criticized the windjammers gave an honest nod of approval.

During the 1980s, I constructed a large, two-story, three-unit retail space and connected it to the spar shed with a European-like arched bridge. The new building had a Victorian flair, very much in keeping with the ambiance of the area. We put together a Victorian-style tower on the ground, and fired up old Lula Belle to lift the whole works—shingled roof, painted trim, and all—high atop the building. It was ornamented with a beautiful cupola and a fully rigged schooner weathervane crowning the top. I traded an old anchor for two eight-foot theater stage-prop columns and sawed them in half on the big bandsaw. Now, with four halves, we adorned the façade of the building with elegance.

We were putting knees and dentil molding across the face when a tourist came along and, after watching our progress for an unfathomable amount of time, she suddenly blurted out, "Excuse me, sir, when was that old building built?"

I answered with a fake Maine accent, "No idea, ma'am. Probably afore the turn of the century."

"Oh," she said, "it's a wonderful restoration! Keep up the good work. It is so nice to see you are saving all the good parts!"

As the years passed, I continued the insanity. I took the five-bay antique car shed, jacked it up, and built a first floor underneath for more retail space. I also continued to expand my shop with another garage building, hooking it onto the Wham Bam Building. It had taken many years and seemingly endless effort, but by 1990 Sharp's Wharf was finally promising me my retirement.

Chapter 21

Europe Tugs at My Sleeeve

In spite of the hopes and dreams for a solid second marriage, in 1983, my frenetic life with boats again took its toll. Pat and I, after six years of navigating alternately serene waters and stormy seas, went mutually on our separate ways. Again, I was deeply hurt but, trying to learn from my past experience, I decided to do whatever necessary to avoid melancholy. Needless to say, my thoughts turned to a new boat! Yet, there was no more room at my dock in Camden. What then?

Seven years earlier, after my divorce from Louise and at the end of the windjammer season, I had become intrigued by reading and hearing about the veritable highway system of canals crisscrossing all of Europe. Having traveled abroad with my parents as a youngster, I then got this crazy idea to go over and look for a little boat to explore the fantastic network of waterways in France.

Well, I thought, this will be a shot in the dark, as I had no idea where to start. My cook at that time, Dee Carstarphen, a chef supreme, became hooked on the idea of a boat in Europe and offered to go "Dutch" and prepare the victuals. The cheapest fare we could get that autumn of '76 was to Brussels, where I rented a camper van at the airport. Then Dee and I drove north along the Belgian canal system exploring all the boating nooks and crannies towards Holland. I had heard there were more boats in Holland per capita than anywhere in the world—a Sharp kind of country if ever there was one!

In Belgium, we started poking in marinas, commercial yards, and private docks all along the way. At night, we parked the camper in gravel pits, in fields, in deserted ocean overlooks, and once in a Belgian potato field. The next morning, at the crack of dawn, the farmer arrived with his rifle and an angry dog. He pounded on the side of the camper. I went out with a big smile on my face, hoping it would disarm him, and tried to explain in very broken French that we were very harmless, dumb tourists. He went on and on about stealing his potatoes and waved his rifle in the air. The more I smiled, the more the dog growled.

It was truly a circus trying to get our point across. Nothing would satisfy him until I invited him to enter the camper to look under the bunks, high and low, and in all the cabinets for new and dirty, freshly dug potatoes. A close inspection ensued and, finding none, he calmed down and broke into a big, toothless grin. He then welcomed us as if we were old cousins and enjoyed coffee and conversation *avec beaucoup gesticulation*. Ah, an international truce established!

Four days later in a small boatyard in Holland we stumbled across an ex-German police boat of about 38 feet (12 meters). It was all mahogany and teak, had a galley, head, cabin heater, and a little four-cylinder Mercedes engine. It was clean and in good condition for a World War Two–era patrol craft. *Resi* was her name, and the Dutch guilders converted to dollars to the tune of $2,900. It sounded just right, so I requested they launch it for a demo. We ran up the canal and back a half mile, and when starting into the slip I threw her into reverse, and there was the clunk of a sudden disconnect. No power fore or aft!

We threw a line ashore and pulled her in to the dock. I yanked up the floorboards to look at the drive shaft, dropped her in gear, and saw that the shaft was turning merrily. I knew immediately that she had spun off her propeller when we reversed the engine. I asked for a rake. First, I had to get a pencil and paper and draw a picture. How do you say "rake" in Dutch? (How do you say anything in Dutch?) We weren't long in raking up the prop, hauling the boat, fitting the prop back on, and then I excused myself to go to the WC. No, I only had to get at the big bucks that were sewn securely into a pocket buried deep in my underwear. We loaded all our gear, including a couple of Flemish potatoes donated by the Belgian farmer, fit *Resi* out with Dutch food, turned in the van, and got underway towards the first of a multitude of fascinating locks, villages, canals, and countries to the south in my first real European canal boat.

The big question was how to handle the Douane (customs) at the border of Belgium. They took one look at these American yachties and wanted the value added tax paid on the worth of the vessel. I was a dumb tourist. I turned right around and went back and took us down a small side canal well after hours, closed my eyes, crossed the border, and kept right on going. Amazingly, we were neither arrested nor questioned as we entered into France. There we locked down through the twenty-six French locks of the Ardennes Mountains staircase. Unfortunately, this was the year they suffered a long drought in Europe, and we found the canal system closed to the south of Paris. They just didn't have water enough to operate the locks. We were disappointed at that news, but the trip was a huge success, if only as an appetite whetter. We could tie up at almost any little positively charming thousand-year-old French village, stay as long as we wished, shop at the open market, and buy most elegant French wine for a song.

We negotiated dozens of ancient, hand-operated locks, some built before Napoleon's time, and enjoyed a thousand kilometers of the alluring French countryside for almost three months. Then I returned to the boatyard where we started and contacted the affable, personable Dutchman who sold me *Resi*. I said, "Please haul her, store her, and sell her in the spring for me." I flew to London, did my Christmas shopping, and flew home to Maine. The old Dutchman came through for me. In June, he sent me a check for $5,000. What a great way to see Europe—all expenses paid and a profit besides! I decided then and there that I would just have to return someday, spend more time, drink more wine, and live the European canal experience.

Now, years later, the memories of that 1976 cruise kept coming back like a nagging post-nasal drip. Sitting around the table with a sales listing of Dutch boats, a taste of French wine, and a whiff of Gouda cheese, my old friends Hal and Barbara from the *Malabar* days in Florida were soon won over by the lore, the fascination, and the advantages of sailing the canal system in Europe. They agreed to my crazy idea of purchasing a boat in Holland and using it for soaking up Europe's sights and diverse cultures. In those days before the European Union, what with the closed borders, different currencies, different customs, and border restrictions, the idea of taking a vessel from country to country was something unheard of.

Since I was busy on the old schooner in the summer, Hal would use our floating "Chateau in Europe" during the summer season when all the tourists were milling about, and I would enjoy it the rest of the year. Boat shopping is a hoot! Nothing excites this addict more than hunting up a new boat. It is even more exciting when one goes shopping in a foreign language and in a foreign place like Holland, where they are simply swimming in boats. We packed up and went off on a shopping spree!

Hal, Barbara, my cook "Georgia"—the handle I had hung on Shelley Johnson—and I flew into Amsterdam and were soon driving through the tulip fields and flower farms. We zeroed in on Enkuizen on the Ijsselmeer, where the great brown fleet of windjammer cruise boats is located. Here, if anywhere, we would find our European dreamboat. After a few rejections, the broker suggested a 16-meter (50-foot) Friesland *tjalk* (old-style sailing cargo canal boat) located in an antique village on the other side of the Ijssel called Kampen. Soon we were following the strange Dutch signposts over bridges, around locks, and past restored old windmills dotting the made-land behind the dikes. Down a cow path of a farm road we bounced until we came to Nesweg 13, where the round bow, sweet sheer, round stern, and well-painted cabin of an 88-year-old iron hull delighted our eyes.

Receiving no answer at the door and having driven far to get here, we decided to sneak aboard and have a quick look around the deck. We peeked in the windows and, liking what we saw, I discovered an unlocked hatch over the head (toilet) forward, lowered myself down on top of the commode, and was soon opening the main door so we all could "ooh and aah" over the varnished mahogany main cabin. She had all the mystique and charm one would expect to find in a classic foreign workboat and was befitting of her strange Dutch name, *Hoop Op Zegen*. They told me it means "Hope springs eternal" or something fairly close to that—it just doesn't translate to English literally. Putting all to rights, we went ashore before the owner would discover our illegal entry, and then Hal and I sat down for a session of pros and cons. We batted it back and forth a bit, but this addict's enthusiasm prevailed. We decided to go for it!

Why not? Here was just the ticket for our European junket. Built in 1898 of the finest wrought iron, she had carried every cargo from pungent, odiferous fertilizer to the pretty red tulips it fertilized. The old *Hoop* had traded all over Holland and had such an aura of history about her that you could almost hear the clunk of the captain's wooden shoes as he stomped around the iron decks. The vessel still resounded, seemingly haunted with the shouted directions from captain to wife as she, trudging the tow path, drew the loaded vessel ahead in a calm, tugging at the towline affixed to the decorated strap around her ample bosom, pulling with her every fiber, straining to do what was expected of Dutch mariners' wives. *Hoop* had done this before automobiles, before trucks, before airplanes, before two great wars—and she just seemed to be the essence of all history. I looked at her with a reverence.

We hauled her and surveyed that old riveted wrought-iron plating. After applying a thickness gauge, we decided her plates must still be sound. She was planked up and fitted with 80-year-old felt in the seams of the riveted hull to make the overlapping plates tight. Those felt strips still looked like new. In spite of the neat, efficient, reliable B.M.C. truck engine in her, *Hoop* was very slow under power, so we replaced her old prop with a reconditioned oversized one, resulting in a nice turn of a speed.

After two coats of coal tar were applied to the bottom (in the fresh water of the canal system, a coat of black tar lasts about five years), we paid the balance to former owner Herr Van' T. Hul. He was fast becoming our best friend in all of Holland, and he agreed to moor the vessel at his dock for this season, keeping her safe from vandals and storms until our return. We took a little toot in the area, cruising only a fraction of the myriad of water systems in that traditional part of northern Holland, but thoroughly seduced, we craved for more and more. It was hard to leave the attractiveness of the country and the hospitality of the Dutch people, and

Hoop Op Zegen *absorbs the exotic charm of the French countryside.*
(author's collection)

especially the alluring, magnetic fascination of the old *Hoop Op Zegen*. We
flew home to the 1984 season of Maine-style schoonering.

By the mid-'80s, I recognized that changes, some subtle and some not so
subtle, were occurring in my life. Captain Orvil had already eased out of
the *Roseway*, giving the younger but totally capable Captain Alan Talbot
the responsibility for the operation and management of the vessel. I myself started to mull over the idea of retirement. I felt 25 years would be
enough and I would make the '88 season my last. This windjammer business, after all, is a young man's job.

The years of hard work, the sleepless nights, the responsibility, the
pounding on huge pieces of heavy oak in the winter, and the stress of
the busy summer season were all telling on my body and especially my
legs. Besides, I had that wonderful old canal boat in Holland just looking
for someone to guide her through the calm, placid vineyards of southern

France. My friend Hal had had second thoughts about the old boat, and I looked forward to returning to *Hoop*, now as sole owner, after the 1985 season.

Then I met Meg Gunther. She lived on the other side of the pond from "the ranch." I had never formally met her before that day—Mother's Day 1985—but we shared a common "Maine-style" driveway. By "Maine-style drive," I mean a drive that is one series of potholes that will shake your bones into oblivion, knock your wheels out of alignment, and bog you down in the spring mud season. Particularly disconcerting is the thaw because, after plowing the snow off the frozen gravel all winter, the warm weather turns the entire drive into a quagmire. The only solution is to haul in more fill and dress the many, abyss-like ruts.

I shared this spring-swamp and winter ice rink driveway with three neighbors, and I decided to drum up their support for the repairs. At the same time, exercising my active imagination, I thought it only reasonable to start with Meg, whose blonde hair might add a bright spot to the gray, muddy day. Her house was a white-painted lakefront cottage surrounded by large old-growth pines. A knock on the door brought her warm smile from within the well-painted, homey-looking kitchen. When I broached the subject of the old ravaged road, she said, "Well, come in and have a cup of coffee. We'll talk it over." And I did.

Later, the memory of that brief meeting stuck with me. I couldn't figure it. But there was something, something about this green-eyed schoolteacher that retained my attention. Still, with the crush of outfitting and the busy summer season, I hadn't much time to get to know Meg any better. However, two months later, with the memory of our brief chat still haunting me, I had the perfect opportunity to call her.

Throughout my years with the *Adventure*, I had never forgotten those incredible color movies, slides, and black-and-white images of my old vessel that John Clayton had showed to me and Captain Hynes. I had taken all of these materials, together with my own collection, and dumped the whole mess on author Joseph Garland's living room table one spring day in 1985. "Can you make a book of this stuff?" I asked Joe.

Meg 'n me in a Ford Model T—my 1923 Tin Lizzy. (photo: Bangor Daily News*)*

He said, "You bet I can!"

And he did. *Adventure, Queen of the Windjammers*, was written by Joe in only twelve weeks and published in 1985. To commemorate the event, I decided to have a huge book-signing party aboard the old vessel. We invited everyone we could think of around town, out of town, and all the people in the fishing industry. Looking for a little political handle, I even invited my very good friends, the United States Coast Guard. I thought the book signing might be of interest to Meg and invited her aboard, too. We served champagne and munchies, had happy, toe-tapping Dixieland music, and got writer's cramp from signing the new volumes. My passengers quickly gobbled up the finished product as it came aboard in boxes hot off the press.

At the party, I found myself feeling proud to introduce Meg to my sister and all my friends. Why proud? I didn't know her that well. I had only met her in the spring over the old driveway we shared. I was a little baffled. Still, it was a nice feeling. Watching her circulate, being congenial and engaging, but displaying a reserve, refinement, and charisma, surely impressed me. I was quite taken by this Miss Gunther. To escape the schooner on summer weekends, I found myself looking forward to Meg's frequent dinner invitations, enjoying many an outdoor barbecue under the pines.

And that is how, in the fall of 1985, I decided to invite Meg Gunther, my "across-the-pond neighbor," to accompany me to cruise on the old Dutch canal boat *Hoop Op Zegen* waiting for me in the champagne country of southern France.

Chapter 22

The Lady's Birthday

Seven million people! Can you imagine seven million people at one birthday party? Well, she is *the* most important lady in the United States. She was to be 100 years old! It was the Statue of Liberty's rededication, and on July 4, 1986 there was to be the biggest Tall Ships rendezvous—the biggest Operation Sail—that New York City and most of the world had ever seen. This would truly be a colossal gathering of the most impressive sailing vessels from all countries of the globe, making the '76 event, which we had also attended, pale in comparison. Now, aboard *Roseway*, with a full complement of passengers and crew, we were on our way, but first we had to fight our way through a hellacious gale of wind!

It swooped down on us the first black night. We were fresh out of Camden and no one had as yet acquired "sea legs." There were some things in the galley that had not been safely put away, and I could hear the periodic crash when a sea would pick poor old *Roseway* up and deposit her headlong on top of a steep, dark wave. We had our halyards pre-coiled and ready to run, and I, fighting the wheel, shook out the crew to get on deck and furl the mainsail. By the time we were putting the last of the gaskets around that big sail, the wind had jumped to about 40 knots and sheets of spray were blowing horizontally across the decks.

It was not what you would call fun, and the night was as dark as the inside of a pocket. The dull glow shining from our running lights and the wink of the lighthouse at Monhegan Island flashing now and again back on the horizon were the only lights to see. The old weather folk wisdom "Wind before rain, clearing will soon come again" didn't seem to work that night. The rain followed the wind, and came in a torrential cloudburst and hung on until dawn. It was soon trickling down behind my oilskins, and my sou'wester hat had blown back on its tether like a kite and was creating a funnel steering the pouring rain in a stream directly down my back. It was a long, wet night.

Roseway was a queen with her red sails, white hull, and especially the 10-foot, rich-looking, gilded, spread-winged eagle Captain Orvil had hand-carved for the cutwater of the bow. Orvil, ever the master craftsman, had carved an amazingly beautiful eagle for me back in 1964 when he was on the *Stephen Taber*, a finely conceived solid mahogany creation I have cherished all these years. I proudly display her now on my office wall. The colossal, golden *Roseway* eagle was carved to fit around her stem with the head and beak plunging forward under the bowsprit and the long wings sweeping back along both bows and flashing in the sun and spray. It is by far the biggest and best of Orvil's carved eagles.

Back in 1976, when prepping *Roseway* for that year's Operation Sail, I had decided she needed more sail area. The first thing we needed were mastheads. I came up with the idea to create tapered mastheads out of steel, pick them up with Ichabod, set them on top of the steel caps presently on the masts, weld them in place, and relocate the peak and throat halyard blocks higher up. That would provide height enough to get a full mainsail and give us the ironwork to mount a main topmast. We hired Red Franklin, a talented tin knocker, to fashion the new mastheads and we built a stage around the masts that we could hoist up to work on site, 80-some feet above the deck. Red did a beautiful job on the mastheads and we sent them out for galvanizing, gave them a fresh coat of white paint, and mounted them. We then went into the woods, felled a tree to fashion into a spar for the topmast, and were soon planing it round and fitting it. Our new sails were bent just in time to start the season.

Now, ten years later, we had faced up to the fact that, despite our efforts, *Roseway* was slow—too slow! She has such a beautiful hull, a deep fisherman model, so she should really be a smart sailing machine. I used to go screaming by her with the old *Adventure* and damned if *Roseway* didn't act like she was dragging some kind of an anchor. You could see the water boiling with turbulence coming from under her stern and creating eddies and whirlpools in her wake. It was that five-foot, five-bladed propeller she was lugging around behind her, a leftover from the days when she was a pilot boat in Boston.

That wheel gave her plenty of speed under power, but under sail it was a terrible drag. She needed a feathering wheel. I suggested we try out one of the new Luke feathering-type propellers. I was sure that in spite of the expense, *Roseway* would be much more exciting to sail. We took the plunge and installed the new wheel. "*Rosie*" deserved it, and it made all the difference. She immediately became one of the faster vessels in the fleet, making her captain smile and tip his hat to the pokey old coasters he was passing. The old *Adventure* would still sail past her, but do so much more slowly and without destroying any of *Roseway's* dignity in the process.

For this Operation Sail, *Roseway's* fifth as a representative of the state of Maine, we had fitted her as before with a pine tree at the masthead. Also, we had signed on our own special Scottish piper, a passenger named Peter Parks. He, marching in his kilts, had piped us gloriously out of Camden Harbor, but we soon chastised him for stirring up the weather gods with that ungodly clamor and bringing on this "gale o' wind." Only the hullabaloo of bagpipes could be so inspirational as to raise the wrath of wind and wave to this extreme, where so many had to down a fist-full of Dramamine pills and hold their tender tummies against the tumult. Fortunately, Peter was a good sport and we all had a rousing belly laugh in the sun the next day on our run to Gloucester Harbor.

Away we went crossing Massachusetts Bay and dove into the Cape Cod Canal, waving to the spectators lining the shores. Block Island Sound was clear and kind to us, and the horizon was peppered with masts and sails of ships nosing into Narragansett Bay. Peter, our piper, gave us a rousing rendition of "Scotland the Brave" as we made our grand entrance through the fleet and into Newport Harbor. There we found, as in 1976, a harbor full of the most magnificent square-rigged training ships from all over the globe, as well as literally hundreds of schooners, sloops, ketches,

Originally built as a yacht along the lines of a Gloucester fishing schooner, Roseway *was a "looker." The addition of topmasts and a feathering propeller made her a fast sailer, too. (author's collection)*

yawls, and rigs of all description, from Chinese junks to Dutch canal barges and even Eskimo kayaks.

As we plunged into the hubbub, to my total surprise, my passengers skipped below and each donned a newly purchased bright red T-shirt emblazoned with the name *Roseway* on both sides, and our grand entrance was soon enhanced with uniformed crew placing us in the same social echelon as the finest windjammers of the event. We saluted all, sailing back and forth through and around the anchored ships, dodging the small craft and proudly sporting *Roseway's* red sail canvas and our spectacular fancy uniforms. Sleep came hard, for the excitement of the day and the constant movement of boats and their high-reveling crews seemed to extend through most of the long night.

Each and every vessel in Newport got underway in the forenoon bound for the Big Apple. To me, this was always the most impressive sight of the entire Operation Sail. The stream of Cape Horn beauties, upping anchors, bo'suns' pipes screaming, mates barking orders, crews swarming aloft, sheeting home topsails and standing off to sea, each surrounded with a gaggle of wonderful small sail flitting from tack to tack like children at a kindergarten recess. . . I loved it.

We went the Long Island Sound route, enjoyed a guitar concert at Fishers Island, tried for Northport but found it too shoal, and finally anchored in Cold Spring Harbor. The Cold Spring Yacht Club launch with its uniformed representative immediately put out from their private dock with special invitations for our whole complement to attend a private bash, which they had planned for that evening. All took advantage of the gala affair, and Peter piped a proper goodnight salute under the full moon when we returned to our schooner.

Donning our T-shirts, we hot-dogged our way, with a fair current, through Hell Gate in company with 200 other vessels bound for the parade. Our orders were to accompany the controversial, 370-foot, four-masted barkentine *Esmeralda*, the Chilean naval training ship, that under the dictator Pinochet had been a prison ship with a long record of torture.

We decided that, in spite of her country's human rights record, we would give her a real state o'Maine welcome, and delivered three hearty cheers and a bagpipe snippet of "Scotland the Brave" as we passed, and then took up our position on her starboard quarter. In her assigned place to port was the schooner *Pilot*. She was of about the same size and a sister to *Roseway* when they were both employed in the pilot service for Boston's commercial shipping. As we started up the Hudson River, we passed the aircraft carrier *John F. Kennedy* just as President Reagan arrived by helicopter, and we gave him a blast with our cannon. It may have been our imagination, but with the report, the security people seemed to crowd more closely around the president and glowered at our little puff of smoke.

With a nice southerly blowing us upriver, we sailed wing-and-wing, often overtaking the *Esmeralda* and backing down with the engine to stay in line. Pretty much behaving ourselves, we paraded until we got to the turnaround at the George Washington Bridge. With such a seductive breeze making up, I couldn't stand the powering any longer. So, turning around, we started down the river, tacking back and forth, beating up-wind as sailing vessels are wont to do. Powerboat parade be damned, I was determined to sail my ship. We would cheer each vessel we passed with three hearty "hurrahs," tack across their bows, admire their crew standing strictly at full attention but surreptitiously smirking down at us. If their watch officer wasn't looking, they'd return our salutes, waves, and thumbs-up.

Pretty soon the Coast Guard came with blue lights a-flashing. I had a vague idea what they wanted, so I called on my chief piper to bring his bagpipes into action. He struck up the longest rendition in all history of "Scotland the Brave." Certainly a standing Guinness record, it lasted until the "Coasties" got frustrated trying to communicate and damn near ran square into the side of us. What a bunch of boat handlers they were! I waved them off, and soon there were so many other boats around us they got confused, gave up, and cautiously went away.

We were assigned to a berth behind a "parkateria" where we would see nothing of the proposed unbelievable array of fireworks over Lady Liberty. I would have none of that and moved to an anchorage reserved for small spectator boats over on the Jersey side. Sweeping the way ahead with my 25-foot bowsprit and nearly skewering the rigging on what we affectionately called a Clorox bottle (fiberglass boat), I barged right into the illegal anchorage. That gigantic sprit, threatening to dismast the little sloop, intimidated their crew into upping their anchor and moving elsewhere, enabling us to enjoy their anchorage with a beautiful, unobstructed view of the famous statue.

As precursor of what was to come from the planned blitz-works, my crew passed out a fist-full of sparklers to every passenger, and our decks were soon aglow with tiny lights. Never have I seen such a sight. The pyrotechnics arcing over the Lady in an almost continuous bombardment must have cost a small fortune, for they lit up the sky without a pause for more than an hour. There was an accompanying musical score, and a full orchestra played from a barge anchored out in the middle of the

Hudson. When they struck up the national anthem for the grand finale, it masterfully went hand-in-hand with a totally uninterrupted and freshly presented barrage. We had a shipload of gapers! They stood in awe with jaws hung in absolute stupefaction at the entire spectacular as burst after incredible burst spread light and color over the entire New York skyline and the Lady's crown.

We never went into the city. Our passengers had no interest in downtown, and all voted to depart the city stuff and go sailing. We high-tailed it for the unpolluted waters of the Sound and a cleansing swim over the side. It was a fantastic birthday party. We were privileged to be a part of this awesome spectacular that will probably never again occur in that same rich, extravagant, style. The new century, terrorism, a much more dangerous world, and the stringent rules of Homeland Security have changed the face of New York Harbor. I doubt that we will ever see a repeat of such a wondrous collection of wind ships parading majestically under the torch of Our Lady of Freedom.

The trip home was a great downwind sail made interesting with stops at Huntington, Orient Harbor, Greenport, Vineyard Haven, and then, with a stint of deep-sea sailing for a day and a half, we glided into Owls Head Bay, Maine. It was a salty bunch of sailors that were piped onto the wharf at Camden, home from one of the great adventures of 1986, and, you guessed it, "Scotland the Brave" was wafting over the waves. (In all fairness, Peter—a truly accomplished piper—knew a slew of bagpipe medleys, but just to be ornery and to pull his kilt, I called his every tune "S. the B.")

Back in Maine, Captain Orvil Young, that long, lanky, Down Easter I so admire, was now enjoying his semi-retirement, but had, true to his loyalty, jumped in to run the *Adventure* for the two weeks we were in New York. Captain Alan Talbot, *Roseway*'s regular skipper, had been mate for me for this Tall Ships voyage and now slipped again behind the helm of "Rosie." He took command so naturally that I never even noticed so much as a blink in the operation. I went immediately to the quarterdeck of my old

Adventure to sail her for the rest of an exciting '86 season. That fall, I again pursued a life full of tugboats, canal boats, and any other type of boat I could jump in, or on, or around—anything to feed my habit.

Many, many changes were in store for the next two years. Captain Orvil was tickled with his short-lived leisure. However, very soon responsibilities concerning the health of his wife Andrea became a growing concern, so in 1987 we quietly put *Roseway* up for sale. A prospective buyer soon came into the picture and started sniffing around asking all kinds of questions about the business and seemed serious about owning our queen with the tanbark sails. He spent most of the winter researching the project and by spring was ready to offer.

By then, Meg, taking a winter sabbatical, was with me in Castelnaudary, a medieval village in the south of France. We were gloriously cruising the circuitous Canal du Midi on the *Hoop Op Zegen*, and enjoying visiting the local wineries, filling up on good Bordeaux wine and true French cassoulet (a melt-in-your-mouth, gourmet bean-and-goose repast). In the States, it was April Fool's Day 1987, and we were waiting for a prearranged phone call outside the maroon-colored European telephone booth—the only one in the entire town—when it rang as expected.

Orvil's familiar voice came booming out of the funny-looking French receiver, drowning out the noise of the French cars crowding past the intersection, honking with impatience at their neighbors. "He countered our asking price, Jim," Orvil explained, "and I told him to forget it. I said, 'She's too good a boat to give away to the likes of you.' Then, he darn soon came around all peaches and cream, and was chummy as a cousin when he signed the agreements!"

Meg and I scratched around and found a secure berth for *Hoop*, packed up, and high-tailed it on the first airplane home. Somehow, I understood that, with *Roseway*'s sale, a big change in my life had begun. But, as Meg and I winged our way home, I had no idea just how big it would be.

Chapter 23

The Tears of '88

"See," he exclaimed. "I told you there was rot in that schooner, and I was right, wasn't I! See—right there!" The United States Coast Guard inspector announced his findings in an authoritative, loud, booming voice to all in earshot.

That April day had dawned with a leaden sky and gloomy forecast, both in weather and mood. We opened a topside plank on the old schooner so the Guard officer could get a beady eye on her timbers. His findings were right, of course, as any boatbuilder, seaman, sailor or just about any knowledgeable person could have told you. These vessels were probably built with some rot in them when they were new. *Adventure,* more than sixty years, would most certainly have rot in the timbers somewhere. It was, naturally, a consideration of degree. *Adventure* had been built in the Essex fashion by the James Yard, one of the best builders of Gloucester fishing vessels, using the very finest materials available. Her oak frames were a huge 12 by 12 inches and closely spaced. Her planking was also oak, three inches thick and in great, long lengths. Her ceiling, that near-perfect, beautiful inner planking, was four inches thick, long-lasting, rot-resistant hard pine and mostly in lengths of greater than 40 feet.

The schooner had been built to withstand the worst kind of weather the old North Atlantic could dish out in the dead of winter. She'd been built to load thousands of pounds of fish in her hold and race through great seas to deliver them to market. Now, in her after-market years, she loaded only people and sailed only coastal during Maine summers. That didn't matter to the Coast Guard inspector. Logic was not part of the formula. There was the *rot*. And yet, a "zero-rot" policy had never been part of the requirements of inspection.

In the past, I always did what I had to do to satisfy the inspectors during their annual inspections of the schooners, even if it seemed trivial. But I had long since come to believe that the system of vessel inspection we have is backwards. In my experience, the inspectors simply didn't possess the training or background to survey wooden vessels, yet they had to justify their existence. One inspector, while crawling around inside the huge cypress water tank we had under the galley floor, complimented me on how clean my bilge was and how good the inside of the vessel looked down there. I don't know where he thought the frames and ceiling were, but he was convinced he was looking at the inside of *Adventure*'s bottom.

Another wished to pull a trunnel (one of the wooden dowel-like fastenings that hold plank and frame together) to check if the fastening was *corroded*. Once, an inspector drove his icepick into a piece of cement and exclaimed how hard the wood was in that spot, and then, when it came time to inspect aloft where the danger really could be serious, he looked up in awe and asked, "How's everything up there, captain?" Them climb aloft? No way.

Each year, they would try very hard to find a life jacket in the pile that would fail the inspection. They would jerk with vengeance on the straps as described in the Coast Guard manual to make sure they would not rip or pull out. I had an obviously new jacket that the zealous inspector yanked on so hard it ripped the material of the jacket and made a sizable hole. He, realizing what he had done, quickly put it down and didn't say another word. Next year, that jacket failed the inspection because of the rip. From then on, we would sneak some old jackets in the pile that would always fail and could suffice for the "jackets that need replacement" requirement.

Whatever the issues with inspections, I had always been able to comply and renew and repair as necessary. But this time it soon became clear, that negotiation was out of the question. This inspector unequivocally proclaimed *Adventure* too weak and rotted to sail the summer season. I, frustrated, blurted, "You, as a ship's surveyor, are hardly worth your salt! My vessel, built more recently than many of the other older vessels, is far stronger and more able than most." That statement was, of course, a big mistake. He, in an effort to enhance his rank in the bureau, was insisting on a "zero-rot" policy. That was unreasonable to me, but I was now fighting city hall.

Some of the older windjammers, those built before the turn of the century, as the *Taber* was, were going through a rebuilding process. Some others were put on a schedule of renewing and reconditioning over several years, and I tried to offer that alternative. It was ignored. Then I learned from a trusted friend and longtime member of the Maine windjammer world, that he'd overheard a conversation between the inspector and a rival operator detailing where the *Adventure*'s timbers could be at question.

I demanded of my friend, "Why would anyone do that?" He suggested that the *Adventure* was a big carrier with a large capacity, popular, and a threat to those with empty bunks. My friend was impartial. He had no particular axe to grind, and when he described the interview in great detail, he convinced me of the total veracity of his statements. I prepared to do battle.

Just as you don't want a street-corner policeman with an auto manual inspecting your car's equipment, I didn't want to have to accept the opinion of one person with a shiny rulebook passing judgment on my vessel. So, gathering five knowledgeable heads, I set to work analyzing the condition of the frames. I was assisted by three schooner captains who had rebuilt many old vessels and were shipwrights themselves, and a professional marine surveyor familiar with wooden construction. I removed planking from both sides of the vessel, exposing the vessel's massive frames.

We all took tools to sound the condition of each and every frame and analyzed the percent of bad wood in each. We wrote down our numbers so we could compute an average from each. The sum total of the perfectly sound timber was 75 percent. She was about one-quarter-rotted. Interestingly enough, that result showed the percentage of good, sound timber in the *Adventure's* hull totaled 25 percent more in volume than the total wood used in the construction of my good friend Captain Buds Hawkins' new schooner *Mary Day*! The massive size of the timbers used in the frames and planking of *Adventure* spoke loudly for her strength. I was so sure I was on to something that I appealed the decision to the District Commander, U.S. Coast Guard Headquarters, Boston. I drove to his office and laid out all the computations, graphs, drawings, and logic of my appeal. He listened, but only to be courteous.

From my standpoint, the decision now seemed even more unreasonable. I asked for a limited certificate for only the 1988 season. Denied! One mile from shore? Denied! For only Penobscot Bay? Denied! I asked for only in winds of less than 10 knots. Denied! They wouldn't even consider another boat tied up alongside as a safety precaution. A vessel built for the North Atlantic in the winter was denied sailing across Penobscot Bay. It was heartbreaking. Once this decision was made, there was no way in hell it would be reversed without a congressional edict. I was spinning my wheels.

Both the month of April and my Coast Guard certification were now running out. Come May, I had no choice but to send the following message to all those wonderful, devoted people:

Dear Shipmate,

I guess this is probably going to be the last "Dear Shipmate" letter you will receive from the old schooner *Adventure* and me. I regret to say the bureaucratic Coast Guard has taken another good boat out of service. Three weeks ago, one officer in Portland decided that the vessel is too old to continue operation. I appealed for my last season and was denied. It seems such an injustice, as those of you who have sailed on her know that she is a strong and stout old girl.

This is the end of an era and a shame. I can't believe it myself. I keep thinking a congressman or someone with some clout could bring the Coast Guard to some sense, but wooden vessels—they just don't understand. I had planned to donate the *Adventure* to the City of Gloucester at the end of the season, to become a national exhibit to marine history. Hopefully they will be able to restore her and she will live for many years to come.

We have an alternative—the *Roseway*, with top-notch Captains Alan Talbot and George Sloan. The *Roseway* will be cruising the regular schedule. There is limited space, but if you can call me right away, I will try hard to place you on the *Roseway* or another schooner of your choice. If I don't hear from you, you will automatically receive your deposit back by return mail.

I had a wonderful 24 years with the old lady, and many of you have shared many of those years with us. Thanks to all of you and fair winds, good shipmates.

Sincerely
Capt. Jim Sharp, Ret.

I was desolate. My cook and good friend Georgia, aka Shelley, came to my assistance and did all the mailing and organizing of the return of deposits, saving me a ton of mental anguish. Meg propped me up to keep my depression from overwhelming me. I just couldn't bear to see the *Adventure* at Sharp's Wharf in Camden, a dead ship, though still able but with no passengers. Seeing the *Roseway* busy with my old passengers and her new owner and watching all the other windjammers going in and out would just be too painful. I had to have another place to put her—to hide her from sight—to shut her in a closet somewhere so no one, especially me, would see her and be forced to answer questions all summer long. I called the Maine Maritime Museum in Bath. They agreed to have her at their dock on display until fall.

Depressed, broken, dejected, and morose, I dredged up enough courage to get the old vessel underway for the solemn one-way voyage. It was like a funeral procession. It was the last time the vessel would see Camden. I felt I was one of the pallbearers taking my best friend off in a floating casket. With an uncertain future, I half-heartedly sailed her west to the Kennebec River, powered upriver to Bath, and was met by a representative of the museum. Since there was a hazard near where we were to tie, he was to direct me safely to the dock. Then he promptly set me right on top of the only rock in the river. With the current swirling in eddies around the hull, the keel grinding away on Maine's granite, my little yawlboat pulling this way and that, we finally managed to drag her off the ledge.

At last we got to the dock and tied her, set her fenders, and tidied up for the last time, but I could hardly bear to look back as we walked to where Meg waited with the car. I went off leaving my poor vessel there to fend for herself, abandoned and forsaken, when I knew she was still a sound vessel with many more years of excitement in her stout hull. We were one melancholy bunch in the car heading back to Camden.

I finally took stock of myself and sought the flip side. For several years, thinking ahead about *Adventure*'s ultimate fate, I had been considering the idea of donating the vessel to an appropriate organization. Now, that old idea reoccurred. Well, there is always some glimmer of hope in a bitterly depressing day. As I had hinted to my passengers in that terrible letter, since we couldn't go sailing this season, I would try to find a way to offer her for preservation as a monument to the fisheries. I had felt that if *Adventure* could be returned to Gloucester and if Gloucester was capable of saving her as a representative of its maritime heritage, it might be a fitting way to conclude my tenure with the old girl and provide for her future.

Author Joe Garland was just the man to orchestrate such a move. Since that happy day in 1985 when Joe's book about the *Adventure* had been published, Joe and I had gabbed many times about the logic of Gloucester someday again being home to the *Adventure*. He was a well-respected mover and shaker on the Gloucester waterfront. The pieces all seemed to fit. Now, fighting my way out of dejection, I called Joe.

Good old Joe! He was able to quickly mobilize a group of enthusiasts and form a non-profit organization, and, as September approached, I got the vessel ready for the trip from Bath to Cape Ann's famous seaport. My faithful cook Georgia, Meg, and I set to bending on sail, a horrendous job with so few hands. Scouring some additional help from the Bath Museum crew, we finished outfitting, and after loading some Gloucester guests excited about the sail west, we caught the ebb tide to the mouth of the Kennebec River.

Adventure, with a strong sou'wester and a good-size sea running, proceeded to beat offshore, leaping from wave to wave, throwing spray and driving hard as if she were coming home from Georges Bank. Tack—tack—tack, she blew all the way to the Piscataqua River just below Portsmouth in an all-day exciting sail to windward. The poor old thing! Condemned by the Coast Guard as unfit to handle Penobscot Bay, and here she beat offshore all day in a hard breeze and didn't even leak.

I slammed her into a cove for the night and dropped the anchor on the fly, impressing the hell out of the crowd of small-boat sailors from Gloucester. Sailing on to Cape Ann, we picked up Captain Leo Hynes and Joe Garland from a launch and made our grand entrance into Gloucester Harbor under full sail. There, with a crowd of enthusiasts on the wharf, we had a wrenching ceremony in which I transferred the ownership of my old schooner to the Gloucester *Adventure,* a nonprofit organization incorporated in Massachusetts.

The entire day was an emotional wringer. I could only hope that the group's members would be able to do some good for the old girl and keep her well in her third career, this one for the education and enjoyment of the public. They would be looking at more than a million-dollar restoration project, but the old *Adventure* would be worth it—every penny!

A little more than a week later, we entered her in the 1988 Mayor's Cup Schooner Races against six other large schooners in the ocean off Cape Ann. Again, with a good smart breeze blowing, the *Adventure* stepped out and showed her stern to the competition, coming in easily a half mile ahead. I guess, when you think about it, we had an unfair advantage as *Adventure* and I had had twenty-four years of testing each other and we both knew what the other was about. She's a sailing machine. I gave her the reins. She took the lead. The other vessels just didn't have a chance. Unfit for Penobscot Bay!

As we made our approach to the inner harbor, the breeze puffed up until it was blowing a good hat-full-o'-wind right into the harbor. We were entering a cul-de-sac and, even though I had dropped all sail long before entering the narrows, she was gaining speed from the wind pressing against the bare masts. My son Topher was at the controls of the yawlboat and I told him to put her in neutral and just let the schooner coast with only the wind pressure on the rigging. She kept gaining. We then put the yawl boat in reverse to create drag. *Adventure* continued to gain headway.

By the time we were squared away for the city fish dock, our designated berth, she was still making knots. There, ahead of our bow, right in our sights was the much-admired and famous Gloucester fisherman *Ernestina*. She's elderly, she's handsome, and she's a very historic vessel. Having at various times in her life been a Grand Banker herself, and an Arctic exploration and research vessel under Captain Bob Bartlett, she was later converted to a freighter sailing from the States to the Cape Verde Islands. Now *Ernestina* is a showpiece for the state of Massachusetts, and colliding with her—a vessel crowded with spectators—would indeed be embarrassing. Since she was equipped with an inboard engine, she had managed to slip in first with her powerful machinery while we were parading at the finish line, taking our bows.

The spot behind her was ours. Stopping cold, just off her stern with only our little yawlboat would be a challenge. I knew our only chance to stop those 230 tons of oak and iron would be the quick and delicate maneuver of reversing the direction of the yawlboat. The idea of a "tow back" is to apply power so that little boat could pull in the opposite direction and eventually destroy the momentum of the schooner. There was no room in this basin to turn the schooner around. We were long since committed. It was do or die.

I hand-signaled Toph: "Turn the yawl around backwards to tow by her stern." He was familiar with this unorthodox stunt and executed it with dispatch. I looked up and saw the *Ernestina*'s stern, crowded with spectators, looming larger and larger as we bore down on it. I sent my most-experienced man, the mate, John McBride, to the anchor, and he hung the flukes in readiness. He knew the importance of his position and understood immediately what was at stake.

With John on the foredeck, I felt I had done all I could to turn this imminent disaster-in-the-making into something from which we could walk away proud. I signaled to Toph to start pulling. When he revved up the engine, the yawl stood up on its stern and started to immediately broach as the relentless headway of the schooner pulled obliquely against the towline, showing no mercy, threatening to trip her, fill her, and drown my son. I was ready. I had the towline in my hand. I cast it off in one motion and, with the next, I signaled to John to drop the anchor.

Knowing the harbor was probably dredged to bare ledge and the anchor would probably not find anything to hook to, I signaled to John to bail out more chain and more chain. If the anchor hooked prematurely and fetched up, the chain would break and we would cut the *Ernestina* in half. I saw the horror of it all in my mind's eye. Our bow, climbing her rail, would come smashing down through the deck and deckhouses amidships, scattering screaming people in all directions. That was the image. More chain, John, for God's sake, more chain! The more chain we let out, the more drag and interference to her momentum; the more drag, the less inertia, the less inertia—until we could finally, painlessly check her.

The chain box was more empty than full by the time we stopped. Topher came up in the yawl under the stern and hooked on. He dragged the schooner sideways to the berth and we tied up, pretending all the while the whole operation was planned that way. Most onlookers thought we were pretty good. I got a bunch of gray ones under my hat that day. Toph, knowing just how close he came to a capsize, said, "Thanks for dropping me off, Dad."

"No prob, Toph. Thanks for a good job."

I sailed her again the following year in the Mayoral races. The weather didn't cooperate the way we all would have liked. It was calm, ghosting conditions with a big swell running, and none of the big schooners were able to finish the prescribed course. But again *Adventure* left all contenders in her wake astern, and when the race was called off, we were so far ahead they had to send a towboat to fetch us and drag us back to Gloucester so we wouldn't miss the celebratory dinner speeches. Without enough wind to keep our sails full and with the groundswell rocking, rolling, and crashing us about, there was many a seasick sailor who was not at all interested in that dinner until they felt solid ground under their toes. Admittedly, when racing my lovely schooner, I had no time for compassion for the ailing.

In the more than twenty years since its founding, the Gloucester *Adventure*, Inc. organization has gone through the vicissitudes to which many non-profits are subject. At one point, the alliance came unglued and dissolved. All those on the Board of Directors quit, so that the entire association fell to pieces. There was a period when the group owed lots of money and the poor vessel suffered terribly for several years, but somehow the phenomenal luck of the *Adventure* seemed again to pull her through. When things seemed at their darkest, a savior named Marty came into her life.

By a phenomenal stroke of luck, Professor Martin Krugman came on board to head up the *Adventure* organization. No, he was not an expert boatbuilder, nor a white-bearded schooner man, nor a shipwright squinting over his glasses. Marty was an Associate Professor of Psychology at Salem State College. He is one who knows how to talk to people and could take the *Adventure*'s case into their pockets. He took hold of this project and tenaciously clamped down like a bulldog to see it to fruition. When things in the organization looked about at their worst in June of 1997, I happened to be passing through Gloucester on my motor vessel *Maine*.

Meg and I were on the last leg of a 6,000-mile cruise through the Erie Canal, Great Lakes, Mississippi, Gulf Coast, and East Coast in our shapely Stanley 44, a typical Down East–style lobster boat hull that we had lovingly converted to a private workboat/cruising yacht. Roaring into Gloucester and being "hot-under-the-collar" concerned for the welfare of the old vessel, I stopped to give 'em hell and demanded to know where they were putting their energy and how they were spending the few donations generated.

The looks of the schooner attested to a serious lack of maintenance. They weren't properly caring for her. I sat and talked to Marty for almost an hour. He, ever so subtly, calmly took the wind out of my sails. By the time he was finished straightening out my attitude, my anger had gone and I pledged a sizable donation to help the project!

He has since raised well over $2 million. Restoration of the hull is realized and new energy, new zeal is now being funneled into the remaining details. *Adventure* has been designated as a National Historic Landmark and will be a showpiece to illustrate and educate the world about Gloucester's amazing history. So, in spite of the reversals I suffered with the Coast Guard, and the vicissitudes *Adventure* survived in Gloucester, I'm confident my old vessel will again grace the waters of New England. I wonder if it all boils down to a better bit of heaven for her in her third career.

Perhaps fate did us all a favor.

Afterword

Mulling over the almost twenty years since my retirement, I have become rather philosophical about the surprising outcome of my career. Had I not been shut down, it may have meant several more wrenching years negotiating the sale of my *Adventure* to a strange hand. Any new operator would have had to be a very special person to satisfy the likes of me. As it was, Meg and I had time to become a couple and get comfortable with each other. I bought a ring for her pretty finger in 1990 in Bangkok on an exciting world voyage aboard a Russian freight and passenger ship. We were married a year later, emotions soaring, on the top of Mount Battie overlooking Camden's spectacular Penobscot Bay on a spanking, crystal-clear Maine day.

We have since traveled, cruised, and visited many lands all over this Earth, boated together through almost every canal, river, and lock on the European continent, and navigated through hundreds of waterways in and around these United States. Meg still insists that if I had two good legs, she would never have been able to keep up. What a mate! My two sons, of whom I am boastfully proud, have gone West to seek their own fortunes. Topher became a respected doctor at Stanford University Hospital and was married to a beautiful Hungarian gal, also a doctor, in the medieval Castle of Vesprem, Hungary, on Mother's Day 2002. Strangely, that was the same day sister Chris passed away in North Carolina. The two docs recently honored us with our first grandchild, a hale and hearty little girl. Zeb is (like his pop) a free spirit, hiking with his dog, bursting through snowdrifts on a snowboard, biking over the mountains, and working in security for the University of Nevada.

As for Sharp's Wharf, the twenty-some rentals I had created for my retirement reduced me from shipwright to landlord. It became more of a chore and a bore, much less fun than when we'd been banging and crashing with the dooryard filled full of a variety of vessels—so I sold it in 1997.

Of course, I am still addicted to the sea and run the *Maine*, my 44-foot lobster boat-type yacht from Camden in summers. In winter, we're usually aboard the *Funky-Old-Thing*, a 47-foot shoal-draft river trawler, in Southern waters.

Although I am now more than three score and ten and leaning hard on my cane and my dear wife, I realize that my early retirement at fifty-five years was a blessing. The post-polio syndrome (early deterioration of the nerve cells destroyed by my polio) was setting in at that time and the legs were already starting to weaken. It was time to hand the opportunity over to the younger generation. The big-schooner business, no matter how you slice it, takes a vast amount of energy and is taxing even for the able.

However, in looking back over fifty years of schoonering and messing about in boats, I come off with a wondrous feeling of contentment. I think I have never been happier except, perhaps, on one of those bygone summer days when standing proudly at the wheel of my old *Adventure* with a hat full o' wind in that ungodly mainsail, thumping the knots off and throwing spray all over Penobscot Bay—totally infected with reckless abandon.

Addendum

And Then I Flunked Retirement

I still can't figure out what happened. I was busy, happily dragging Meg all over the world in this boat and that, cruising and sailing from the canals of Europe to the lakes and rivers of the United States, from Paris to Bordeaux, from Texas to Toronto, New York to the Smokey Mountains and to Florida; we put on thousands of kilometers and miles over almost 20 years and at age 75, I flunked out.

One of the few beautiful pieces of waterfront left on the Maine coast appeared, and to me, was almost irresistible. If you remember, I was interested in developing a museum back in the days of the old *Bowdoin*, and, since this beautiful 2.5+ acres included three large buildings and a commercial dock, and, since my old head was still full of dormant dreams of imaginary museums, I, with the same old recklessness, jumped at the chance to have at it—the ink was hardly dry on the contracts when the economy went seriously south.

Never look back at impetuous decisions—always plow onward (more whimsical philosophy). I renovated the buildings to accommodate a large professional office complex with spectacular ocean views, installed a boat building and repair shop, and in the "museum building" assembled a full floor of magnificent maritime artifacts, at the same time supplanting the first-floor storage with both a children's museum, nonpareil, and a rowing club all stirred into the non-profit mix.

My old M/V *Rekord* came home—again. That grand, old, 60-foot, 1914 Norwegian freight boat had been bouncing back like a boomerang since 1978. She had gone through three or four owners and was languishing, going to pieces, up the Connecticut River. Her owner could no longer do for her and called me for help. He donated her; we brought her home and set about her restoration, making her the stately flagship for the museum. Then, just to complicate life to the fullest, I rented, renovated, rebuilt and outfitted a city-owned shed on the adjoining property to make a down-home lobster take-out/eat-in restaurant. Reckless indeed!

The Sail, Power & Steam Museum is surely one of the most exciting things I have done. It may not be quite as enticing as sailing a big windjammer, but it has turned into a most fascinating, all absorbing, and rewarding kind of project for a 77-year-old duffer. Starting with my own collection of maritime artifacts, once the doors were open, enthusiasts came forth to donate many invaluable treasures from their barns and coffers and with each one a story of spectacular historic interest. The museum, after only a year and a half of operation, has become too small and our new antique engine house is presently under construction. We have many educational programs, demonstrations, momentous music programs, and a wide variety of displays of special interest filling the museum summer calendar.

If you journey to Maine, you must stop for a look at the Sail, Power & Steam Museum of South Rockland. Come in—set a spell—I'll spin you a yarn—maybe two—and you may go home a bit more nautical than you came.

—Captain Jim Sharp

www.sharpspointsouth.com
ssmuseum@midcoast.com
Sail, Power & Steam Museum
75 Mechanic Street, Rockland, Maine 04841